AF763224

THE ROLE OF IMAGINATION IN UNDERSTANDING LEADERSHIP

This book presents a series of fascinating investigations into the role that the imagination plays in studying and practicing leadership. It explains how using the imagination is integral to both the study and practice of leadership itself.

Each study presented began as distinct and conceptually separable and is eloquently tied together by the author through the lens of imagination. This volume outlines the role of the imagination in understanding (a) one's self, as well as other people, (b) the social groups to which one belongs, (c) the dynamics by which these groups change, (d) the conceptual structures we use to determine boundaries, and (e) the role of ritual ceremonies such as legislative committee hearings. In so doing, it offers novel insights that will encourage the reader to consider their own understanding and study of leadership.

The Role of Imagination in Understanding Leadership will appeal to scholars and advanced students in the field of Leadership Studies, including graduate students studying leadership.

Nathan W. Harter has taught Leadership Studies since 1989, when he began at Purdue University in the State of Indiana. Today, he serves at Christopher Newport University in Newport News, VA. He is the author of several books, numerous articles, and book chapters on leadership.

THE ROLE OF IMAGINATION IN UNDERSTANDING LEADERSHIP

The Forgotten Dimension

Nathan W. Harter

Routledge
Taylor & Francis Group
NEW YORK AND LONDON

Cover image: © Getty Images

First published 2024
by Routledge
605 Third Avenue, New York, NY 10158

and by Routledge
4 Park Square, Milton Park, Abingdon, Oxon, OX14 4RN

Routledge is an imprint of the Taylor & Francis Group, an informa business

Library of Congress Cataloging-in-Publication Data
Names: Harter, Nathan, author.
Title: The role of imagination in understanding leadership : the forgotten dimension / Nathan W. Harter.
Description: New York, NY : Routledge, 2024. | Includes bibliographical references and index.
Identifiers: LCCN 2023031303 (print) | LCCN 2023031304 (ebook) | ISBN 9781032449869 (hardback) | ISBN 9781032449852 (paperback) | ISBN 9781003374831 (ebook)
Subjects: LCSH: Imagination. | Leadership.
Classification: LCC BF408 .H31635 2024 (print) | LCC BF408 (ebook) | DDC 153.3/2—dc23/eng/20230927
LC record available at https://lccn.loc.gov/2023031303
LC ebook record available at https://lccn.loc.gov/2023031304

ISBN: 978-1-032-44986-9 (hbk)
ISBN: 978-1-032-44985-2 (pbk)
ISBN: 978-1-003-37483-1 (ebk)

DOI: 10.4324/9781003374831

Typeset in Times New Roman
by codeMantra

To Bob Colvin and Paul Trible, men of vision

CONTENTS

ACKNOWLEDGMENTS

During the writing of this book, I enjoyed the encouragement of many people, only some of whom I can name here: Willy Donaldson, Marvin Kalb, Tony Middlebrooks, Madden O'Neill, John Pratt, Ben Redekop, Qingyan Tian. Furthermore, the film analysis was invigorated by the anonymous reviewers at the journal *Leadership and the Humanities*. The many professionals at Routledge have shepherded this project through to completion, with special thanks to Zoe Thomson, Maddie Gray, Christina Chronister, and their anonymous reviewers, who did me a great kindness by reading and commenting carefully on an earlier draft. As has been my practice for over ten years, I have shared these topics with my Private Study Group at Christopher Newport University in Newport News, Virginia, a gathering of selected undergraduates whose practice of dialogue is the professional highlight of my week. To be sure, the faults in this book are mine alone.

To God be all the glory and to Karin daily, this heart.

1

ON THE POWERS AND PITFALLS OF THE IMAGINATION

Introduction to the chapter

> Life has more imagination than we carry in our dreams.
>
> – *Christopher Columbus*

Students of leadership approach their investigations in a variety of ways. These investigations require the use of many methods, including observation, logic, and abstract theories. A thorough understanding depends upon all of these powers working together. This is one reason that Leadership Studies stubbornly persists as an interdisciplinary project: it draws from so many different methods. This fact should not be surprising inasmuch as the practice of leadership draws from a comparable array of attributes. Nobody leads for long without such powers. It is my contention in these pages that the central attribute – and one that students of leadership ignore at their peril – is the imagination, a sometimes-vague capacity to represent what is not present to the senses.[1]

The imagination operates by means of images and stories. What does such a statement even mean? This chapter begins to answer that question, beginning to explain what the imagination contributes, as well as acknowledging (at least in part) some of its limitations. The imagination contributes to our understanding but only to the extent that it participates with our other attributes or powers. In fact, it is possible to use these other powers to examine the imagination itself – to

1 What I am offering here is a stipulated definition for provisional purposes. In an appendix, I examine three terms more closely: imagination, imaginary, and the imaginal.

DOI: 10.4324/9781003374831-1

put it under the microscope, as it were, as we do here. Be forewarned, however, that what we have is a slippery topic that loves to hide, eager to hop into the thicket and run away.

This chapter therefore outlines the content of the book, introducing some of its themes and giving to you, the reader, a kind of roadmap, a way through that proverbial thicket, through the hazel and hawthorn, in pursuit of our quarry.

Several years ago, during a visit to my university, the inestimable Barbara Kellerman met with the leadership faculty to discuss our curriculum. She asked where we were incorporating the arts. We admitted that we had not really done so. Chastened, we subsequently found ways to do as she had suggested. Kellerman's question indicted me personally, for I had neglected to consider works of the imagination in any systematic way. I needed to inform my aesthetic understanding of leadership as a performance – or what the experts call a dramaturgical approach. Thus began several unrelated efforts in this regard. The following book is a product of these efforts.

Images and stories

Scholars have already addressed the role of images and stories in understanding leadership. I owe a special debt to Bruce Mazlish (1990) and Howard Gardner (1996), respectively, for helping me see this. There is no reason to cite a bunch of equivalent examples.

I too have previously written about the importance of images in understanding leadership (see, e.g. Harter, 2020, ch. 1; 2014, p. 80; 2007, ch. 3). Alongside the more analytical portions of these prior publications, in parallel, I also tried to cite real-world exemplars from history, in part to illustrate what I was writing about but also in part to make the argument more plausible. I wrote for example about Socrates, Clovis I, St. Francis of Assisi, Martin Luther, Abraham Lincoln, Alexander Solzhenitsyn, Jan Patočka, and the twenty-first century U.S. military. In assorted articles, I also took a closer look at Shays Rebellion (Harter & Clark, 2020), Franklin Delano Roosevelt's court-packing scheme (Harter & Downs, 2017), and post-conflict Sierra Leone (Miller & Harter, 2015), not to mention the struggles of William F. Buckley, Jr. to make sense of the Civil Rights era (Harter, 2022).

I find that I keep writing about images and stories, using the imagination as a lens through which to extend and refine my understanding. Periodically, as a classroom instructor, I resort to works of the imagination, including cinema, novels, paintings, music, and stage plays. It is probably no coincidence that like anybody else I am a frequent consumer of the arts and that sometimes I try my hand at writing poetry and fiction – bad poetry, perhaps, but at least I understand the impulse to express myself creatively. You don't have to be a connoisseur to grasp the importance of the imagination in ordinary life.

This capability I am calling the imagination is more than ornamentation, a superfluous feature of the good life, adding a few grace notes during an otherwise humdrum existence. I have been persuaded that human understanding – including the hardest of sciences – absolutely requires the use of the imagination. It does us no good to pretend otherwise. To be sure, works of the imagination also *threaten* our understanding, constructing things that aren't even there, i.e. falsities, fabrications, oversimplifications, and rank delusion. Such threats come with the territory. Better to take them head-on, explicitly, rather than adopt the fiction that we can do without them, as though we can escape to some pure, ethereal realm of intellectual lucidity without having to rely on the imagination.

One phrase that I often use when talking about teaching leadership is "populating the imagination" – by which I mean the process of accumulating images and stories, adding to the storehouse from which we can subsequently draw. If all we possess is a single image of leadership, then we will be like the guy with only a hammer to whom everything is a nail. By enriching the reservoir in this fashion, by populating the imagination, we can subsequently recognize a broader array of leadership and likewise aspire to our own unique version. A heavily populated imagination opens us up to greater variety and reduces our insistence that there is only one right way to do things. And if I've learned anything about leadership, it is that there is no one right way to lead.

Leadership education includes exposing the student to leaders and episodes of leadership. By the time a student enters the workforce, he or she will have experienced dozens of classroom teachers, several athletic coaches and band directors, a handful of summer employers, club presidents, parish priests – in addition to parental figures. He or she will have watched hundreds of television shows and films and will have read about leaders in books and articles. The formal study of leadership very likely included a range of historical figures, from Moses to Margaret Thatcher – many of them saints and heroes, with a genius or two thrown in among them. Education has traditionally provided introductions to eminent persons, whether apocryphal anecdotes, like little George Washington chopping down the cherry tree, or full-scale analysis, using complex theories to make nuanced assessments. At the very least, it helps when teaching a lesson to give concrete examples. "Do you want to understand X from the syllabus? Let us watch somebody who actually did X."

As Barbara Kellerman (2004) astutely noted, sometimes you have to populate the imagination with counterexamples, i.e. bad leaders, those who fail for one reason or another. We learn as much from their example as from those who succeed. Ultimately, of course, the highest form of such biographical study is recognizing the duality in each leader, the good and the bad, the strengths and the weaknesses, accepting that every single leader is a complex – as each one of us is. A leader such as Mao Zedong has left an ambiguous legacy. Rare are the paragons who always wore the white hat. Nobody is perfect. The most responsible posture for any student is to see both sides of the ledger, doling out praise and blame parsimoniously, as the evidence warrants.

Let me take this one step further. The imagination is populated by more than individual human beings, like characters in a drama. We can imitate what clothing others choose to wear, a facial expression, a gesture, a cadence, a tone of voice. We notice even fragments of a moment. It might be subtle and fleeting, not even conscious, yet we notice and remember. Later, we might draw from this storehouse of disembodied features, techniques, and other choices. We associate a particular automobile or entrée at dinner or fabric such as silk with a life of success. We certainly pick up phrases and cusswords liberally from our surroundings. Our own choices in life originate from all of the snippets and samples to which we shall have been exposed. It follows logically that presuming to lead means that you are projecting yourself onto the imagination of others, and this includes whether you habitually laugh at your own jokes, for example, or mow your own lawn. Everything you do is fair game. As we live our lives, we are all populating one another's imagination, in large ways and small. Leadership is simply a more elaborate (and predominately intentional) attempt to do so.

Imagination plays a central role in a number of leader **traits**, such as empathy, in which you can imagine what another person might be going through, as well as playing a role in a number of typical leader **behaviors**, such as conducting games of strategy, in which you anticipate what the other side is going to do. Also, imagination plays a central role in more than one leader **task**, such as adapting to unforeseen challenges (i.e. creativity) – let alone the task of foreseeing challenges to begin with. Persuasion is another leader task, in which you must anticipate the arguments and reasons the other person will find compelling.[2] Leaders must resort to their imaginations in order to function effectively.

Russell Kirk, paying a debt to Edmund Burke (1981), once wrote of three forms of the imagination – namely the **moral** imagination, the **idyllic** imagination, and the **diabolic** imagination. The moral imagination portrays human nature as it is. The idyllic imagination portrays human nature only as we might like for it to be. Diabolic imagination revels in the subhuman, the less-than-human, the bestial nature that resorts heedlessly to cruelty, violence, and gratification. Kirk was arguing that all three forms of the imagination would pertain as well to leadership ethics.

Not just leaders, but followers as well use their imaginations. Leaders sometimes use the followers' imaginations against them. Michel Foucault found the notion of Jeremy Bentham's Panopticon to be a mechanism for social control, whereby those in authority implant in the occupants the fear that they are

2 Television producer Fred Friendly observed two successive U.S. presidents up close, Eisenhower and Kennedy. He admired their scrupulous attention to maintaining their public image as a key attribute of a successful politician (1968, p. 146).

continuously being "surveilled" by faceless warders (Elden, 2017, p. 152f). Here, the leader instills into the imagination of subordinates the murky possibility that they are always being watched...and for them to behave accordingly, whether in fact there is anybody staffing the observation posts or not. This idea of the Panopticon is a version of admonitions to children that God (or Santa Claus) sees all, i.e. to raise the specter of constant scrutiny, which H.G. Wells so adroitly depicted in his novel *1984* and which security forces such as the Stasi and the KGB (Committee for State Security of the Soviet Union) perfected in the Soviet Union (see, e.g. Scott & Flagg Taylor, 2014). This intimidating form of "impression management" is another way that leaders exploit the imagination of the follower.

As a student of leadership, I am more than a consumer of images and stories. I pass them along to other people through my lectures and published articles. Scholars, no less than leaders, traffic in them. This is not to suggest that a well-told tale is enough. There must be room for analysis, the sober logic of cause-and-effect. Nothing I am saying here is intended to disparage or ignore the importance of data, reasoning, and abstract theory. The imagination is only one of several necessary faculties. Still, let's be honest: even Euclid's geometry is beautiful.[3] It just seems imperative to make sure that leadership scholars give the imagination its due.[4]

The literary critic Walter Benjamin (1963) once offered a distinction between the local storyteller who remembers the lore of one place and the wayfarer who tells of adventure from other places. Each brings something of value from a distance, whether distant in time or distant in space. Their tales feed a desire in all of us to become part of a larger narrative – offering context, to be sure, so that we have a greater sense of where we come from and what lies beyond the far horizon. Maybe more importantly, however, they can be said to fuel the imagination, enriching what seems possible tomorrow.

The following might sound like an extravagant claim, but in my estimation, every episode of leadership begins in the imagination. Let me say that again: *every episode of leadership begins in the imagination.* And the study of leadership consists of these stories. Nobody leads who doesn't believe that we can do better, if only we take our dreams, rise up, and enact them. Leadership is less about the gross execution of a plan and more about opening ourselves to the future, seeing what happens, being a part of the pageant. I would go so far as to suggest that we are at our best *living* the stories our grandchildren will want to

3 For a colorful examination of the origins of geometry, grounded in the imagination, see Serres, 1995/2018.

4 James March (2014) made the case in a colorful video for the Stanford Graduate School of Business, titled *Passion and Discipline: Don Quixote's Lessons for Leadership*. For an extended treatment of his work on the intersection of leadership and the imagination, see March and Weil, 2005.

hear.[5] In this sense, therefore, every society must gather everybody around the campfire to hear edifying tales.

In 2018, John von Heyking published a book on the politics of Winston Churchill, where he made the argument that for Churchill (and others, going back to Aristotle), politics is in essence living together *as a story* and sharing stories with one another. Doing great things is not enough; one must then give an account, for this is the "mode by which political actors explain and judge political action… (p. 165)." We go out in the world to have our adventures, then sit around afterwards talking about them. This for example was a function of King Arthur's fabled Round Table, where knights listened to one another spin their yarns.

Politics occupies a space between the concrete fact (science) and abstract principle (philosophy). No matter what else the political leader pursues, foremost he or she seeks to live a life consisting of uplifting exploits (von Heyking, 2018, pp. 165169). John Keegan wrote that "Churchill the war leader was literature in action (2002, p. 16)." Looking forward, then, we can say that one version of a story inspires a leader to act (vision); whereas looking backward, another version completes that action. At its best, it is a story in which others fully participate, a story that we enact in concert and then recount afterwards. Citing Hannah Arendt, Thomas Mann, and Eric Voegelin (among others), von Heyking writes that leadership is fundamentally a story-producing activity (2018, p. 168f). Even the rituals we observe, such as laying a wreath on the tomb of the unknown soldier, dramatize something about us collectively (2018, p. 88).[6] Images and stories go to the meaning of things.

I have been anticipated in drawing attention to the importance of using the imagination to lead and to teach leadership. The idea is not original with me. Let me acknowledge, for example, a recent article by Nikolaos Raptis et al. (2021) titled "Imaginative Leadership: Imagination as a Central Characteristic of Effective Leadership" in the *International Journal of Educational Organization and Leadership*. The authors assert that "all types of leadership possess or involve imagination… (p. 84)." Indeed, they go one step further to refer to "the centrality of imagination, as a characteristic of effective leadership… (p. 85)." Yet they call for more scholarship to bring that fact to the forefront, and I am happy to oblige.

Raptis et al. begin their article by acknowledging the importance of the imagination to human thinking generally. Then, they emphasize two functions in

5 In the same spirit, Carol Pearson (2021) has written about leadership as the enactment of a plot originating in our imagination. She then identifies 12 archetypes that leaders enact, such as warrior, lover, and magician.

6 Foucault examined the role of ritual executions in another era, known as *supplice*, as an exhibition of sovereignty that is no longer practiced – probably for the best. The exhibition of cruel authority "must be stunning, spectacular or explosive (Elden, 2017, p. 144)." Foucault famously offered a gruesome example in the opening pages of *Discipline and Punish* (1977).

particular that we often associate with effective leadership. One of these functions is visioning, when the leader provides purpose and meaning (2021, p. 86). One must be able to imagine and help others imagine a desired future state, even an ideal (2021, p. 87). The key word here is possibility. Leadership originates from the capacity to imagine multiple possibilities. The other function they emphasize is empathy, which involves adopting the perspective of the other person (2021, p. 88). An effective leader must be able to appreciate how other people feel. Together, these functions explain that what they are calling imaginative leadership is, in their words, "a type of leadership that focuses on human possibility… (2021, p. 92)."

In 2022, Kelli Pearson published her own account of "imaginative leadership" as a book chapter in *Co-Creativity and Engaged Scholarship* (Palgrave Macmillan). She defines this type of leadership as "the ability to understand and consciously influence the symbolic/metaphorical dimensions of self and others that are linked to specific values, mindsets, worldviews (p. 167)." In a subsequent passage, she tries again: "the ability to influence, evoke, or shape the mental models, metaphors, and cultural narratives that people… use to make sense of the world (p. 176)." She agrees that one facet of imaginative leadership would be envisioning scenarios, both what *could* happen and what *should* happen (p. 174), so in this respect she aligns nicely with Raptis, Mousena, and Kouroutsidou. She then highlights the function of *altering the imagination of others*. That is to say, not only the leader herself is imaginative, but she also influences the imagination of others. This activity is a different – and no less significant – function of leadership.

Limitations

I just admitted in the previous section that reliance on images and stories can be risky. Scholarship has to mean more. Before working through a series of studies about imagining leadership, it is incumbent on me to acknowledge some of these limitations. Like any good teacher, I give with one hand and take with the other, placing ultimate responsibility on the reader/student to live with the uncertainty – an uncertainty that, from my vantage point, seems inescapable.

Perhaps the place to begin is with the humble realization that images and stories serve as surface representations of a far more complicated depth. As I have had reason to mention in prior publications (Harter, 2020, ch. 1), José Ortega y Gasset first examined a simple schema of surface and depth in his *Meditations on Quixote* (1914/1961). Part of the utility in images and stories is that they omit a lot of distracting detail. One does not have to know literally everything, such as where the candle sat on the mantle and how long the bologna sat in the fridge. An image or story is a distillation, a product of selectivity. And it may be that something omitted turns out to have been crucial. At the very least, indulging in images and stories leaves the (false) impression that there is nothing more. There is no forest … just trees.

Politicians are all too happy brushing a lot of the details under the rug. Nothing to see here. After all, it is one of the most infuriating moments in the life of leadership: when somebody in the back says, "Yes, but…." Part of the merit in systems thinking is the holistic vision of reality, reminding us that everything is connected to everything else. Occasionally, the butterfly effect teaches us that the little things sometimes have big consequences. The words "simplicity" and "simplification" come from the same root, as does the epithet "simpleton." Reality is always more than any one of us can grasp. Images and stories can seem grotesque (or childish) by comparison.

"Yes, well, it's more complicated than that…." And it always is. Always.

An acknowledgment of the depth of reality gives the faint of heart an excuse to do nothing. Presuming to lead in such a bewildering context can be daunting and probably should be. Nevertheless, we require leadership that takes up the sword and shield. This includes the intellectual adventurer, girded for the quest, with a merry song in his heart. Images and stories are akin to language itself in this respect: to make much headway, one must use them despite their imperfections. The attitude that seems to work best is called fallibilism, by which one accepts the possibility of error (see generally, Menand, 2001). Is there more going on than we can possibly solve? Absolutely. That, however, is not an excuse to quit. So yes, the imagination reduces the complexity in order to accommodate our bounded rationality. It is just that we have no choice.

As I understand it, the right hemisphere of the brain generates possible patterns, extending what a person experiences into what might be the case. The imagination takes hints and cues and generates possible explanations. This can be detrimental, of course, especially in neurotics when a person tends to "catastrophize" – that is, to inject the worst possible version of things, as though it were true. You find an ant in the kitchen and immediately conclude that the walls of the house must be infested with them. You begin a road trip, wondering if you'll get into a car wreck on the highway. You get rejected by someone on a date and go home convinced that you are unlovable, forever doomed to loneliness, found dead in your apartment one day surrounded by starving cats. And so, with this tendency to imagine the worst, the brain starts to "read into" things, wondering what a simple fact might signify. The brain gets ahead of itself, in other words, leaping to worst-case scenarios. In short, the imagination can convince you about *what might go wrong*, even if that outcome is unlikely.

To be sure, part of the leadership advantage of depressives is that they tend to be more realistic about reality; they have shed the unreasonable optimism most humans feel (e.g. Ghaemi, 2011). A Winston Churchill could penetrate to the threat that was Hitler because he was able to foresee the nightmare that was to come, whereas his fellow politicians dismissed these alarms. On occasion, yes, the pattern-seeking part of the brain detects a genuine threat. Part of leadership is anticipating and preparing for these threats. Nevertheless, it is a limitation of using the imagination to generate dire possibilities that have little or no chance of occurring. Leaders cannot afford to be alarmists. How does one guard against possible threats without becoming unduly anxious?

Previously, I have written about the state or condition of liminality, which is that in-between space where it is unclear what's going on (e.g. Harter, 2016, pp. ixxii). Writers have spoken of the *metaxy*, liquid times, permanent whitewater, chaos – the wilderness between Egypt and the Promised Land. I have gone so far as to ask, as a matter of epistemology, whether reality is all liminal and not an interim phase on the way to greater stability. Is stability itself an illusion? If liminality is the forest, the underlying reality, the condition wherein we must live and move and have our being, then maybe we should walk around suspicious of every assertion, every solution, every pose. Maybe images and stories are fundamentally falsifications, coping mechanisms for our bounded rationality, not unlike sheltering habitations carved out of the chaparral. Perhaps even *to think* is to distort reality.

Images and stories are indeed partial or incomplete. To some extent, they are also probably mistaken about one aspect or another, or even false! Sometimes, a good story fudges the data. Sometimes, of course, the image or story is an outright lie.

In addition, an image or story intended to represent an underlying reality might persist long after that underlying reality has changed. That is to say that it might have been accurate and useful once upon a time, but no longer – like an outdated map.

Often, the image or story exists because it would be impossible to get behind it and comprehend the reality on which it is based. It had to be reduced to an image or story because the truth is just too much to handle, e.g. too strange, too wonderful, too overwhelming. In those instances, the image might be all you get. I am reminded of the lawyer asking the Rabbi, who is my neighbor? Rather than provide a cogent and succinct definition, Jesus told a parable instead, and "The Good Samaritan" had to suffice. The story said more than any treatise could.

Human beings are pattern-seeking creatures, rewarded for recognizing them. Part of learning is taking some pattern and using it to overlay an unfamiliar situation. We see this happen often, even with rudimentary arithmetic and reading. Parents rejoice once the infant connects certain sounds with various objects in the room, beginning (let us all hope) with "mama." Patterns are good to detect. But then, no two sonnets are alike, except for the abstract form, such as 14 lines of iambic pentameter. Quartets and sonatas, portraits and plinths, classical versus baroque – the arts frolic among patterns. My wife and daughter can devote hours to mixing and matching colors and design when they shop for clothes. In my field of study, we do much the same thing, scrounging around among all of the real-world activities, seeking patterns that work, patterns that fit, patterns we can possibly replicate. Students look to us for credible patterns. At the most abstract level, therefore, the human mind can find patterns across domains. This was in part the genius of Leonardo da Vinci, to see these patterns in disparate things. I admire Michel Serres for doing the same thing (see generally Watkin, 2020). But be careful, though: just because you see a lamb in the cloud formation up in the sky does not mean there is one. We are so wont to detect patterns that we find them where they don't exist.

This capacity to imagine realities that do not in fact exist led Eric Voegelin to caution his reader not to replace reality with these second-order narratives (1990, ch. 3). One must still account for the world as it is and work with the processes by which it operates. The goal is not to escape reality but to find one's way through it. Fantasy and fiction have their place (Voegelin was an avid reader of detective novels); but leadership still occurs in paramount reality, where people struggle, strive, and suffer. Leadership detached from mundane existence never ends well.

Human understanding relies on a vast and hidden web of knowledge that Michael Polanyi referred to as tacit (2009). Over the course of our lives, we accumulate information, impressions, and ideas and constellate them as best we can, piecemeal, sometimes almost haphazardly. We adopt little schemas about this and that, implicit theories about people, places, and things and how the world works. These chunks of knowledge accumulate and gather in a part of our mind that does not require full consciousness. In fact, we learn how to take things for granted, operating as though it were so, without further scrutiny. They operate in the background. We discover later that we were mistaken about some of these things, of course, and it is only rarely that we bother to integrate these little schemas into anything larger and comprehending, trying to make sense of the whole. Whatever the origin of this tacit knowledge, whether from personal experience directly or second hand, it impinges on decision-making unless and until the world gives us reason to question any of it. And even then, we may be reluctant to revisit what we already took for granted, accepting as true what the evidence would cast into doubt.

This web of tacit knowledge includes a lot of images and stories that turn out to be mistaken, or partial, or misleading, or inapplicable to the situation at hand. They may not fit together into a coherent whole. Nevertheless, we go about our business oblivious to the inadequacies of our own knowledge, and in this way, we cling to works of the imagination without taking any further responsibility. We just know things, you see, even when they are not so. The same applies both to students of leadership and to practitioners.

This entire book must be read with such caveats in mind.

Structure of this book

The following studies are distinct, conceptually separable. Each one began as a unique investigation. Only later was I able to constellate them in what I hope will be a coherent framework. For this reason, together they do not constitute a seamless argument, with one part building upon another. Nevertheless, there is indeed a forest behind these discrete trees, which it is now my purpose to describe briefly.

The best way to structure this material is by a series of distinctions, beginning with the difference between images (on the one hand) and stories (on the other), one of them static and the other dynamic. This book treats them as different species of the same genus. That is one distinction I wish to make. Here is another. There is often a distinction made between studying leadership and practicing leadership, although in these pages, I group them together, inasmuch as many of the same observations apply to each. Nevertheless, I am writing predominantly to students of leadership. Another distinction of particular relevance to investigations regarding the imagination is between looking at something from the outside-in, which I call the exterior perspective, and from the inside-out, which I call the interior perspective. More on this distinction later.

The next chapter takes up the idea that images and stories of various kinds turn out to be integral to science, as dogma, hypotheses, and fictions. Relying on the work of Hans Vaihinger, I try to make the case that we cannot understand leadership without them. In the second chapter after this one, I examine the importance of playfulness, as a central feature of culture. The trick is finding the right balance in life, preserving a spirit of playfulness into adulthood, in even the most serious activities, which I discuss in terms of a cult film by George Romero titled *Knightriders*. *Knightriders* is a story about leadership, where the "king" of a little traveling troupe must contend with various challenges. Together, these first two chapters highlight the importance of the imagination to both science and culture.

In Leadership Studies, we are interested in the images we possess of one another. As followers, how do we imagine leaders? And how do they imagine their followers? What they imagine about other people influences how they treat them. But each of us also imagines ourselves. We walk around with a self-image. And we base many of our decisions on these images. In leader development, the person going through maturation not only possesses a self-image, he or she also gradually develops an image of a future self, as a leader. The student learns over time to approximate some ideal, so it matters a great deal how they craft this image. The term I use for this image of a future self as leader is the *imago*. Thus, the imagination influences how people regard one another as well as themselves. I devote a chapter of this book to that topic.

People also possess images of their collectivities, the groups to which they belong, for example, the community or nation. Charles Taylor called these representations "social imaginaries" (2007). These images influence many leadership decisions. How do we imagine ourselves, together? Are we the good guys? Do we enjoy a particular status? Going one step further, leaders possess an image of what the collectivity *can become*, the future ideal state we are trying to reach together. In the literature, we call that vision. Visioning is an essential leader task. So, there is on the one hand the descriptive imagery of who we are and, on the other hand, the prescriptive vision. How a person imagines these things will influence the decisions he or she makes today. In a chapter about these social imaginaries, I describe an image that, in my opinion, promises to enrich our conversations about life together, and that is the labyrinth, where we can identify at least three distinct roles for leaders: those who construct the labyrinth (the artifex), those who demonstrate how to make it through the labyrinth successfully (the exemplar), and those who accompany the follower along the pathways, offering words of encouragement (the guide). Each of these three is a different leadership function.

The imagination informs who we are as individuals and in collectivities. It also informs the dynamics by which we function. Over 100 years ago, Gabriel de Tarde tried to establish the field of sociology upon the simple operation we call imitation. He wrote that everything we call society is comprised of imitation, including paradoxically innovation and opposition. We consult one another for the simplest things. That is (to use a phrase I introduced previously), we populate one another's imaginations, constantly glancing sideways to see what others are doing. I think that Tarde made a strong case, which it will be my purpose later to summarize. Leaders need to operate with some kind of image of how to bring about change. Tarde offered one possibility when he wrote about imitation. And imitation involves the imagination.

Leadership takes place within different kinds of boundaries. These boundaries become increasingly important to successful leadership, where leaders resist incursions, yet welcome innovation, even venturing beyond the ordinary, now and then, in a never-ending search. In a previous book, I argued that leadership can be "imagined" as an operation of bringing something of value into a circle or enclosure, literally influencing one's community by managing the boundary that defines it – defending its identity while at the same time infusing it regularly with ideas and meaning borrowed from outside the circle (Harter, 2020). Leaders go out and return, like a deer hunter who ventured into the forest and returned with bounty for his neighbors. He or she is literally extraordinary, which according to Sverre Spoelstra (2018) means beyond the ordinary, i.e. beyond the prevailing order everybody else knows. This management of the boundary, literal and conceptual, resisting adulteration and admitting wholesome novelty, can be depicted using humble symbols. For our purposes, in the penultimate chapter, I adopt the imagery of the hazel and the hawthorn, two wild plants believed in Celtic lore to manage the border, the threshold, the fence line between two worlds – only one side of which we know well: that which is "ours."

The final chapter opens out onto a broad and conceptually daunting field of possibilities. Modern history routinely provides theatrical exhibitions of authority, in such venues as judicial trials and investigative hearings. The examples in the final chapter will be drawn primarily from recent United States history, even though the same principles should apply elsewhere, wherever communities gather information (such as evidence) in order to make collective decisions. On such occasions, one finds a drama in manifestations of power, even at the most intimate level; yet the final chapter introduces examples that were truly consequential, largely because the interest in these proceedings had become widespread. People wanted to know what was happening. In fact, such widespread interest shaped the sensibilities of the participants, in full awareness that the world was watching. In these tense confrontations, in forms of communal deliberation, where does leadership lie? And what might be required of participants and audience alike, if not courage? For courage as a virtue presupposes an imagined risk, a capability of foreseeing possible harm. A leader proceeds knowing the risk, for the sake of something higher – even if it means possible ruin. At the center of this concluding chapter will be an account of the exemplary broadcast journalism of Edward R. Murrow and his response to McCarthyism.

As I said, these are separable studies, each one of which promises to contribute to one's understanding of leadership. Nevertheless, they conform to a larger, comprehending framework that it will have been my mission to elaborate. First, I address the relevance of the imagination to both science and culture. Second, I argue that images we possess of ourselves as individuals and as collectivities shape the decisions that we make going forward. Third, I use the imagination to depict the dynamics by which leadership operates, both by means of imitation and by means of managing boundaries. Fourth, I conclude by examining leadership as theatrics by writing about civic ceremonies such as televised congressional hearings.

Nothing written in these pages is conclusive. In fact, the opposite is the case. I am hoping that the reader finds reason to conduct their own studies, populating the imagination of students and scholars in our mutual efforts to understand this phenomenon we call leadership.

Concluding thoughts

The study of leadership can be conducted using multiple methods, from within multiple academic disciplines, at multiple magnitudes, and from multiple perspectives. Rather than set out to negate existing arguments in the literature, my purpose is (in imitation of Michel Serres) to generate a smorgasbord of alternative possibilities (Watkin, 2020). I do not seek to negate what somebody else has written about leadership, except when they claim to be in sole possession of the truth. Everybody operates by relying in part on the imagination, yet the thing about the imagination is that the same reality can be imagined in multiple ways. It will have been my purpose in these pages to illustrate what I mean by that.

Serres explained that reality is a multiplicity comprised of multiplicities *ad infinitum*. We experience our bewildering reality by means of unities that we imagine. We have to. "This is a tennis ball. That is a doughnut. We are a team." Nevertheless, at some point, it is imperative to question the unities we experience and see behind them to the multiplicities of which they are comprised and to the encompassing multiplicities of which they are a part, if for no other reason than that these unities do change over time. Permanence is an illusion, albeit a necessary illusion that we must occasionally outgrow. We can understand reality only if we engage in using the imagination. But the paramount lesson I hope to impart is this: leadership itself is fundamentally a product of the imagination. It must be. So perhaps it will repay to take a closer look at what this might mean for both students and practitioners.

References

Benjamin, W. (1963, WinterSpring). "The story-teller: Reflections on the works of Nicolai Leskov." *Chicago Review*. *16*(1): 80–101.

Elden, S. (2017). *Foucault: The birth of power*. Polity.

Foucault, M. (1977). *Discipline and punish: The birth of the prison* (A. Sheridan, trans.). Pantheon Books.

Gardner, H. (1996). "Leadership: A cognitive perspective." *SAIS Review*. *16*(2): 109–122.

Gardner, H., & E. Laskin. (2011). *Leading minds: An anatomy of leadership*. Basic Books.

Ghaemi, N. (2011). *A first-rate madness: Uncovering the links between leadership and mental illness*. Penguin.

Harter, N. (2022). *Cultural dynamics and leadership: An interpretive approach*. Cambridge University Press.

Harter, N. (2020). *Leadership across boundaries: A passage to aporia*. Routledge.

Harter, N. (2016). *Foucault on leadership*. Routledge.

Harter, N. (2014). *Leadership and coherence: A cognitive approach*. Routledge.

Harter, N. (2007). *Clearings in the forest*. Purdue University Press.

Harter, N., & C. Clark. "Eric Voegelin on the seemliness of symbols: Shays' Rebellion." In K. Bezio & G. Goethals (eds.). (2020). *Leadership, populism and resistance*. Edward Elgar.

Harter, N., & D. Downs. (2017, Winter). "FDR, presencing, and the Court-Packing Plan of 1937." *International Leadership Journal*. *9*(1): 56–70.

Keegan, J. (2002). *Winston Churchill: A Penguin life*. Viking Book.

Kellerman, B. (2004). *Bad leadership: What it is, how it happens, why it matters*. Harvard Business Press.

Kirk, R. (1981). "The moral imagination." *Literature and Belief*. *1*(1): 37–49.

March, J. (2014). *Passion and discipline: Don Quixote's lessons for leadership.* Stanford Graduate School of Business. Retrieved 3 June 2021 at https://www.youtube.com/watch?v=NYmbiv_cbn8.

March, J., & T. Weil. (2005). *On leadership*. Blackwell.

Mazlish, B. (1990). *The leader, the led, and the psyche*. Wesleyan University Press.

Menand, L. (2001). *The metaphysical club: A story of ideas in America*. Farrar, Straus, Giroux.

Miller, W.M., & N. Harter. (2015). "Liminality and chieftaincy leadership: Transitioning leadership in postconflict Sierra Leone." *International Leadership Journal. 7*(1): 3–22.

Ortega y Gasset, J. (1914/1961). *Meditations on Quixote* (E. Rugg & D. Marin, trans.). University of Illinois Press.

Pearson, C. (2021). "The power of leadership narrative intelligence." *ILA Intersections*. Retrieved 1 July 2021 from https://intersections.ilamembers.org/member-benefit-access/interface/field-reports/2021-the-power-of-leadership-narrative-intelligence.

Pearson, K. "Imaginative leadership: A conceptual frame for the design and facilitation of creative methods and generative engagement." In Franklin, A. (ed.). (2022). *Co-creativity and engaged scholarship: Transformative methods in social sustainability research* (ch. 6). Palgrave Macmillan.

Polanyi, M. (2009). *The tacit dimension*. University of Chicago press.

Raptis, N., E. Mousena, & M. Kouroutsidou. (2021). "Imaginative leadership: Imagination as a central characteristic of effective leadership." *International Journal of Educational Organization and Leadership. 28*(2): 83–96.

Scott, C.E. & F.F. Flagg Taylor, IV (eds.). (2014). *Totalitarianism on screen: The art and politics of "The Lives of Others."* University Press of Kentucky.

Spoelstra, S. (2018). *Leadership and organization: A philosophical introduction*. Routledge.

Taylor, C. (2007). *Modern social imaginaries*. Duke University Press.

Voegelin, E. "The eclipse of reality." In Voegelin, E. (1990). *Collected works* (T. Hollweck & P. Caringella, eds.) (vol. 28, ch. 3). Louisiana State University Press.

von Heyking, J. (2018). *Comprehensive judgment and absolute selflessness: Winston Churchill on politics as friendship.* St. Augustine Press.

Watkin, C. (2020). *Michel Serres: Figures of thought*. Edinburgh University Press.

2

FICTIONS IN THE STUDY OF LEADERSHIP

Applying the philosophy of "as if"

Introduction

Tough-minded investigators might squirm at the suggestion that part of Leadership Studies relies on works of the imagination. They might regard anything "imagined" as false by definition and beyond the pale of credible science. The imagination itself promises to be a difficult terrain to domesticate, full as it is with chimeras. How precisely is a conscientious investigator to observe and measure what happens there? Worse, it defies quantification. The imagination would seem to occupy a private space, inaccessible to third parties and necessarily outside the field of common sense, no more reliable for purposes of research than one's evanescent dreaming.

Scholars and educators must take these reservations seriously. Nevertheless, there seems to be no escape from the importance of the imagination in both the study and practice of leadership. Human beings are imagining creatures, and it will be my contention throughout this book that images and stories play an integral role in anything we hope to understand as leadership. Fortunately, we have access to a few academic disciplines dedicated to archetypal psychology, mythology, and the arts – not to mention sober accounts of madness, dreams, and drug-induced consciousness replete with figments of the imagination. Kenneth Boulding, an economist of renown, once published a short book (1961) urging the disciplines to come together in order to discuss the importance of images in their scholarly work. I concur.

Doing so would not require drawing the conclusion that there is nothing for us but imaginary constructs and that we have no access to something we might refer to as paramount reality. Taking the imagination seriously does not have

DOI: 10.4324/9781003374831-2

to commit us to a radical, postmodern turn that denies common sense. It might seem condescending to say that clearly reality includes the human experience and that the human experience includes the imagination, whatever it might mean for our shared understanding. The following study takes a look at an early attempt to fit the imagination into the practice of science especially. We are not required to adopt everything that Hans Vaihinger asserted a hundred years ago for us to recognize that he had something of value to say. This chapter is best understood as an exercise, asking the reader to consider the integral role played by the imagination in science itself.

Vaihinger is translated from the German as using the term "fiction" to cover an array of imaginary constructs, ranging from abstract models (such as charts and graphs) to bald-faced lies. He conceded that there are many other terms that could serve a similar function in his philosophy,[1] so it would be useful to read him in the spirit he intended. He was not denying reality. He was not denying that we can know reality. He was not questioning science. He was simply hoping to examine the role that the imagination plays in doing science properly.

Hans Vaihinger

To the extent that Leadership Studies aspires to becoming scientific, scholars will adopt some version of the scientific method in order to determine what is true about leadership. Every step in that direction presumably liberates them as a field of study from intuition, fables, myth, self-serving memoir, and guesswork, not to mention findings obtained by trial-and-error and the proverbial school of hard knocks. Using the conventions of proving some hypothesis or other, scholars believe that they are drawing closer to knowledge and away from illusion, cant, and wishful thinking – of which there has been plenty.

The position I wish to take in this chapter is that creditable science is itself replete with fictions and that perhaps leadership is an illusion, albeit a necessary one. The basis for these bold assertions relies primarily on an old book written by Hans Vaihinger (1852–1933), a neglected philosopher whose reputation in the philosophy of science and modeling has in fact been rising of late (see Adair-Toteff, n.d.; Appiah, 2017; Fine, 1993, p. 15f).[2]

Born in 1852 near Tübingen, Vaihinger was, like so many German philosophers, the son of a Lutheran pastor. He completed his dissertation in 1874 and spent a career in academe before going blind, losing all of his investments to

1 The term "fiction" often denotes works of literature, but for our purposes, we shall intend a broader meaning.

2 The edition of Vaihinger's book most readily available in English is a faulty re-formatting of C.K. Ogden's translation from 1925. The original manuscript was published in German back in 1911, although much of it had first been composed some 30 years before.

the Russian Revolution, and burying a daughter due to suicide in 1918. He died in 1933 (Stoll, 2020). For some time thereafter, his reputation languished, having run afoul of the Nazi regime in the short term and being marginalized ever since by the very movement he had named, i.e. Logical Positivism (Fine, 1993, pp. 2ff).[3] A restoration of his reputation lately is generating new perspectives on the scientific method, with intriguing possibilities for the study of leadership in particular. The last section of this chapter will develop thoughts inspired at the Carus Lectures of 2013 by Kwame Anthony Appiah and subsequently published by the Harvard University Press in 2017, where Appiah set out to bring Vaihinger back to academic respectability.

The philosophy of "As If"

Vaihinger accepted as a premise that rationality is bounded (1911/1925, p. xxvii). Reality as a whole is too complex to understand, which is why human beings need to simplify it (1911/1925, p. 15). One's capacity to simplify a complex reality is an important contribution to evolutionary success, since rational thought is a product of nature's evolution – originally developed to aid in survival. That is to say that rationality serves an evolutionary function.

In the struggle to use rationality, human beings have frequently adopted fictions in order to understand their experience. We think of myths, for example, as immature attempts to understand the world (1911/1925, p. 61f). We also consider the utility of metaphor. A mundane example is saying that the sun rises or sets, when in relationship to the earth the sun is immobile. A person does not refer to the sunrise as a way of making a scientific claim. That is not its purpose. Metaphors of this sort abound because they aid in communication (1911/1925, p. 22; see generally Alvesson & Spicer, 2011). What Vaihinger would assert, however, is that science itself is not only full of fictions, but that *fictions turn out to be an essential element in the practice of science*. That is a much stronger claim.

To begin, then, Vaihinger wrote that "fictions are mental structures [or] thought-structures" (p. 9). These fictions are not only unverifiable (1911/1925, p. xxvi), they contradict reality. They are indeed fictional. And not only do they contradict reality, but they also reveal themselves to be self-contradictory (1911/1925, p. 12). Nevertheless, the fact that they are unverifiable, contradicting reality and even themselves, is part of their value. No doubt, this assertion sounds strange to the modern ear. Even so, it is, in his opinion, a misapprehension of science to think that contradictions disqualify a fiction. He called it a prejudice of the misinformed to believe otherwise (1911/1925, p. 48). *Of course* fictions are contradictory; the best ones are riddled with

3 For a summary of Vaihinger's philosophy, see Stoll, 2020.

them (1911/1925, pp. 35, 73). To expect them to be free of contradiction is to miss their utility. And please notice that for Vaihinger, utility is far more significant than truth. Ultimately, the author put it this way:

> [T]oday scientific thought makes use of the same imaginative faculty that created the primary elements, and conceives other more generalized cases which can be thought of in abstract terms, such as a space with *n*-dimensions.... This device is not only the basis of scientific progress but of the whole practical progress of mankind.
>
> *(1911/1925, p. 40f)*

A fiction is a means to an end (1911/1925, p. 14). It is not an end in itself. To be sure, Vaihinger conceded that not all fictions are equally useful. Some turn out to be bad fictions we are better off without (1911/1925, p. 67). Worse, people sometimes forget or ignore their fictive character and treat them as hypotheses about reality, which they aren't (1911/1925, p. 15); or as absolute truth, through a process of hypostatizing or dogmatizing (1911/1925, pp. 21, 28).[4] A fiction is neither a **hypothesis** about reality nor **dogma**. On the contrary, a fiction is a deviation from reality (1911/1925, pp. 26, 60). In daily usage, though, a fiction can certainly resemble either a hypothesis or dogma, so it is prudent to make the "as if" explicit (1911/1925, p. 71). Vaihinger identified a slew of equivalent terms such as invention, conceit, fantasy, stratagem, contrivance, schema, and shortcut (1911/1925, p. 72f). He also mentioned "conceptual and ideational aids" (1911/1925, p. 131). Also, based upon Kant, "heuristics" (1911/1925, p. 202). Who imagined that scientists were so dependent on the subjunctive mood?

The better fictions in the sciences do invite closer scrutiny (1911/1925, p. 45). That is their job. A fiction aids with understanding in part by enabling critique. He called a fiction of this sort an "expedient" (1911/1925, p. 44). After all, to repeat: it doesn't have to be true to be useful (1911/1925, pp. 17, 74, 79). In other words, people talk and operate "as if" it were true (1911/1925, p. 31). He wrote that a fiction is both imaginary and necessary (1911/1925, p. 171). In many instances down through the ages, many of these fictions have had to be discarded, but it was in the process of discarding these fictions that we learned so much. He called these "fruitful errors" which serve our purposes – better certainly than harmful truths ever could (1911/1925, p. 34). A commentator on Vaihinger named Arthur Fine (1993) called these "eliminative" fictions, like temporary

4 Vaihinger differentiated a fiction from a hypothesis on pages 64–68 and again on 197–199. We judge a hypothesis by its probability; we judge a fiction by its expediency (1911/1925, p. 67; see also p. 198). Thus, one *verifies* a hypothesis and *justifies* a fiction (Fine, 1993, p. 7). When a person treats as real what is merely the mental construct intended to communicate about the real, he commits a fallacy (1911/1925, p. 78; see also pp. 91, 199). To this extent (and probably more), Vaihinger can be labeled as a realist.

placeholders, provisional explanations that one knows to be false, but serviceable until a better explanation comes along. Nevertheless, some fictions remain because they serve an ongoing purpose, such as a kind of shorthand among experts. Fine (1993) called these "instrumentalist" fictions (p. 2).

Arthur Koestler published a book in 1959 titled *The Sleepwalkers* which details the transition from a Ptolemaic vision of the solar system (geocentric) to a Copernican vision (heliocentric) – both of which depended on multiple non-existent epicycles that (so far as we can tell) neither man believed to exist. They had quit expounding on what exists and instead pursued the geometric, a set of fictions. They also relied on other fictions to make their case, and then as the scientific world labored to improve upon their findings, men such as Kepler and Galileo invented their own fictions. Kepler suggested that planets orbit around different non-existent shapes; one planet whirled around a pyramid, another around a cube, and so forth (1959, p. 251). Even by the mid-twentieth century, Koestler asserted that scientists had already given up the notion that at the center of the atom is some lump of matter we call a nucleus (1959, p. 542). We still speak as though there is such a thing, knowing full well that there isn't.

The process by which this happens is not unimportant. At some point (going back to Vaihinger), the eliminative fiction has to yield to scientific understanding (1911/1925, p. 74). Vaihinger wrote, "In a large number of fictions… they are first adopted as hypotheses and the realization of their fictional nature only develops later" (1911/1925, p. 74). They can serve as "points of transition" (1911/1925, p. 75), as for example a taxonomy of types (red buttons, blue buttons, green buttons, and so forth). We use the types in order to sort and organize our experiences, even though with sufficient exposure to reality, we should not have to insist on the boundaries within the taxonomy. Beyond a certain point, we are talking about the concrete objects themselves (1911/1925, p. 89). The classification drops out of our consideration (1911/1925, p. 90). It had served its transitory purpose. Every taxonomy is at heart a fiction.

Vaihinger offered a dynamic model about how fictions become hypotheses which in turn become dogma and (in reverse) how dogma becomes hypotheses, which in turn become fictions. It can go either way.

Fiction → Hypothesis → Dogma

Dogma → Hypothesis → Fiction

Dogma means ideas that are taken for granted as true. We might even say that they constitute common sense. Hypotheses are ideas that might be true. Fictions are most definitely *not* true. He called this process of going one way or the other the Law of Ideational Shifts (1911/1925, pp. 92–99). He even referred to this as "the life-history of an idea" (1911/1925, p. 95).

We have seen this shift or process in Leadership Studies. For instance, the so-called Great Man Theory was apparently dogma for many centuries, until Carlyle (1902) noticed it was actually more of a hypothesis – a hypothesis he was eager to champion. Subsequently, as it turns out, leadership scholars rejected the Great Man Theory as a hypothesis, for sound reasons. Nevertheless, it still helps to explain certain real-world phenomena, so that it survives in ordinary usage even though we know that as a scientific theory it is riddled with contradictions. That example of the Great Man Theory illustrates the process from dogma-to-hypothesis-to-fiction.

Working the other direction, i.e. Fiction → Hypothesis → Dogma, the imagery of systems thinking was adopted to help leadership scholars think about certain dynamics. It is unclear, for example, just how far Margaret Wheatley (1992) was prepared to extend systems thinking beyond offering it as a compelling metaphor. Yet soon enough a number of scholars such as Mary Uhl-Bien et al. (2007) decided to treat it as a hypothesis, which they are in the process of testing, even today. A number of writers, such as Barbara Kellerman (2016) and William Donaldson (2017), have concluded that in fact systems thinking is fundamentally "true," i.e. dogma. Dogma, hypothesis, and fiction – science includes all three.

It might be helpful now to consult Vaihinger for a number of concrete examples of fictions. Vaihinger identified many. For example, in statistics, one speaks of "the mean" – which has no necessary corollary to reality (1911/1925, p. 17). Approximation is another process using a fiction (1911/1925, p. 18). He continued describing a variety of schemas, paradigms, utopias, and types (1911/1925, p. 19). He wrote about the idea of "the simple case" in which the scientist sets forth a wildly abstract scenario that could never possibly exist, such as the three-body problem, the atom (1911/1925, pp. 52f, 161–165, 250f), or the extravagant fiction of supply and demand, as though the universe were nothing but the one commodity (widgets) in a society of rational maximizers (1911/1925, p. 19). Economists know this to be a fiction. It is simply a handy one.

Jurisprudence routinely resorts to fictions, such as "corporations as persons" and the so-called reasonable man (1911/1925, pp. 24–26). He illustrated how this works on the occasion when a purchaser takes delivery of some object that is defective. Vaihinger wrote that "goods not returned to the sender within the proper time are to be regarded *as if* the recipient had definitely authorized and accepted them (1911/1925, p. 26)." Additionally, there is the entire corpus of the criminal law which is built on the fiction that human beings have free will. Otherwise, how could we hold anyone accountable? Free will itself is, in his opinion, a critical fiction under the law (1911/1925, pp. 32–37). In addition, crimes were regarded "as if" committed against the king himself (1911/1925, p. 110; see Elden, 2017, p. 63). They called it the king's peace, even when the flesh-and-blood king took no notice whatsoever of these infractions.

In political thought, Vaihinger named utopian schemas and ideal states such as Plato's as fictions (1911/1925, p. 103). He detected them in Jeremy Bentham's politics (1911/1925, p. 139). But then any thought-experiment can be regarded as fictive (1911/1925, p. 112, n. 1). One thinks for example of John Rawls' "veil of ignorance" (1971). In economics, of course, money itself is a fictive object to be treated "as if" it had real value (1911/1925, p. 119). Otherwise, the system cannot work. Legally, currency is a token, a promise to pay with something concrete such as gold. Vaihinger devoted space to emphasizing Adam Smith's use of fiction, such as the infamous Invisible Hand (1911/1925, pp. 136–139). Matt Ridley has added that market equilibrium of any sort is a fiction (2011, p. 249). In health care, experts frequently speak as though the patient were a solitary being passing through its environment, beset by infection and risk (1911/1925, pp. 142–144). A fiction lies at the center of Kant's ethics, to act *as if* one's action could serve as universal law (1911/1925, p. 216). Another fiction in the realm of ethics is the ideal self toward which one is presumably striving (Appiah, 2014, p. 217, n. 9, quoting William James). Vaihinger's book went on to cite other luminaries who knowingly adopted useful fictions, e.g. Descartes, Pascal, Leibnitz, Kepler, Faraday, and Archimedes.[5]

Vaihinger asserted that Newton knew that gravity is a fiction (1911/1925, p. 27). Hume held that causation is a fiction, albeit an extremely useful one (1911/1925, p. 28). Any ideal is a fiction (1911/1925, p. 36), as is infinity (1911/1925, p. 46f). So also anything we call "the world" (1911/1925, p. 47). If we were honest, we would find that ideas such as "matter" and "force" are fictions (e.g. 1911/1925, pp. 146f, 159). Every object, isolated in the mind for attention – a clock, a hammer, or a chicken – is a fiction, inasmuch as it has been ripped out of context as though it *had no context* (1911/1925, pp. 124, 144f). Vaihinger wrote, "There are no partitions in nature … all our divisions are artificial and … no natural dividing line can be detected (1911/1925, p. 136)." Not only isolated objects, but their properties such as sweetness, redness, and coldness (1911/1925, p. 149) – fictions all. Just to emphasize the breadth of its applicability, Vaihinger mentions "equality" and "permanence" as two additional fictions (1911/1925, p. 259). Any natural law, according to Vaihinger, is what he called a summational fiction based on a series of experiences (1911/1925, p. 160).

At this point, Vaihinger seems to be getting carried away, taking that lamentable postmodern turn away from paramount reality, apparently contending that all of reality is a fiction, such that we all live in a dreamscape that is fundamentally, essentially untrue.

5 Archimedes adopted the fiction of a center of gravity that is obviously impossible. The "center of gravity" for a ring, for instance, exists in the space that is not occupied by the ring, at the center that is in fact empty (1911/1925, p. 166).

Vaihinger would peek behind the fundamental division between (a) reality, which we refer to as nature, and (b) our conceptualizations about reality, whether expressed in terms of science or the arts. The division Vaihinger was trying to portray is grounded in a lie, a fantasy, at so rudimentary level as the zero (in mathematics), equality (in geometry), classification (in science), and even the language of "things." Science is in the same predicament as the arts. These abstractions, which are of such utility to scientists, exist only in the minds of human beings, i.e. the product of an apparatus we call the nervous system. They persist because they work – they work within the larger, encompassing system of thoughts and ideas (otherwise, we would be right to doubt them); but they also work in the struggle with reality. When they cease to work and even jeopardize our lives and everything we love, then the mind has further work to do.

At this point, the reader might wonder to what extent Vaihinger did not take a postmodern turn so much as he accepted an epistemology known as pragmatism. He certainly seems to be at least sympathetic with the tradition popularized by William James, Charles Sanders Peirce, and their confreres (see Menand, 2002).

Experts are not deluded. Educated people know them to be fictions. Mathematics is chock full of them (1911/1925, p. 38f). Just think of perfect circles, negative and imaginary numbers, the square root of 1, or 1 as a product of 1 times 1. How can anything singular be a multiple? In algebra, of course, they use letters as numbers, "as if" they were numbers (1911/1925, p. 110f). These fictions rarely trouble mathematicians. Geometry and the Calculus are basically fictional, as Vaihinger meant the term.[6]

Vaihinger was a noted scholar of Kant's philosophy, whom he credited with much of his training (see generally 1911/1925, pp. 201–235). He cited Kant for the fiction that separates between subject and object (1911/1925, p. 43). Scientists need that distinction, even though it does not work ultimately as a hypothesis about reality. Vaihinger credited Leibnitz with another idea that has considerable applicability to science generally. Science deals with compossibilities, which are multiple possibilities for the same phenomenon (1911/1925, p. 41). One thing might be possible (e.g. that A causes B), but at one and the same time, other things might be possible as well (e.g. that B causes A or that A causes C). Science can tolerate these compossibilities. Just think of light behaving both as particles and as waves; each is compossible. Or think of Schrödinger's cat.

To the uninitiated, a fiction can sound ludicrous or mystical (1911/1925, p. 40). It would be, if it were being used as a hypothesis or as dogma; but in the right hands, it is neither. With an apt appreciation, fictions turn out to enable our transitions from confusion to understanding. More importantly, they help us to function.

6 Vaihinger mentions the fiction that "a circle is an ellipse whose two foci have a distance 0" (1911/1925, p. 42; see 1911/1925, p. 175). By this reasoning, one might wonder to what extent leadership is a process by which two persons's purposes come to have a distance 0.

Finding applications of "As If" to Leadership Studies

Leadership Studies operate or function in the real world as though certain things were true, even when we know them not to be true. The task for scholars appears to be three-fold: recognizing when we are using a fiction, discarding the bad fictions, and generating new ones as they are needed.

If anything in leadership qualifies as a fiction, it is the **aim**, **purpose**, or **objective** toward which groups and organizations are striving. Such an imaginary state of affairs does not yet exist. It is akin to what Vaihinger referred to as an ideal or utopia. Thus, it is a fiction in one sense, even as it possesses causal properties. The same can be said for leader development in which an individual works to become something they are not yet. They are realizing a vision of themselves, an *imago*, as it were, operating in accordance with a useful fiction, an image that is by definition unreal because it hasn't yet come into existence. The problem is that these examples do not quite fit Vaihinger's definition, inasmuch as we would not be taking action if we were to proceed *as if* they were already so. We are doing the exact opposite of his "philosophy of the as if": we are saying that we are taking action because it is *not* so and should (in our opinion) become so. That is a different usage of the term "fiction" than Vaihinger was writing about. The only way these imaginary states fit is when a leader behaves *as if* this vision of the future exists in reality and only needs us to participate in its emergence. In other words, *as if* it were true already in some mystical sense, such that leadership participates in disclosing its existence. It exists in the minds and hearts of the participants, one might say.

Taxonomies of leadership, of which there are many, fall prey to the criticism that they are fictions, inasmuch as they categorize and classify based on types. Types are fictions, wrote Vaihinger. And yet taxonomies serve a purpose, even when we recognize that some leaders fall into more than one category (both/and) or into none at all (neither/nor). To classify is to render a useful fiction. It is not necessarily wrong to do so, even when the lines get blurry. A fairly typical such taxonomy appears in the so-called Managerial Grid (Blake & Mouton, 1964).

But then, the same thing could be said about subsequent theories, such as Trait Theory, Situational Theory, Path-Goal, and so forth. The trick would be sorting which of these are in fact hypotheses (and therefore something different) and which are fictions. It is certainly the case that sometimes a *failed* hypothesis persists as a fiction, such that people say that they are fully aware of its contradictions, yet it serves a purpose of some kind to keep referring back to it. The test of its value, once again, is not its truth value.

Consider one's implicit leadership theory (or ILT), which is by definition implicit, unexamined, something of a proto-theory (Schyns & Meindl, 2005). It emerged over time in response to a variety of demands, from infancy onward, gradually becoming fleshed out and smooth; yet after a certain point, it proves to be inadequate in actual practice. It is incomplete, confusing, mistaken, or limited in some fashion. If one's ILT were in any sense correct, then there would be no purpose for Leadership Studies. Let us conceive of an ILT therefore as a coarse construct, something to build on or replace with a better alternative. Except that as an educator, my job is not to tear it down and install in its place knowledge of what is real, i.e. the **truth** about leadership. Vaihinger would not have it so. I am not in the business of dismantling fictions altogether. In fact, I am not even in the business of providing a more sophisticated and useful fiction for students to adopt. It goes a step further than that. My job is to expose the entire charade so that students can become shrewd consumers of fiction. I am not having them trade one model for a better model. I am urging them to become the master of their own illusions, and this process begins with recognizing that these are indeed what they are. Once a leader comes to recognize that beliefs (beliefs about what is true and good, etc.) serve as a *scaffolding* for leadership, then the real work can begin.

It is not my purpose to make the obvious claim that leaders and followers use fictions in their dealings with one another. It could be the benign fictions of etiquette and play-acting (a la Goffman, 1978), in which the participants share in the ruse, or it could be outright fabrications to deceive one another (a la Machiavelli). These are instrumental uses of fiction for the purpose of enacting leadership. Instead, I am emphasizing the role of fictions in trying to understand leadership as a phenomenon, the fictions that scholars adopt for the sake of analysis.

We know that leadership involves more than the individual we call the leader. That is why Leadership Studies started to examine the relationship between the leader and led (Harter, 2007). This approach proved to be an advance on more leader-centric models; yet once again the leader–follower (or leader–member) construct proved to be a fiction – useful though it might be – not unlike the relationship of subject and object in Kant or the atom or "the simple case" that Vaihinger was talking about. Any relationship is an abstraction from a far more complex reality, but we can isolate relationships for formal study and "bracket" the rest of reality for the sake of investigation (for social relationships, see, e.g. Simmel, 1971).

Perhaps the obvious thing should not go unsaid. One has to wonder to what extent the whole idea of leadership is a fiction. Given the complexity of social dynamics, with myriad strands of influence – especially if, as Vaihinger claims, causation itself is a fiction – maybe the attempt to isolate somebody as the leader is a convenient fiction, an expedient. We speak *as if* leadership occurs. As conscientious scholars, we recognize that more is going on in any specific context, but we choose the fiction because it seems to make a wholesome difference.[7] In addition to the possibility that leadership is a fiction, we should notice that to the extent that leadership presupposes free will, Vaihinger would posit that it is based on a fiction. This is not to say that we would be wrong to analyze social dynamics in terms of leadership, any more than astrophysicists are wrong to plan interstellar probes based upon the fiction of gravity. Nevertheless, we must resist the temptation to hold these fictions either as hypotheses or dogma.

Supposing leadership itself to be a fiction, full of contradictions yet useful (if not necessary), what then of the field within which leadership takes place? That is to say, what is culture, if not the storehouse and development of fictions – an entire network or web of fictions by which humanity contends against the uncertainties of nature (Vaihinger, 1911/1925, p. 255)? Many voices have declared the split between nature, on the one hand, and culture, on the other. And in a sense, that distinction would resonate with the philosophy of "as if," inasmuch as Vaihinger wrote of the mind's creative function when it invents thoughts and ideas about reality in order to aid human beings in their evolutionary struggles, even when those thoughts and ideas (and logic itself) prove to be a falsification, illusory. In other words, consciousness represents a break with reality, an opportunity in order for human beings to turn around and ponder reality.

Leadership, like so many things, is an artifice that serves the imperative to live. Otherwise, good riddance … or what's the point?

Thoughts inspired by Kwame Anthony Appiah

In 2017, Kwame Anthony Appiah published his own book on the philosophy of "as if" where he claims that an understanding of fictions "matters in all the major areas of the humanities and the sciences and in every life (2017, p. x)." The reason is that "sometimes, in thinking about the world, truth isn't what you need" (2017, p. xii). He summarizes Vaihinger thus: "Very often we can reasonably proceed as if what we know to be false is true *because it is useful for some purpose to do so*" (2017, p. 3). In fact, he writes, "treating a thought as if it were true is treating it as if it were true for some purpose and some contexts" (2017, p. 16). Regardless, however, that purpose is not to lie or misrepresent or deceive anyone (2017, p. 4). The philosophy of "as if" was never intended to mislead. In some instances, the fiction helps one to manage a complex reality, as a kind of convenient shorthand. In other instances, it forms an ideal toward which one

7 Sergio Tonkonoff (2017) explores a tradition in sociology credited to Gabriel de Tarde, Gilles Deleuze, and Michel Foucault about accepting the multiplicity of variables and the infinitesimally subtle dynamics that take place every day to shape society, as a myriad of streams going in a bewildering array of directions, with varying intensities, in a totally uncoordinated fashion, such that thinking one can isolate leadership as a distinct object of study would be practically impossible.

might travel. It might serve to explain functions as though they were designed by some creator, even when we know that is not the case. Children readily adopt fictions when they play make-believe (2017, p. 106). Often, when creating and using a model of reality, such as a theory of leadership, it does no harm to omit elements of reality that turn out to be causally irrelevant (2017, p. 55), with the result that the model is found to be useful despite ignoring parts of reality.

Things get interesting when Appiah introduces lessons from Frank Ramsey (2017, ch. 2), a precocious philosopher who died tragically at 26 years of age. Ramsey had pointed out that it was naïve to think that belief led to action, when in fact an entire web of beliefs contributed to the likelihood of action (2017, p. 63). Rarely is human action driven by a single motive. And we cannot state with confidence that belief (no matter how many of them, in fact) literally *causes* action, like one domino knocking into the next. Instead, we must understand human behavior more probabilistically. Persons with such-and-such beliefs tend to take such-and-such actions – all other things being equal. Whatever it looks like for an individual human being, this "web of beliefs" includes many beliefs that are simply incompatible with one another (2017, p. 69). It would be unrealistic to presuppose that everything a person believes fits logically with everything else one believes. There will be moments when a social actor feels consciously torn or unconsciously contradicts himself or herself. In short, a web of incoherent beliefs makes certain decisions more likely than not. Thus, predicting what will happen in a single instance becomes risky. Nevertheless, we can make predictions over time, knowing that there will be exceptions and countervailing conditions.

Certain kinds of people, as for example older citizens, might vote a certain way more often than not with a great degree of consistency, but certainly not uniformly as a bloc; some older voters deviate from the pattern. Furthermore, these same citizens might vote otherwise if, for example, a particular candidate who would ordinarily enjoy their support becomes embroiled in scandal. As a way of conducting analysis, therefore, one might construct what Appiah calls "cognitive angels" – which are imaginary beings with full knowledge and full rationality. Appiah calls this imaginary being "a computationally perfect agent" (2017, p. 91). In our example, we might call that cognitive angel an "older citizen" and analyze what to expect on election day. But what we are really analyzing is an avatar, a fiction. We can use these cognitive angels to predict behavior knowing that human beings aren't so pure and unrelenting in their decision-making. Businesses operate using a model of likely customers. Architects design homes for people they can only imagine. Statistically, we can live with some variation. And we can factor back in intervening events that might otherwise throw off our calculations.

Picture two persons standing side-by-side. One is a concrete human being with flesh-and-blood … somebody with a unique history and a name. The other is the avatar, a cognitive angel, a simplification of the human being. Multiply these pairings to reflect groups of people – that is, a literal crowd of human beings, on the one hand, and a cluster of their avatars, on the other. A social scientist can set aside or bracket the living, breathing crowd temporarily and study the cluster of avatars, making useful inferences about what to expect. Economists do this routinely; they call this cognitive angel *homo economicus* (see, e.g. Schreck et al., 2020; Urbina & Ruiz-Villaverde, 2019). No one in reality is *homo economicus*. In the law, one thinks in terms of the reasonable man (see, e.g. Saltman, 2017; Green, 1967); they ask, what would a "reasonable man" do in this situation?

Ramsey took this idea of the cognitive angel and extended it across time. In other words, there is a cognitive angel for you at age 25 in one situation and another one for you at age 50 in a completely different situation. You can be portrayed by a series of avatars, depending on the situation you are in (Appiah, 2017, p. 88). Then, a social scientist can compare these avatars to one another, even though none of them is in any sense real. Here is what a 25-year old under these conditions is likely to do, whereas here is what a 50-year old under those conditions is likely to do. All of them fictions. All of them potentially analytically useful.

In actual practice, however, a computationally imperfect agent who tries to make decisions in an effort to approximate the cognitive angel could easily make mistakes. In fact, that is what it means to be computationally imperfect. Aspiring to perfection when you are not perfect can result in disastrous choices. Better perhaps to acknowledge one's limitations and work within what Herbert Simon (2000) called our "bounded rationality." Given that a person is not computationally perfect, is it truly advisable to pretend that you are? Appiah wrote that "aiming lower and succeeding can leave you better off than aiming too high and failing, and those may be the only serious options we face (2017, p. 126)." Later he puts it this way: "the best is the enemy of the good" (2017, p. 164). None of which diminishes the utility of thinking as if one were a cognitive angel. Appiah calls it a paradox: "the recognition that our decision-theoretic picture is an idealization comes with the recognition that it is of no use, for us, as an ideal at which to aim" (2017, p. 97). He concludes, "Our knowledge of reality is held, then, in pictures of the world, each of which has something wrong with it but is good enough for some purposes" (2017, p. 110). Thus, "the great skill in managing our cognitive lives is figuring out which pictures to use for which purposes" (2017, p. 111).

A thespian, for example, can pretend to be somebody else. A role is a fiction. Here, though, Appiah adds a crucial dimension of direct relevance to Leadership Studies, which is that the audience pretends as well. They don't rush the stage to prevent Romeo from killing Tybalt. Audiences are complicit in the ruse. And so a dramaturgical approach to leadership, in the spirit of Erving Goffman (1978), means that everyone in the relationship adopts some version of the fiction, that leadership is literally an enactment. Because neither the leader nor the audience is a cognitive angel, instead they are governed by heuristics, i.e. rules or guides to action that make life manageable (2017, p. 113).[8]

Leadership education that urges prospective leaders to act as cognitive angels would be a mistake. Judging leaders in the real world by the same impossible standard would be a mistake. We would be advised to work with what Immanuel Kant called the crooked timber of humanity, which is the way we figuratively are (see Berlin, 2013). Appiah is especially exercised by the attempt to see other people in terms of identities, which are fictions with potentially ghastly consequences (2017, p. 143). This includes identities as they pertain to leaders (women leaders, young leaders, black leaders, and so forth), and also identities as they pertain to followers. Perhaps the most pernicious of these is forgetting that one's identity is a fiction – a useful fiction, perhaps, but a fiction nonetheless (e.g. Appiah, 2014). By the same token, Appiah worries that theorists such as John Rawls urge such a complete distantiation from one's actual circumstance, imagining oneself as having no identity whatsoever, that once again the fiction of an ideal (disinterested, abstract) could be unrealistic, if not impossible, leading to worse outcomes than some consideration from within one's identity (2014, p. 153). We must use identities, though not be trapped in them.

Operating within that web of fictions

If culture can be pictured in the mind as a web of useful fictions, or what used to be called just-so stories, characterized as myth, lore, and fable, then leaders would be advised to operate "as if" that were the context for his or her exertions. Some of these fictions might require explicit reinforcement, as for example when Ronald Reagan referred to the United States of America as a shining city on a hill. Other fictions might need to be challenged and even replaced. Nelson Mandela questioned apartheid, the fiction that South Africa was some kind of confederation of warring and underdeveloped tribes requiring that those of European descent must mediate and govern. In many instances, the struggle between any two factions is more accurately understood as a contest over fictions, such as symbols (Harter & Clark, 2020). The Cold War was a massive and intransigent struggle between two ideologies pertaining as much to economic policy as to anything else, a complex and covert reduction to two and only two competing representations.

Scholars do a disservice to leadership when we presume to look past these fictions and instead go in search of hypotheses to observe, measure, and test under objective conditions. Call what we study a hall of mirrors or a charade.

8 Indeed, the leader himself or herself often serves as the heuristic for others.

Still, culture explains much of what we set out to understand. Fictions can be real. People take actions based upon them. Scientists need them to do their work. Culture proves to be a storehouse full of them, many of which are compelling and persistent.

Scholars and educators would be advised to recognize the role of fictions in their understandings of leadership, differentiating them from hypotheses and dogma. They would be right to discard inadequate fictions. They are encouraged to invent better ones. Nevertheless, they must always remember this is what they are, i.e. conveniences, tools over which we should exercise some authority.

References

Adair-Toteff, C. (n.d.). Hans Vaihinger's Kant-Studien. Retrieved 14 March 2020 from https://www.kant.uni-mainz.de/ks/history/adair-toteff.html.

Alvesson, M., & A. Spicer (eds.). (2011). *Metaphors we lead by: Understanding leadership in the real world*. Routledge.

Appiah, K.A. (2017). *As if: Idealization and ideals*. Harvard University Press.

Appiah, K.A. (2014). *Lines of descent: W.E.B. DuBois and the emergence of identity*. Harvard University Press.

Berlin, I. (2013). *The crooked timber of humanity: Chapters in the history of ideas*. Princeton University Press.

Blake, R., & J. Mouton. (1964). *The managerial grid*. Gulf Publishing.

Boulding, K. (1961). *The image: Knowledge in life and society*. University of Michigan Press.

Carlyle, T. (1902). *On heroes, hero worship, and the heroic in history*. Boston: Ginn & Co.

Donaldson, W. (2017). *Simple_complexity: A management book for the rest of us*. Morgan James Publishing.

Elden, S. (2017). *Foucault: The birth of power*. Polity.

Fine, A. (1993). "Fictionalism." *Midwest Studies in Philosophy. XVIII*: 1–18.

Goffman, E. (1978). *The presentation of self in everyday life*. Harmondsworth.

Green, E. (1967). "The reasonable man: Legal fiction or psychosocial reality." *Law & Society Review. 2*: 241.

Harter, N. (2007). *Clearings in the forest*. Purdue University Press.

Harter, N., & C. Clark. "Eric Voegelin on the seemliness of symbols: Shays' Rebellion." In K. Bezio & G. Goethals (eds.). (2020). *Leadership, populism and resistance*. Edward Elgar.

Kellerman, B. (2016). "Leadership – It's a system, not a person!" *Daedalus. 145*(3): 83–94.

Koestler, A. (1959). *The sleepwalkers: A history of man's changing vision of the universe*. Penguin.

Menand, L. (2001). *The metaphysical club: A story of ideas in America*. Farrar, Straus, Giroux.

Rawls, J. (1971). *A theory of justice*. Harvard University Press.

Ridley, M. (2011). *The rational optimist: How prosperity evolves*. Harper Perennial.

Saltman, M. (2017). *The demise of the reasonable man: A cross-cultural study of a legal concept*. Routledge.

Schreck, P., D. van Aaken, & K. Homann. (2020). "'There's Life in the Old Dog Yet': The Homo economicus model and its value for behavioral ethics." *Journal of Business Economics. 90*: 401–425.

Schyns, B., & J.R. Meindl (eds.). (2005). *Implicit leadership theories: Essays and explorations*. Information Age Publishing.

Simmel, G. (1971). *On individuality and social forms* (D. Levine, ed.). University of Chicago Press.

Simon, H.A. (2000). "Bounded rationality in social science: Today and tomorrow." *Mind & Society. 1*(1): 25–39.

Stoll, T. "Hans Vaihinger." In Zalta, E.N. (ed.). (Spring 2020 Edition). *The Stanford Encyclopedia of Philosophy*. Retrieved 7 April 2020 from https://plato.stanford.edu/archives/spr2020/entries/vaihinger/.

Tonkonoff, S. (2017). *From Tarde to Deleuze and Foucault: The infinitesimal revolution*. Palgrave Macmillan.

Uhl-Bien, M., R. Marion, & B. McKelvey. (2007). "Complexity leadership theory: Shifting leadership from the industrial age to the knowledge era." *The Leadership Quarterly. 18*(4): 298–318.

Urbina, D.A., & A. Ruiz-Villaverde. (2019). "A critical review of homo economicus from five approaches." *American Journal of Economics and Sociology. 78*(1): 63–93.

Vaihinger, H. (1911/2015). *The philosophy of "as if": A system of the theoretical, practical and religious fictions of mankind* (C.K. Ogden, trans.). Random Shack.

Wheatley, M. (1992). *Leadership and the new science*. Barrett-Koehler.

3

HOMO LUDENS ON MOTORBIKES

Negotiating play in George Romero's *Knightriders*

Introduction to the chapter

The following chapter includes four interrelated parts. The first part embeds this chapter within the rest of the book – that is, within the encompassing project at the intersection of Leadership Studies and the imagination. It does this by turning a previous chapter's treatment of images (such as pictures, models, and representations) into stories, which are – in a manner of speaking – complex depictions of dynamic images across time which have a shared meaning. Stories are constructed of interwoven images. Of particular relevance to leadership, it is my belief that the telling of stories is a form of play, which leads to the second part of the chapter, namely a brief analysis of the 1981 feature-length film by George Romero titled *Knightriders. Knightriders* is a fanciful story about leadership and about the significance of playfulness in communal life. One way to make sense of this film is through the lens of playfulness. The third part of this book chapter then considers the film as a theater of archetypes, characters, and tropes that keep recurring in Western culture, going all the way back to prehistory. These archetypes exemplify themes in surprising ways, for the archetypes enact familiar dramas that would appear to convey meaning. Stories blend both playfulness and a message. Finally, the concluding part of the chapter consults Johan Huizinga's landmark study of the element of play in human culture (1938). One can discern lessons in *Knightriders* that implicate Huizinga's work.

Ultimately, the chapter suggests that leadership itself is a form of play that must in some sense straddle two things: both paramount reality, on the one hand, and the life of the imagination, on the other. It will be my contention that leadership exists in part to maintain a healthy balance between the two.

DOI: 10.4324/9781003374831-3

Leadership in stories

Stories are images in motion – moving pictures, as it were – with an internal coherence or meaning. Leaders traffic in them every day. Leaders tell stories about where we are as a society and where we are going. Stories are also told about leaders. Often, leaders are the story.

Neuroscience indicates that human beings may be "hard-wired" to comprehend and think in terms of stories (see, e.g. Suzuki et al., 2018; Swart et al., 2015; Gardner, 2006; cf. Lee et al., 2012). At the very least, even as children, we are steeped in stories, in mythology, lore, anecdotes, fables, and a thousand narratives about how the world works. We expect other people to tell us stories: "How was your day, honey?" Each life is a biography. It is preceded by an epic tale known as history, once upon a time.[1] And we often fantasize about where it is all headed, whether in an apocalypse, followed by eternal silence, or on the sunny uplands, happily ever after. We find ourselves surrounded by heroes and villains, struggling over good and evil and locked in immortal combat. Stories are the signature of time as it blows through our lives.

The study of leadership is ultimately an investigation into a certain kind of story that we tell about the meaning of social change (see, e.g. Wright & Dziak, 2016; Campbell, 2013; Gardner & Laskin, 2011, ch. 3; Forest, 2006). Participation in leadership is living such a story, complete with characters and a plot. We step into the second act of a three-act play and try to figure out our parts impromptu, all while advancing the storyline.

The following chapter looks at the importance of storytelling as a form of play, a participation in that never-ending cavalcade, without which life loses its meaning. As with so many classic tensions in the field of Leadership Studies (see Collinson, 2014), human beings occupy an in-between or liminal state – neither completely lost in fabrications untethered to reality, detached in a world of make-believe, nor immersed so grimly in the base mechanics of staying alive, scrambling around in the dust, preoccupied by labor. We occupy a space, as it were, where both can be true. We need both.

Educators in the field of Leadership Studies often resort to telling stories, ranging from brief case studies from the workplace to full-blown epics about Truth, Justice, and the American Way (e.g. Judson, 2023; Callahan et al., 2007; Danzig, 1999). These stories can be drawn from a variety of sources, real and imagined, from the distant past or science fiction. The simplest of these will present (A) antecedent conditions, (B) human behavior, and (C) mixed consequences, i.e. past, present, and future. It might be extravagant to put it this way, but leadership is the story. Furthermore, leadership takes place by means of storytelling,

1 Alex Rosenberg (2018) uses findings from neuroscience to dispute the value of studying biographies in particular and history in general, although at present his skepticism is not mainstream.

as I had reason to mention in the introduction to this book. Stories gather up disparate information and give it all unity, direction, and meaning. Thus, we might be able to say that stories are the means, the outcome, and the purpose of leadership, without which we are left with mere data and raw experience.

One of the most powerful media for delivering stories to the viewing public is the cinema. The cinema shapes so many of the implicit leadership theories by which ordinary people operate. Let me use the next part of this chapter to introduce one particular film that not only exhibits the role of the imagination in telling its story, but it also addresses the topic of using the imagination to shape culture. That is to say, it is a work of the imagination about the importance of the imagination. That film is the 1981 cult classic *Knightriders*.

Romero's film

Director George Romero confessed more than once that *Knightriders* is one of his favorite films and (in his words) "closest to me … most personal" (Williams, 2011, pp. 152, 176). He reflected on the making of *Knightriders* in this way.

> Basically, it's a film about idealism. It's about a group of people who are trying to live their own lifestyle completely separate and apart from the rest of society. They are all members of a traveling Renaissance fair. They travel from town to town, holding jousting tournaments on motorcycles. Instead of searching for the Holy Grail, their quest is to keep themselves uncorrupted, despite the media's attempt to commercialize them.… That's what *Knightriders* is about – about people trying to live by their own simple code, independent of the rest of society.
>
> *(Williams, 2011, p. 84f; see also p. 69)*

In 1981, Ed Sikov wrote a more pungent precis for *Cinéaste*:

> *Knightriders* is the story of a troupe of misfit bikers who tour the countryside of Pennsylvania dressed in neo-medieval armor and perform jousting tournaments for the locals. Featured in the Arthurian fellowship are a king, a Guinevere, a Black Knight, a Merlin, and assorted courtiers, all of whom openly admit their association to be a reaction against the plasticity of a decidedly unheroic America.
>
> *(p. 31)*

King Billy, the leader of this little troupe, knows the likely audience for his traveling pageant. He calls them all "suckerheaded American driftwood" and complains that it becomes too easy for these people just to give up on life. They get tired of their diets, he says, "their exercises, their marriage or their kids or their jobs or themselves. Or they get tired of their God." They have no real sense of purpose. They show up, spend money, watch the staged violence, and go home again, amused. Instead of such a dissolute life, Billy wishes to offer to the troupe itself an alternative that Tony Williams describes as "community, professionalism and chosen exile in an increasingly contaminated and commercial world" (2015, p. 119). Billy and his companions are to live on the margins, by their own rules. The film examines their struggle to achieve this purpose.

Billy presides over a small group of merchants, performers, technicians, and mechanics who migrate from one small town in rural Pennsylvania to another, setting up camp and selling tickets to the locals for what amounts to a kind of Renaissance fair, where folks will buy food and trinkets and see a demonstration of prowess by combatants on motorbikes. The knights joust in a tournament, tilting against one another while riding their bikes, until one of them finally wins.

Billy is the king and apparently the founder. He has a queen. There is a Lancelot-type named Alan, who sees it as his duty to protect the king. Like the original Lancelot, he also finds himself attracted to the queen, although unlike his legend, there is no overt betrayal. Instead, he tries hooking up with a townie … which doesn't end well. Opposing the king throughout the story is the infamous Black Knight, Morgan, who has been challenging Billy for the crown for some time. Morgan is plainly superior as a combatant, but he is also arrogant, narcissistic, and comfortable with compromising his ethics. There are other knights who split roughly into two groups: supporters of Billy and supporters of Morgan. That split will become more pronounced as the plot unfolds. Billy is also advised by an older man, Merlin, who is revealed to be a licensed physician, as well as something of a mentor to Billy.

The film clusters around three of these little festivals. The first one, while revealing some of the tensions within the troupe, primarily introduces the characters and the nature of their sport. It also sets Billy on a collision course with a local Sheriff's deputy who tries to shake them down for a bribe, which Billy flatly refuses. The second festival occurs once the divisions within the troupe come out into the open. Morgan the Black Knight has decided to break away and start his own troupe by following a sleazy impresario promising booze and sex and fame and money. He tells his supporters at this second festival in the middle of the film that once it's over, he intends to leave. Everybody's nerves are frayed. Safety precautions are neglected, so that a motorbike strikes a young mother in the audience. And a few local toughs show up on their own bikes in homemade gear ready to challenge the knights. The ensuing confusion results in destruction, alarm, and a parting of the ways. Morgan takes his buddies to go enjoy the high life. Alan the Lancelot character takes his teenage hookup and one of his friends up into the hills to think things through. Because so many key players have left, Billy has to shut down operations and brood.

The third festival toward the end of the film is closed to the public. It is not meant for the "suckerheaded American driftwood." By that point, all of the departed have returned, having seen the error of their ways. They pledge themselves to the ideals embodied throughout the film by Billy, but they also agree to one decisive contest between the allies of Morgan and the allies of Billy – winner-take-all. In the morning mist, the two sides face one another, revving their engines. And so the final battle begins. After many feats of derring-do, one knight survives and only one: Morgan. Morgan wins. Billy accepts the outcome of the trial by combat, passing his crown to his erstwhile rival. He releases his queen to find succor in the arms of Alan. He then bids everybody goodbye and leaves. In his absence, Morgan accepts the crown, picks a new queen, and rejects the impresario who had earlier promised him so much. The show as they had known it must go on.

It seems appropriate here to introduce a distinction between finite games and infinite games. James Carse (1986) famously wrote about games as fictional worlds that we construct within a set of rules, partly to escape our mundane existence, but mostly to infuse our mundane existence with drama. We enter into the game and play, trying to win while having fun. These games all take place within a very different kind of game, which Carse called the infinite game. The infinite game is the extended story of human life – a game you win only by carrying it forward to the next generation. In the film, then, each festival is a finite game, where knights win or lose, but at last, they understand that the infinite game is paramount. It does not matter so much who wins and loses, so long as they preserve the community. I mention this distinction because leadership takes place within the context of each kind of game. There are finite games where the leader is hoping to win, such as courtroom trials, surgeries, battles, and getting legislation passed; then there is the infinite game, which no leader wins except by means of stewardship. Morgan the Black Knight in the film had been routinely fixated on winning the finite games, which he did regularly, but he had to learn the truth that as a leader he would also be responsible for the infinite game. Once the defeated Billy saw that Morgan finally understood this, he could walk away, assured that the community was left in good hands.

The presence of archetypes

Film analysis can take many forms. I choose to concentrate on the presence of archetypes.

Romero consciously drew from the field of archetypal psychology when writing *Knightriders*. Archetypal psychology lends itself to the medium of film, where images predominate. James Hillman wrote, "Archetypal psychology *axiomatically* assumes imagistic universals ... that is, mythical figures that provide the poetic characteristics of human thought, feeling, and action ... [*emphasis supplied*]" (2013, p. 21). One observer put it this way: "a [film's] meaning is shaped by cultural and psychological myths. Archetypes are the unknowable basic forms personified or concretized in recurring images, symbols, or patterns which may include motifs…" (Delahoyde, n.d.). Romero's *Knightriders* relies heavily on archetypes, even as he playfully tweaks them.

The most prevalent archetype in the film is the Arthurian legend, hearkening back to the medieval romance about a virtuous king who assembles brave knights in order to undertake the quest for the Holy Grail with chivalry and courage.[2] Arthur presided over a time of peace and prosperity, along with the cultivation of the arts – that is, until Morgan le Fay insinuates herself into this fragile paradise and wrecks it all by exploiting the king's vulnerabilities. After a furious battle of good versus evil, Arthur lies slain in a ship bearing the corpse to Avalon. His magic sword, submerged with the Lady of the Lake. Sorrowful listeners of the tale are promised a return of that glorious epoch, one day, should a prince with sufficient virtue win the favor of the fairy gods and regain Excalibur.

The protagonist in *Knightriders* embodies an ideal, presiding over a little troupe that adheres to a strict code, even when there is no audience to pay admission. They live each day according to a hierarchy, with archetypal roles, such as king, queen, knight, jester, and madrigal. There is even a Merlin, Arthur's enchanted tutor. At one point, the character Merlin entertains the king with a retelling of the Arthurian legend. When Merlin injects a note of cynicism part way through his account, Billy turns and pleads with him to finish the story correctly. "You're supposed to believe in this stuff, man."

The antagonist, as we saw, is named Morgan. When somebody at the beginning of the film teases him that the Morgan of legend was a woman, the hypermasculine Morgan is supposed to be insulted by this literary detail, but he replies that he "was never into this King Arthur crap." Morgan and his buddies threaten the spirit of comity by pushing the limits of violence in order to win, by paying unsentimental attention to the business side of things, by braggadocio, as well as an affinity for the temptations of the outside world. Morgan even speculates that Billy has gone mad. His suspicion of Billy's state of mind gains traction within the troupe. Slowly, others begin to wonder the same thing. Both Billy's wife and his heir apparent (Alan) separately presume to upbraid the king, as though he has become at the very least unreasonable. Merlin too has to rebuke his ward from time to time. And the brewing conflict between Billy and Morgan culminates in a council meeting to which he – the king – is not invited, where everybody worries that the entire enterprise will soon fold. Despite not being invited, Billy does show up anyway, however, bleeding, sleepless, furious, berating the lot of them

2 Sabino et al. (2022) analyzed a batch of feature-length films about King Arthur for the *Journal of Leadership Studies*, but they did not include "Knightriders." Neither, I might add, did they include "Monty Python and the Holy Grail."

for going behind his back. If ever he does look unhinged, as people were starting to suspect, it is during his tirade. One might say that he reinforces the impression at this moment that he has lost his mind.

After this tense episode, about two thirds of the way through the film, Morgan takes his buddies (and a pleasure-seeking Friar Tuck) and starts his own kingdom in the fleshpots of the city. The heir apparent Alan rides off into the mountains to get some critical distance. These two choices present the viewer of the film with alternatives. In fact, one sees a vivid contrast between them, neither of which will ultimately satisfy: the hubbub and decadence of the big city (Morgan), with rock music and a party vibe, on the one hand, and the slow-moving, empty retreat into the hills (Alan), where they sit around in idle, philosophical speculations (and where his teeny-bopper girlfriend becomes openly bored), on the other hand. This contrast illustrates an in-between status of the original troupe on the outskirts of small-town America, neither lost in a sensual, urban landscape (Morgan) nor withdrawn to a cerebral, remote cabin (Alan), but a vital community of its own. The contrast reveals something of the tension that Billy had helped to create and sustain. His leadership represents neither extreme, neither metropolitan excitement nor rural isolation. Instead, he represents home. Despite the comfort of home, however, under tremendous strains, the troupe had to suspend operations. There is nowhere now for them to go. Billy is left to wander through what remains of the camp, waiting and hoping for the return of his "lost sheep."

Speaking of "lost sheep," a second recurring motif in the film is Christianity more broadly speaking. Morgan alludes to Billy's crown as "a crown of thorns, if you know what I mean." Themes of holiness, as in being set apart, apply to the troupe as a whole and to Billy in particular. Billy flagellates himself kneeling and prays using his sword as a makeshift prie-dieu. Friar Tuck is ostensibly a monkish figure. Indirectly, of course, the spirit of the Middle Ages that the troupe tries to re-create was itself infused with Christianity.

Romero was not content to adopt these themes without poking fun at them. Friar Tuck is the monk who loves to cuss and get drunk and fornicate wearing a headdress of devilish horns. Romero also exhibits lifestyles that many Christians in the 1980s would have found at least questionable, including an interracial marriage, one gay and one lesbian relationship, a mild tolerance for smoking pot (which Billy forbids only to prevent giving law enforcement grounds to persecute them), the occasional swear word, premarital sex (with nudity), and a number of what I will call occult overtures. Conventional Christians circa 1981 would have had many reasons to be appalled. The protagonist Billy himself rarely indulges in these questionable behaviors, but he also seems mostly tolerant, because it is not these things that offend his sense of honor. If he is a Christ-figure and he can accept these things, then he seems for all the world like the Jesus of Nazareth who mingled with sinners, drawing rebukes from the religious leaders of his own day (see, e.g. *Matthew* 9: 10–13; *Mark* 2: 13–17; *Luke* 5: 29–32).

The most significant of these "occult" overtures is the appearance part way through the film of the Black Bird, a Native American identified in the script only as "the Indian" who is a local male dressed in armor showing up on his own bike after a show. In the hero's quest, as many remember, the hero encounters many fabulous creatures, some of whom mean him harm; yet often the very one who seems to mean him harm blesses him instead and turns out to be helpful. Billy had been dreaming about a black bird of some sort since the opening scene of the movie, as though it was destined at last to vanquish him. That was his interpretation of the dream. Now, in the swirling dust of the remnants of a tumultuous show, with everything in chaos, this unknown personage rides up with a black bird painted on his chest plate, and Billy construes this to be the character from his dreams whom he is destined to confront. Despite the fact that the entire camp is in disarray at this moment and Billy is still severely injured, the two of them do battle on their bikes, surrounded by a general mayhem. Although Billy barely wins, he is so injured and exhausted by the ordeal that he collapses, requiring stitches for a neck injury that will afflict him for the rest of his days. Nevertheless, this strange (and always silent) adversary known as the Indian not only yields to Billy as a result of their battle but also promptly paints his black bird blue, accepts being dubbed a knight at the hands of Billy, and accompanies the king everywhere he goes, up to and including a fatal accident on the highway. This mysterious character, who in quiet moments would cast small bones in some pagan ritual of prognostication, was more loyal to Billy than to the others, since he leaves the troupe behind in order to accompany Billy on his final foray after the last battle. He has a personal stake in the person of the king. To be sure, after Billy's death, we see "the Indian" at the funeral with the rest of them, and he expresses his grief in a pagan way by smearing mud across his face. He is presumably hereafter part of the troupe.

The character Merlin is also something of a throwback to pagan magic, a strange amalgam of scientific-minded, fully licensed medical doctor who previously treated gall bladders before tattooing himself with butterflies, donning a magician's robe, and spouting freelance poetry, accompanying himself with a harmonica. There is something Celtic about Merlin, with one foot in the mists of pre-Christian Europe. He also possesses more education and wisdom than any of the rest of them. He even explains at one point that his rationality helps him to foresee the future, cause-and-effect, such that to everyone else it seems uncanny. "It's nothing to get excited about," he says dismissively. Knowledge can seem like magic to the uninformed. In a film punctuated by jarring contrasts, this character of the medical doctor who believes in magic seems to be one of the director's most edifying.

At the heart of the film's archetypal journey is the quest for identity, the individuation that Billy especially must undergo (Blanch, 1991, p. 62). He begins the film in command, erect and certain – despite indications now and then that he had been losing his grip before we are permitted to join the story. Billy pushes everybody to the brink, challenging anyone who fails to live up to his ideals. He shows little tolerance for dishonor. Merlin watches this intensification happening, as Billy tries to live up to some unrealistic *imago*, a sainted knight tilting against the dragon. Or against a black bird. Later, as the troupe disintegrates, Billy responds violently, more than indignant that no one else seems capable of living up to his high standards. In his quest for purity, he was gradually losing any sense of fun.

His mindset at that moment is revealed in an exchange around a campfire with a lawyer Steve (the realist), Merlin (the fantasist), and Bagman, a former hippie who just got beat up by local cops. This late night conversation reveals a lot about Billy's state of mind. Bagman explains that he sees the world as two fights, one of them for ideals and one of them for survival. In his view, high ideals don't mean anything if you don't survive. Survival is the most basic struggle. In the darkness, Billy has to contemplate this way of thinking, then later he wakes up Bagman to tell him that he disagrees. There is only one fight, he says. He characterizes it as a struggle for survival, yes, but a struggle for the survival *of the ideals*. You might perish, that's true, he says, but the ideals live on. In short, to borrow that distinction from Carse, Billy switches from the imagery of a finite game to be won or lost, on the one hand, to the infinite game, on the other. He can now see beyond his own well-being and his tenure as king. With this clarity, he rides on ahead to resume his reign, only to find things falling apart in his absence.

Those around him blame Billy and his fixations in part for the collapse. And so he broods, mustering apologies for neglecting folks and waiting like the father of the Prodigal Son for everyone else to return. When everybody does return, of course, he accepts the terms of one final battle and then accepts the outcome, even though his "side" loses. The finite game is lost. But he is assured that the infinite game continues once he sees Morgan, now the *legitimate* successor to the throne, embrace those same ideals. Billy can take his leave and go tie up a few loose ends, smiling. The film ends with the troupe intact, in good order, driving the byways of Pennsylvania, continuing the quest without him.

The quest for individuation ends by his yielding to the perpetuation of the community after he departs.

Huizinga's *Homo Ludens*

In the 1930s, Dutch historian Johan Huizinga wrote *Homo Ludens: A Study of the Play-Element in Culture* (published in 1938 and translated into English

12 years later).[3] The title derives from a Latin ascription for human beings not as *homo sapiens* (or *homo faber*, for that matter), but as the being who plays. This book reframes many aspects of culture, far more than literal playtime, playacting, games of every sort, athletics, recreation, and sports, theater and pretending, competition and gambling, and other temporary suspensions of life's anxiety. These are familiar outlets for the impulse to play. Huizinga went further, arguing that almost any activity can be regarded as play-like, including business, manufacturing, technological innovation, courtship, electoral politics, gardening, litigation, bargaining, surgery, carnival, driving a car, swimming at the beach, hiking a trail, making a feature-length film, studying for a class, and getting an article published in an academic journal.

Play is, in the words of Ruth Benedict (1934), a pinpoint phenomenon, irreducible and frequently a part of the constellation of motives surrounding more complex cultural activities. Just as marriage is about more than gratifying lust and war is about more than pugnacity, she wrote, many of life's activities combine a variety of pinpoints, in much the same way that clothing serves to (a) hide our nakedness, (b) protect our bodies from the elements, (c) attract potential mates, (d) signify status, (e) manifest beauty, (f) provide a degree of comfort, and (g) express our personalities, as well as (h) foster an entire industry. Over time, culture constellates these pinpoints in unique and often bewildering arrays. Huizinga's message is that hidden in many of these cultural "constellations" is an element of play – an element that reveals something about social behavior.

Huizinga saw all of culture through this particular lens and found play permeating our social lives. The sociologist Erving Goffman (1978) adapted the idea of putting on a performance to describe social interaction generally, even so much as getting dressed each morning for work or engaging in frivolous banter at the grocery store. It is not only children who play. To a great extent, life itself introduces an element of play to the grim, impersonal mechanics of physical existence.

"The play's the thing," wrote William Shakespeare. The dramatist famously embedded a play within a play during "Hamlet," a device that continues to pop up in popular culture, such as when Mickey Rooney and Judy Garland decide to raise money by putting on a show or Christian Bale and Amy Adams defraud investors by pretending to be something they are not in "American Hustle." A portrayal of somebody else who is playing is not uncommon. Many artists have depicted the spirit of play in one form or another, such that one could immediately begin listing major motion pictures about characters who play such

3 Readers familiar with my work know that I trust the judgment of philosopher Eric Voegelin. Voegelin concluded his positive review of *Homo Ludens* saying that it is "one of [those] rare great works that advances substantially our understanding of man in historical and political existence" (2001, p. 168).

games as chess, football, baseball, basketball, hockey, poker, and feats of magic. Occasionally, a work of art will address the spirit of play itself, the pinpoint experience so scrupulously examined academically by Huizinga. *Knightriders* is but one example of this.

Huizinga began his study by asserting that play, as he meant the term, is a cultural phenomenon of creating order out of existing tensions, with a discernable objective that constitutes winning according to rules. Huizinga contended that play is actually anterior to culture, in the sense that from out of play human beings construct an elaborate structure that we now call culture. Play is, in his opinion, prior to culture. Even for activities that emerge to satisfy basic needs, such as hunting for food, human beings find ways to turn them into play (p. 46).[4] Participants pretend that they are opposed to one another in competition, for example, when in fact they must collaborate as a community in order for the game to succeed. Huizinga wrote: "Social life is endued with supra-biological forms, in the shape of play, which enhance its value" (p. 46). Today, culture is suffused with play (p. 173).

For the duration of the game, whatever it is, participants escape from paramount reality – i.e. from ordinary life, with all of its serious and mundane dimensions – for the sake of an illusory (or better, an imaginal) outcome. Huizinga called the game "another world" (p. 18) and an "artificial seclusion," without anyone ever literally having to leave (p. 20; Voegelin, 2001, p. 163). During playtime, one gets so immersed in the activity that he or she forgets briefly that it is only a game (p. 51). Needless to say, an audience is often drawn into this make-believe world, however briefly, so that they share in the escape they are witnessing vicariously.

Play injects a kind of manageable drama or performance in which the players participate, enacting a contest. Huizinga called it a process of image-making (p. 25), in which the lawn becomes a field, the ball becomes a projectile, the players dress up and designate themselves by position (leftfielder, catcher, pitcher), on behalf of a colorful team with a nickname, mascot, and history. A banal reality with jumping and running and throwing is thereby construed along a different and entirely fictitious dimension. Paramount reality still exists, and often, it intrudes – sometimes, to disrupt the game, such as darkness or lightning; sometimes, as a condition of play, such as the laws of gravity; and throughout, participants are expected to retain an affiliation with the encompassing collaborative purpose, by remembering to exhibit sportsmanship at all times. A player is both in and out of the game, simultaneously, negotiating the boundary between the two. That is, a player must be (to borrow a phrase from Huizinga) "lightly engrossed" in the game (p. 32). Ideally, then, the activity "has no contact with any reality outside itself, and its performance is its own end. Further [he wrote] it is sustained by the consciousness of being pleasurable, even mirthful, relaxation from the strains of ordinary life" (p. 203).

4 The quarry that one hunts is often referred to in English as "game."

It was important for Huizinga to point out that initially play has no social function. It is not born in order to give participants this experience of "escaping reality." Neither is it born to provide an excuse to exercise or to dominate other players or to make money. Huizinga acknowledged, "Competition serves to give proof of superiority" (p. 63). But that selfish purpose uses the spirit of play to serve its own ends. One can play without deriving any kind of social ranking; one thinks for instance of throwing a frisbee back and forth. Or consider a typical dance floor. It all begins as a spontaneous effort to express a mood, as a kind of ebullience, irreducible to anything else. Huizinga cited Plato favorably for the proposition that play originates in the simple urge to leap (p. 37; see Voegelin, 2001, p. 162).[5] Accordingly, play "lies outside the reasonableness of practical life; has nothing to do with necessity or utility, duty or truth" (p. 158). What Huizinga wrote here is not a minor assertion, especially as it pertains to leadership.

It is important to recognize that Huizinga defined play as:

> a voluntary activity or occupation executed within certain fixed limits of time and place, according to rules freely accepted but absolutely binding, having its aim in itself and accompanied by a feeling of tension, joy and the consciousness that it is "different" from "ordinary life."
>
> *(p. 28)*

Later, he re-stated his meaning as "a contract valid within circumscribed limits, serving no useful purpose but yielding pleasure, relaxation, and an elevation of spirit" (p. 188). From this foundation, Huizinga went on to suggest that culture itself is both a product of play and its habitat. He claimed that most cultural activities manifest elements of play – some of them, such as theater and sports, being more obvious (e.g. p. 196), yet he went to great lengths to show that warfare (ch. 5), business, the arts, flirting, philosophy (ch. 9), politics, law (ch. 4), and mythology (ch. 8) all derive to some degree from, and still incorporate, the spirit of play. Ultimately, he made the case (with Plato) that religion itself is something of a cosmic game. Huizinga wrote, "The ways in which men compete for superiority are as various as the prizes at stake" (p. 105).

Which is not to say that play is orthogonal to seriousness. He tried more than once to refute that canard. Games can be very serious indeed, even deadly.[6] Huizinga alluded to the tendency of every community to subdivide, to choose

5 Martin Heidegger (2018) credited a forerunner of Plato named Heraclitus with this notion that all of life and even philosophy is in many ways a game (pp. 8–16, 18–20).

6 An encomium to hunting by José Ortega y Gasset (1942/1985) explains that hunting is in many ways a diversion from daily living but also an immensely serious undertaking. It is significant that Ortega argues in a manner not unlike as I do here, that the "real world" which one is escaping in order to go hunt animals is the charade, a kind of false existence; thus, the hunting is a restoration of a more primal reality, shorn of civilizational artifice.

up sides, as it were, and demarcate everyone's loyalties – sometimes using quite problematic categories, such as race or gender or social class (p. 53; see Gardner & Laskin, 2011). These rivalries or feuds can become pernicious, ripping families apart, consuming lives and property – hardening, as it were, into that hoary distinction between friend and foe (Schmitt, 1976). Sociology talks about the Other, with a capital "O." Mary Douglas (1966) alluded to the quest for purity that motivates people to resist any contamination by strangers. Ortega y Gasset (1961) noted that each human being is a combination of drives both toward and away from relationships with other people. Play is one way to adapt this societal tension, using it without signaling a desire to obliterate the Other and wreck the superordinate goals that we all might share. In just this way, play serves a civilizing function, helping people who are different to accommodate one another (ch. 3), without pretending that there are no differences. There are such differences, of course, but Huizinga saw the fact of differences as an excuse to play against one another and not to destroy.

Underlying this idea of constructive tensions is the metaphysical posture that all of reality is comprised of beneficial striving (e.g. Heraclitus, Hesiod, Empedocles). The imagery of struggle often provides what Huizinga called a root-principle of existence (p. 116). And why not? Human beings are born into a tension they cannot dissolve: between a complex reality in which they participate, on the one hand, and the words and concepts they use in order to make sense of the world, on the other (p. 133). The only way to bridge the divide, he argued, is by means of the imagination. And the dominant outlet for the imagination is play.

Huizinga made an observation that can be used to analyze the film *Knightriders*, which is that forms of play can lose their status as play. They can be transformed into something the opposite of play, with an infusion of (in his term) over-seriousness (p. 198), in which the sportive or whimsical element becomes reduced to calculation – analysis, moneyball, statistics, business ledgers, playing the odds. In such instances, he wrote, "the virtue has gone out of the game" (p. 199). The drama collapses in a welter of data. It becomes a job. The escape from mundane reality is no longer possible, as paramount reality and its utilities intrude more and more, ruining the transport of one's imagination to another dimension. As Huizinga noted back in 1944, "More and more the sad conclusion forces itself upon us that the play-element in culture has been on the wane" (p. 206). The protagonist in Romero's cult film, Billy the King, finally takes a firm stance against such a sobering transformation of his own bizarre life, where fantasy reigns.[7]

7 A film actually celebrating the transformation of sport into more of a trade and even a profession is *Chariots of Fire*, which coincidentally came out the same year as *Knightriders*, i.e. 1981.

The analysis of *Homo Ludens* concluded with a sustained apologia for play as a civilizing force. And not just play, but play in its purest form, without cheating and without the one we call a spoil sport (p. 211). Everybody still requires play, even if only to retain this thing we refer to as civilization. We must insist upon it, argued Huizinga. We must seriously insist upon playing.

Restoring the balance

The traveling troupe in *Knightriders* pretends to live in another epoch. It performs for the benefit of an audience. The centerpiece of its show are the jousts, which are a strange combination of motorbike and chivalry, designed to result in a champion – a reward of dubious value, even to the knights. The reward is about having fun, bragging rights, and only tangentially the good order of the troupe. Everyone gathers together at the end of the day to share in the food and the laughter.

The performers acknowledge that they are part of the troupe largely to have fun and approximate the fantasy. They are happy to stay just outside the conventional world, on the margins, extending their child-like adventures by dressing up, camping out, and teasing one another. What they offer to the viewer is a game (the joust) within a play (the fair) within a film (*Knightriders*). And what increasingly seems to disturb them most is the intense seriousness of their king, who confesses that he is indeed trying to live according to a strict code of honor and fight some mystical dragon nobody else can see. Billy has transitioned away from the spirit of playfulness, almost like an actor who starts to walk around the set actually believing he is the character. This to many of them is a *faux pas* and a subtle cause for alarm. They see his commitment as a threat to their chance to live the fantasy. He is robbing them of their light-hearted experience. The king is just too serious, too uptight.

Eventually, Billy hears the criticism. He brings a pause to the struggle. He hears what they have to say. He allows the knights to negotiate about the final battle (to be conducted in front of no audience) – a battle that will determine the future of the troupe. He has nothing left to prove. He welcomes them all back, embracing them, smiling, almost as though he had temporarily forgotten why he had started the troupe to begin with. They in turn accept his code and his mission. Everything returns to its playful origins. Billy recovers his own sense of fun. The balance is restored. They will continue to live on the margins, delivering their performances in small-town Pennsylvania, loosely within the fantasy.

And Billy, the founder, accepts the outcome, leaving them to their merriment, as he rides off at the end of the film to settle old scores and restore a sense of rough justice, punishing a corrupt Sheriff's deputy who once beat his friend and also rewarding a small boy of the same name with his Excalibur, feeding the imagination of the next generation (the infinite game). Then, owing no more to the world, he rides away in a dream-like state, yielding to the fantasy so completely that he forgets where he is. In picturesque armor, on a mighty steed, head thrown back with unmitigated glee, he drives headlong into a truck.

During an interview in 2010, Romero was asked, "Are you annoyed when people tend to overanalyze your movies? Are you into that at all?" He responded in part, "I'm certainly not into it. I find, oddly, occasionally you come across something and you say, gee, maybe I was thinking that or maybe this does represent that, but most of the time I think a lot of it's just way overanalyzed" (Williams, 2011, p. 173). One can strip a story of its magic by treating it as an object of academic scrutiny, like a specimen on a slab. Have we done so in these pages?

Film critic Sikov (1981) credits the director with portraying the threat to utopian ideals as coming from within the troupe, from the king, who takes it all much too seriously. In his opinion, the attempt to withdraw from a corrupt society will ultimately fail, because you take the seeds of corruption with you. Trying to start over is a fool's game. Sikov acknowledges that the empty-headed audiences at the jousts provide a disheartening tableau of contemporary America.

> Fat cretins and their brutalized wives, belly-scratching bald neo-Nazis, porcine policemen reaching for payoffs the way zombies grub for flesh – these are the inhabitants of the Allegheny Valley, the fair countryside north of the Steel City. The crowds in *Knightriders* ... are enlivened by a stupidity so great that they must jump up and down in order to express it ....
>
> *(p. 32)*

So it is understandable that the troupe might wish to escape into the margins, away from such decadence. Being in the troupe gives them an excuse to skirt the reality they find so appalling. But Sikov contends that escape is not a solution. The venality of the audience does not make the players any more virtuous. Their desperate tactic to be liberated from all of that is sadly doomed (see also Wilson, 2007).

Robert Blanch (1991) had a different interpretation. He saw the film as an update on the Arthurian romance, a modern day re-telling of an old myth – not to ridicule the ideals embodied by Billy but to remind the audience of a loftier vision.[8] As Blanch put it, the troupe reminds everybody of the importance of one's conscience. Such an ideal is always elusive, as it is in the film, but it is also powerful and meaningful and arguably worth the struggle. Kendall Phillips (2012) agrees that in this film Romero was exploring the archetype of goodness (p. 64) and not portraying the depth of corruption, except by way of contrast. Romero admits that *Knightriders* represents an optimism about the culture, that

8 Romero is quoted as saying that his films are about seeking a better world, "a higher plane of existence, for people to get together" (in Williams, 2015, p. 262, n. 4).

people can recover something of their better selves (Williams, 2011, p. 70). The knightriders in the film did just that.

Tony Williams (2015) offers a balanced assessment in which the director is trying to contrast a flawed reality filled with viscera, vice, and fast-food franchises, on the one hand, with the quest for an ideal, on the other. Billy embodies the ideal with single-minded zeal – probably too much zeal. The rest of the troupe finds his dream fascinating, but they rarely understand it completely. Even so, they appreciate the opportunity he gives them to turn away from a culture in twentieth-century America they can all see has become vulgar and humiliating. It is the character Merlin who has to remind Billy to keep a clear eye on that reality and not become so enamored of magic as to miss the real magic happening around him every day (2015, p. 113). In Huizinga's wording, Billy must remain "lightly engrossed" in the fantasy.

Williams concludes that the film is for Romero about the genuine work of making a film while having fun doing it (2015, p. 107).[9] For example, we see behind the show that the troupe puts on for crowds, at the tricks they use to weave a tapestry for the imagination, all the while fiddling with knobs in the control room, swinging rubber battle axes at one another, and making the lances so that they break easily (2015, p. 112). There is the show, in other words, for popular consumption, which is quite unserious, and then there is the code. Billy represents that code. And in the end, they all pledge allegiance to it. As Billy had said earlier in the film, if you die, your ideals don't die with you. They live on. In that métier of hopefulness, the troupe is last seen riding the backroads together, keeping the faith, their banners flaunting in the breeze.

References

Benedict, R. (1934). *Patterns of culture*. Houghton Mifflin Company.

Blanch, R. (1991, winter). "George Romero's 'Knightriders': A contemporary Arthurian romance." *Quondam et Futurus. 1*(4): 61–69.

Callahan, J., J. Whitener, & J. Sandlin. (2007). "The art of creating leaders: Popular culture artifacts as pathways for development." *Advances in Developing Human Resources. 9*(2): 146–165.

9 In interviews, Romero will reflect on the early days of filmmaking as being fun. "We just said, 'C'mon out, we'll have a ball.' And we always had kegs of beer and a lot of food..." (Williams, 2011, p. 10). Elsewhere, Romero said that he cultivates an informal atmosphere on set, hoping the experience is enjoyable for everyone (Williams, 2011, p. 71). Romero (2001) himself on audio commentary 20 years afterwards talked about having lots of toys and playing "Space Invaders" and pool parties, including skinny dipping. One of the actors can be overheard on the commentary saying, "Greatest summer imaginable." The cast and crew took over a local Holiday Inn over the three summer months they shot *Knightriders*, and Romero sheepishly recalls that the place had to be fumigated after they left. One scene in the film when drunken "knights" with underage girls thrash one another and trash their hotel room was shot at that same Holiday Inn.

Campbell, K.D. (2013). "Mythology as the original framework in the development of leadership principles." *Journal of Leadership Studies. 7*: 48–54. https://doi.org/10.1002/jls.21290.
Carse, J. (1986). *Finite and infinite games: A vision of life as play and possibility*. Free Press.
Collinson, D. (2014). "Dichotomies, dialectics and dilemmas: New directions for critical leadership studies?" *Leadership. 10*(1): 36–55.
Danzig, A. (1999). "How might leadership be taught? The use of story and narrative to teach leadership." *International Journal of Leadership in Education. 2*(2): 117–131.
Delahoyde, M. (n.d.). "Archetypal criticism." Personal website. Retrieved 13 February 2021 from https://public.wsu.edu/~delahoyd/archetypal.crit.html.
Douglas, M. (1966). *Purity and danger: An analysis of the concepts of pollution and taboo*. Routledge.
Forest, H. (2006). "The power of words: Leadership, metaphor and story." *Proceedings of 8th Annual International Leadership Association (ILA) Conference*, Chicago.
Gardner, H. (2006). *Changing minds: The art and science of changing our own and other people's minds*. Harvard Business Review Press.
Gardner, H., & E. Laskin. (2011). *Leading minds: An anatomy of leadership*. Basic Books.
Goffman, E. (1978). *The presentation of self in everyday life*. Harmondsworth.
Heidegger, M. (2018). *Heraclitus: The inception of occidental thinking* (J.G. Assaiante & S.M. Ewegen, trans.). Bloomsbury Academic.
Hillman, J. (2013). *The uniform edition of the writings of James Hillman* (vol. 1). Spring Publications.
Huizinga, J. (1938/2014). *Homo Ludens: A study of the play-element in culture*. Martino Publishing.
Judson, G. (2023). "Cultivating leadership imagination with cognitive tools: An imagination-focused approach to leadership education." *Journal of Research on Leadership Education. 18*(1): 40–62. https://doi.org/10.1177/19427751211022028.
Lee, N., C. Senior, & Butler, M. (2012). "Leadership research and cognitive neuroscience: The state of this union." *The Leadership Quarterly. 23*(2): 213–218.
Ortega y Gasset, J. (1942/1985). *Meditations on hunting* (H. Wescott, trans.). Charles Scribner's Sons.
Ortega y Gasset, J. (1961). *History as a system and other essays toward a philosophy of history* (H. Weyl, trans.). W.W. Norton & Co.
Phillips, K. (2012). *Dark directions: Romero, Craven, Carpenter, and the modern horror film*. Southern Illinois University Press.
Romero, G. (2001). "Audio commentary [DVD]." *Knightriders*. Anchor Bay Entertainment, Inc.
Rosenberg, A. (2018). *How history gets things wrong: The neuroscience of our addiction to stories*. MIT Press.
Sabino, A., F. Cesário, L.J. Andrade, & F. Teobaldi. (Summer 2022). "King Arthur's lessons for leadership and superior performance—From screen to real life." *Journal of Leadership Studies. 16*(2): 56–61. https://doi.org/10.1002/jls.21809.
Schmitt, C. (1976). *The concept of the political* (G. Schwab, trans.). Rutgers University Press.
Sikov, E. (1981). "Review. *Knightriders* by Richard P. Rubinstein and George A. Romero." *Cinéaste. 11*(3): 31–33.

Suzuki, W., M. Feliú-Mójer, U. Hasson, R. Yehuda, & J.M. Zarate. (2018, 31 October). "Dialogues: The science and power of storytelling." *Journal of Neuroscience. 38*(44): 9468–9470. https://doi.org/10.1523/JNEUROSCI.1942-18.2018.

Swart, T., K. Chisholm, & P. Brown. (2015). *Neuroscience for leadership: Harnessing the brain gain advantage* [*The Neuroscience of Business*]. Springer.

Voegelin, E. "Book review. *Homo ludens*: *Versuch einer bestimmung des spielements der kultur*, by Jan Huizinga." In Voegelin, E. (2001). *Collected works* (J. Cockerill & B. Cooper, ed. & trans.) (vol. 13, pp. 160–168). University of Missouri Press.

Williams, T. (2015). *The cinema of George A. Romano: Knight of the living dead* (2nd ed.) (ch. 8). Wallflower Press.

Williams, T. (ed.). (2011). *George R. Romero interviews*. University Press of Mississippi.

Wilson, B. (2007). "Romero, George A." *Senses of Cinema*. Retrieved 19 May 2021 from http://www.sensesofcinema.com/2007/great-directors/romero/.

Wright, R.P., & J.M. Dziak. (2016). "Storytelling as a primary leadership tool." *2016 IEEE Aerospace Conference*. https//doi.org/10.1109/AERO.2016.7500928.

4

THE IMAGO OF LEADERSHIP

Introduction to the chapter

This chapter depends upon two distinctions. The first distinguishes between (a) the individual human being in isolation, as a solitary creature, an organism with a unique name and life-story and (b) collectivities, human beings together in relationships, groups or teams, organizations, or even whole societies. Each can be imagined separately. This chapter will focus on the individual human being. The next will turn to imagining collectivities.

Given the complexity of each person, nobody can know anybody else completely. I would go so far as to say that you cannot even know yourself as well as you might think. Each image that a person uses to identify another represents, but cannot exhaust, a deeper reality about that person, something beyond our ever comprehending, and this includes the fact that people change across time. What you are today may not be what you are tomorrow, so that our images of one another – no matter how elaborate – can soon become outdated.

The second distinction differentiates between (a) knowing from the inside-out, having an interior perspective and (b) knowing from the outside-in, having an exterior perspective (Wilber, 1999). We say that we know what it feels like to be a particular person, what he or she must be going through. Nevertheless, each person occupies a distinct point in social space. You possess a memory of where you have been. You walk around with fluctuating interests and feelings, thoughts and hopes and fears, as you see the world through lenses from a unique

DOI: 10.4324/9781003374831-4

point of view. This chapter will focus primarily on the interior perspective, i.e. seeing the self.[1]

We also go around perceiving (and judging) other individuals, sizing them up, regarding them as not "Me" but "You." We operate according to schemas or models in our head about who they are and what they might mean to us. Are they hospitable or hostile, friend or foe? We take in impressions of them and construct images in our heads about who they are and what they want. Obviously, in many instances, the image we are using is simplistic or even wrong. Nevertheless, we rely on an array of these images in order to make sense of our world. We categorize and sort and label and adopt strategies for dealing with one another. These images are subject to change as we get to know one another more intimately, just as the reality each image is intended to represent can also change. Kids grow up. Spouses grow apart. Nevertheless, I possess an image of my friend, and it is this that I use when interacting with him (Mazlish, 1990).

Leadership as a process therefore includes participants who are making decisions about themselves and one another, separately and together. For it is a hoary truth in social psychology that we treat people based on how we imagine them. This fact puts a premium on imagining accurately. But it also has the effect of making us aware of how we present ourselves to others. We know that other people are doing the same thing about us that we are doing about them. So that if we want them to treat us a certain way, we can (sometimes) take action to make the desired impression. If I want you to believe that I am a nice guy, then I probably ought to do nice things. Leadership includes this reciprocal performance in which we are all trying to manage how others see us (Goffman, 1978). Should they like us? Should they join us? Should they fear us? Should they listen to what we have to say? We all know at a gut level that there are things a person can do to manage these impressions, or at least to make certain impressions more likely than not. Just think of job interviews and first dates.

Further complicating this hall of mirrors is the finding that how I regard you will influence how you regard me. If you know that I esteem you, respect, and otherwise like you, you will in return regard me differently than if you believe that I loathe or despise you. You will base decisions on how to act in part on how you think I look at you. In other words, you have images of how others imagine you! Sometimes, these images are accurate. Sometimes, they are not. As we know only too well, however, we can predict certain reactions from other people once they know things about us – that we belong to a certain race or religion, for example, or that we have an advanced degree from a prestigious school (or not).

1 This operation of seeing one's self goes by many names in the literature, such as self-knowledge, self-awareness, self-concept, self-image, and the like. Often, the use of different names denotes slightly different things.

On many occasions in my personal life, I am told by some clerk to sign a document in order to complete a transaction. When I bend over to read the paperwork, the other person interrupts and tells me, "Oh, that's just a standard form, blah, blah, blah" – as though they are in a hurry. Just sign the thing. I pause, look over my glasses at them, and say, "When I went to law school, I learned how important it is to read anything before I sign it." Immediately, I can see that importunate clerk straighten up at the knowledge that I went to law school, as though they realize maybe they should treat me differently because of that. Why that should be the case annoys me because dadgummit everybody should be afforded the opportunity to read whatever they are being asked to sign; but then I'm not afraid to use the reputation that lawyers have when it suits me. I want you to see me differently, because maybe then you will treat me differently.

I am especially sensitive to the vagaries of perception because of a biblical character who had the same name as I have – a man who made up his mind before ever meeting someone. In the first chapter of *John* (verses 45–46), it states

> Philip found Nathanael and told him, "We have found the one Moses wrote about in the Law, and about whom the prophets also wrote—Jesus of Nazareth, the son of Joseph."
>
> "Nazareth! Can anything good come from there?" Nathanael asked.
>
> "Come and see," said Philip.

We call this prejudice, because Nathanael literally pre-judged someone from Nazareth, without knowing anything further. It was enough that this Jesus fellow right here had come from that place yonder. Yet Philip persisted, asking his friend to penetrate the prejudice, to replace his hasty, lazy stereotype with direct evidence, to upgrade his image with facts.

Who are you?

Each of us walks around with images of other persons, based only in part on what we perceive directly. In fact, we can size somebody up fairly quickly (see Gladwell, 2005). Perhaps with time and further exposure, we can improve that image, elaborating on the details and looking past our hasty presuppositions. But that is not always possible. Sad to say, it is not always preferable. If I infer that you are a homicidal maniac, why would I get any closer to you and remove all doubt? Contrarily, the reason we sometimes prefer not to learn the details about someone is because it would shatter the illusion; we might prefer them as shimmering ideals, pretty at a distance. More commonly, a person does not investigate other human beings beyond a superficial level because he or she has other things to do. Getting to know people is time-consuming and exhausting. City dwellers walk past hundreds, if not thousands, of strangers every day and accept them as such, as part of the background and nothing more. One cannot get to know literally everybody.

As I previously stated, we tend to treat people based upon our image of them. That image might be partial, mistaken, or false; nevertheless, in the absence of better knowledge, the image is all we have to go on. In our selection of someone to follow, we will use an implicit leadership theory (ILT)[2] – or should we start calling it an implicit *leader* image (ILI)? Who looks like a leader? We might have to consult a variety of clues, such as wardrobe, as well as the way that everybody else in the room is treating that person. Maybe they have a pertinent job title, or maybe they exhibit some kind of expertise.

One of the quickest (and cheapest) ways to classify the other person is by this thing called an identity, which is a category generated by society for purposes of sorting humanity into groups by sex, gender, and orientation; race and ethnicity; age; socio-economic class; and so forth (Appiah, 2014). One of today's academic fads is the realization that a single human being can be slotted into different categories at the same time, which they call intersectionality, so that the little girl from India in French designer clothes yet speaking American English might initially confuse the other person. Such a person fits several of these convenient categories. Identity is a heuristic, a convenience that does not always work and is frequently little more than a stereotype. Just because I know your sexual orientation, for example, do I really know much at all about you as a living, breathing human being? In this sense, identity can lead to perceptual errors.

We do the same thing with traits and characteristics (Northouse, 2021, ch. 2). We might be inclined to follow someone older, someone taller, someone with an advanced academic degree. We might be drawn to someone's laughter or deep voice. In short, as followers, we must gather the clues where we find them in order to decide how to respond. And whereas you might be thrilled to pick a woman as your next leader, simply because she is a woman, you might balk if it turns out that her policy proposals run directly counter to your values. Then what? Each leader proves to be a configuration, an amalgam, comprised of a unique constellation that forces the follower to make tough choices. The question arises: What are your priorities as a follower? What is it about the other person that might be a deal-breaker?

Behind the process of making sense of other persons, we possess a variety of templates, in the background, as it were, images of what we think a cop should look like, what a grandmother should look like, what a felon should look like (see generally Hillman, 2019; Polanyi, 2009). These templates (or types) might align with specific social roles, such as leader. What we can do then is compare a template (in one's head) to the actual specimen in front of us. Does this person

2 See e.g. Yukl (2013, p. 233).

fit the profile I would have expected? With time, we build up quite a menagerie of these templates – knowing them to be stereotypes, perhaps, but not always. What do you picture when I say somebody is Italian, a baby, an accountant, a Sikh, or a lacrosse player? Is this process of typing other people fair? Is it fair to superimpose ready-made templates onto the people one meets in paramount reality? Probably not. Still, what else do we have to go on, but our images?

Educators in the field of Leadership Studies frequently expose students to a variety of leaders, in person and in print, from fiction and from history. I call this process "populating the imagination." Let us watch *Rise of the Planet of the Apes* (released in 2011) and examine the protagonist, Caesar, who is indeed both fictional and an ape. Read biographies about Winston Churchill. Analyze a case study. Attend lectures by local community bigwigs. Soon, one can see leadership everywhere, in every shape and size. The broader the array of leaders one has seen, the less likely one is to limit his or her deference to only certain types. Having a diverse collection of examples to draw from means that a follower does not need to insist on only one narrow image. As a follower, the student will be open to a variety.

The same is true about the way that leaders think about followers. It is the same process, only in reverse. Leaders treat followers based upon their image of those followers (Trigg, 1999). Are these followers inherently lazy and unmotivated? Are they stupid, or at least ignorant?[3] The temptation to paint with a broad brush and regard them all the same can backfire, of course. The following leadership theories, cited from the Peter Northouse textbook (2021), share this approach. Situational Leadership, if you recall, put it front-and-center that one must really assess the readiness of followers, individually. Transformational Leadership provided for individualized consideration. Then, LMX (Leader-Member Exchange) spoke about the different ways that leaders bond with followers, thereby creating in-groups.

I would remind the reader here of something I already stated: that any image can become outdated as the reality it represents changes across time. Even if the image had been accurate, once upon a time, or at least sufficiently useful, that may no longer be the case today. Leaders and followers evolve. They grow and mature. Their tastes and preferences can be altered. They lose heart. They fall into moods. They acquire fresh skills. An image has to remain amendable, forever subject to change. Leaders can become corrupted by power, for example, beginning their careers as idealists and ending them in humiliation. Under certain conditions, loyal followers can be incited to rebel.

This lesson about the fact that individual human beings do change often bubbles to the surface in the study of historical leaders. A young Queen Elizabeth I

3 See generally Theory X and Theory Y (https://en.wikipedia.org/wiki/Theory_X_and_Theory_Y).

might lead in a manner different from an older one. Part of this change might be because of experience, or a function of aging, or the changing cast of characters offering her advice. We cannot say that she was the same leader immediately after her coronation as she was on her deathbed. We have to make allowance for her development, her expansion or contraction, her rise or fall.[4]

Students are advised to appreciate the progression, partly in order to manage their own. There is no reason for students to expect that upon graduation they emerge fully equipped to lead, without ever having to improve. We often expect *followers* to make these transitions and improve; in fact, bringing them along a journey is often the metaphor that is used. Change is built in to their social role. Why not also the leaders? Knowing this, leaders can remember to change themselves and attempt to change others, while continually changing the images on which these decisions are based. If everything goes well, the result is a kind of convergence between the image one has of another person right now and the image one has of the future person who develops successfully.

Who am I now? Who am I becoming?

This section of the chapter is about the individual human being as seen from the inside-out. I call this the solitary-interior. People will make decisions while participating in leadership based on who they believe that they are or can become. Self-knowledge might give a person confidence, for example, or doubt. I can always **discover** something more about myself, such as how I handle stress, as well as **inventing** things about myself, such as learning how to speak a foreign language.

The section will address four scenarios.

- Images of the self today in today's situation. (An accurate rendering of the present.)
- Images of the self today in tomorrow's situations. (Possible courses of action.)
- Ideal images of the self in today's situation. (Bracketing parts of myself temporarily.)
- Ideal images of the self in tomorrow's situations. (A future self toward which I am striving.)

4 In the same manner, scholars often must go beyond their interpretation of what some previous scholar thought and instead recognize that his or her thinking probably shifted. In fact, I find myself attracted to scholars such as Eric Voegelin and Michel Foucault who abruptly stopped what they were doing – no matter how successfully — in order to re-think their fundamental position. This shows a degree of humility and openness that makes them more trustworthy as scholars. Thus, it becomes tendentious to assert what any scholar thought, without at least some sensitivity to his or her intellectual journey. Ideally, you would answer not only what they thought, but also when.

Each person has at least one image of themselves. It may be partial, misleading, or even wrong. There may be more than one of these images, imperfectly integrated to make a complete whole.[5] Furthermore, that image of one's self requires periodic upgrading, as a person changes. Part of leader development includes acquiring a more robust image of oneself – one that is forever capable of revision. The objective should be to obtain the *most accurate* images of reality, over and over again (see generally Kegan, 1982).

A person can also imagine future selves. These images might be templates for ambition, for example. It may be that the person I want to become shapes the person I am today. I can overlay this image of a future self to see whether what I am doing today is in any way consistent with fulfilling my dream. Am I becoming what I had hoped to become? In this way, I can compare the reality against an ideal and take steps to correct my trajectory.

These images of a future self might not always be ideals, toward which we are striving. They might be more realistic, possible selves in the present undergoing some future experience. Avatars can be projected from the present into forthcoming scenarios, whenever we ask ourselves, "How would this go if I were to do X, Y, or Z?" In the mind, we send out these avatars to do various things we are considering. We tell a little story about what could transpire. As we internally watch what happens to the avatar, we learn that maybe that's not the way to go. We send out imaginary selves so that we don't have to venture out for real without some idea what to expect. The avatar might flounder or fail or invite some kind of danger. The avatar eats the suspicious berries and gets sick. He takes these imaginary risks so that we don't have to. We can send out thousands of these little avatars every day as part of the decision-making process. Each morning, we ask ourselves what to do. As we ponder the possibilities, we are letting these imaginary avatars conduct little thought experiments. Psychologist Jordan Peterson wrote, "Thinking might in many cases be regarded as the abstracted form of exploration – as the capacity to investigate, without the necessity of direct motoric action" (1999, p. 66).

There is another way that a person can imagine one's self. Instead of imagining an ideal future self to strive for or imagining a present self in possible future scenarios, a person can imagine an ideal *present* self, as though he or she were cognitively perfect, in command of the facts, clear-headed, with complete mental processing power to think things through. This image, which is known as a cognitive angel (Appiah, 2017), is not an accurate depiction of oneself (alas). It is instead the self that is completely rational. (I wrote about cognitive angels in a previous chapter.) This cognitive angel appears when we ask ourselves, "What's the smart thing to do?" We bracket or suspend aspects of ourselves in order to

5 The body itself, for instance, appears to be represented in the neocortex as the *homunculus* (Peterson, 1999, p. 63).

concentrate our minds on the logic. This tactic might require de-centering the self, an exercise in removing oneself from the question. We can call it getting critical distance or distantiation (Harter, 2017). We wonder how we might look at things if we were being objective, disinterested, altogether lucid and shrewd, and not caught up in passions, prejudice, temptation, or noise.[6] Paradoxically, the cognitive angel is an imaginary self shorn of the self, impersonal, coldly calculating, disembodied, occupying a vantage point removed from the concrete particulars of daily life. Leaders benefit from consulting these cognitive angels from time-to-time.

In the next section, however, I prefer to examine the pursuit of the ideal future self, for that image has tremendous implications for leader development. It is my contention that leader development includes the process by which we approximate an ideal future self.

Leader development

Leadership educators like me investigate the process by which people learn how to participate in leadership. We demonstrate an interest in the development of others – that is, we seek to understand how people change, if not improve. With that knowledge, then, we can foster growth, encouraging our students to undertake a journey from where they are now toward some future state that is judged to be better.

The methods by which this can be done are manifold. Educators can be seen to impose, elicit, correct, inspire, monitor, expose, guide, instruct, construct, chastise, suggest, induce, deduce, explore, model, question, and assess (see, e.g. Davis, 2004). Each of these methods has been built on presuppositions about how people change, yet there is no reason to think that with further investigation we will ever arrive at the one true method that works *every* time on *every*body for *every* kind of a lesson. We know, for instance, that students learn in ways that are different from one another (e.g. Gardner & Laskin, 2011; Kolb, 1971) and different from how they had learned at an earlier stage in life (e.g. Piaget, 1961). Not only that, but a consensus in the literature has clustered around the likelihood that using more than one method for the same lesson can improve the results (e.g. Kolb & Kolb, 2013, p. 32).

One way of talking about education is the bringing forth from out of the student something that was there already in nascent form, hidden or crude, so that with the right methods it ultimately emerges and blossoms. The metaphor is not unheard of in the literature on leader development. Explicitly religious articles will refer to one's calling or vocation (e.g. Krispin, 2020; Rothausen, 2017).

6 For such was what Plato described as the so-called Judgment of the Dead, when each of us is to be scrutinized in the next life without distraction (*Gorgias*).

The idea of spiritual intelligence refers to a capability that needs to be accessed in order for spiritual leadership to flourish, a universal identity with the divine that needs to be "wakened" in the individual leader, heeding an "inner voice" toward what is known as a higher self (Fry & Wigglesworth, 2013). Secular research can also rely on similar metaphors, such as the "seeds" of leadership (Murphy & Johnson, 2011). Or the "hidden who" (Seemiller & Priest, 2015). Or prospective leaders simply possess "the right stuff" (Cawthon, 2002, p. 5; citing Kirkpatrick & Locke, 1991). Leaders are to develop in terms of a "professional identity," begun in childhood (e.g. Collay, 2006).

The underlying premise is not new. Plato had indicated thousands of years ago that only certain persons are born to lead, even though their right to lead depends on their subsequent education (Cawthon, 2002, ch. 1). Aristotle would concur, in part (Cawthon, 2002, ch. 2). So would Friedrich Nietzsche (Cawthon, 2002, ch. 10). Of all people, Thomas Jefferson, the author of the *Declaration of Independence*, had written to John Adams in 1813 that he believed in a natural aristocracy (Cawthon, 2002, p. 21). Cawthon then made the remarkable assertion that in the twentieth century, organizational theorists such as Frederick Taylor and Henri Fayol advocated specialization (2002, p. 11), which implies that only certain persons are to be selected to lead. The task is to identify the likeliest candidates, which suggests that only a few people possess the requisite talent. There is, in other words, a preexisting "something" that shrewd managers will be rewarded for detecting and nurturing in others. Otherwise, it would not matter whom you hire or promote into leadership positions.

All of these approaches depend upon the development of something that is already there. The underlying principle goes all the way back to the idea of potential. Scholars and educators sometimes write in terms of (a) finding and uncovering, (b) cultivating and nurturing, (c) realizing and fulfilling this somethng. The schema presupposes a preexisting presence that is imperfectly understood, requiring time and effort to bring to perfection, as though individual human beings experience an inward imperative to become one thing in life and not something else.

The literature offers a range of responses to this possibility. At one extreme, Brent Davis (2004) cast a wary glance at teaching methods that attempt to elicit or draw out something from the student, as though the outcome is already present and simply needs to emerge. He called it mysticism and said that it sounds "implausible" (p. 53). Nevertheless, he saw plenty of evidence in the literature that still, thousands of years after Plato's dialogue *Meno*, scholars and practitioners characterize their mission in these terms. They say that they are trying to evoke something. They see education as helping that which is latent become manifest, as though the student was already "meant" to reach a certain outcome, before the process even began. They speak in terms of a "natural born leader," for example, echoing the tendentious framework of the Great Man Theory (e.g. Harter, 2008). It does not change things, from Davis's point of view, to argue that you believe *everybody* has the capability to lead. He argued that it is still mysticism to believe in something that does not yet exist, let alone that this mysterious something has any normative value.[7]

At the other extreme, archetypal psychologist James Hillman wrote a best-seller titled *The Soul's Code* (2017) in which he made the case for there being a spirit or *daimon* who enters into the life of a child and uses that life to realize its own purpose. Hillman found it useful in his clinical practice to use such colorful imagery when treating patients who didn't know what to do with themselves. He urged them to heed their calling or vocation, precisely because it seems to make claims on the individual, like an inner imperative (Harter, 2014). Some think of it as a voice literally calling them, which is the imagery at the root of the term **vocation**. Hillman even adopted the ancient fantasy of a bevy of angels that drift down to earth, one at a time, from another world at the moment of birth, to possess you as an infant and make an instrument of you, fulfilling themselves and their mission whether you like it or not. But then archetypal psychology often interprets myth – and especially the hero's quest – as a kind of preexisting, universal template for the journey one must take in order to reach maturity (e.g. Neumann, 2015; Campbell, 2008; Peterson, 1999). This narrative is anterior and superior to any one individual person. It summons the student into the darkest part of the forest, to enact once again that archaic tale, such that each of us becomes a hero.

The operative feature of this story, from an educator's point of view, is the student's effort to transition into the character he was always meant to be. What he or she becomes is not random, nor is it necessarily a matter of choice or society's bidding. Neither does the educator somehow implant the dream. The dream in some sense already exists.

If this be mysticism, said Hillman, let's make the most of it.

Situated between these two extremes, the rest of this chapter suggests a version of this same metaphor for leadership education. Whereas I am agnostic whether in fact the student already has a destiny of some sort or a fate (inasmuch as I entrust that question to a person's faith), I want to make the case that using such a metaphor has useful implications for carrying out the avowed mission of leadership education. Students from many traditions will respond to

7 Later in his examination of metaphors for teaching, however, Davis does see merit in complexity science regarding emergent order (2004, ch. 14). The parts or elements of knowledge interact in such a way that a form comes forth from out of multiple iterations to become a whole. And as complexity science tells us, these emergent orders conform to what are known as strange attractors, boundaries within which the resulting system takes discernible shape. The form is somehow embedded in the nonlinear feedback processes. After enough time, the discernible whole becomes one thing and not something else. Looking backwards, it cannot have been otherwise. This, for some reason, Davis finds perfectly scientific and not mystical at all.

the possibility that there is some "thing" they are meant to become, some version of themselves to realize. It is psychologically healthier to believe in one's special calling, and *that* (as William James might say) is often merit enough. Let us suppose therefore (and temporarily set aside our skepticism) that a leader develops in accordance with a form or model of leadership that exists initially and imperfectly in the imagination. That image (or "imago") guides the student's decisions and tugs at his or her attention, lending an air of enchantment perhaps to the process of bringing forth or rendering, growing into, not unlike the acorn that becomes an oak (and not a pansy, let alone a rooster or a clock).

Doing so should not sound alien to leadership educators. In a similar way, we speak of a leader's vision, i.e. a product of the imagination that does not yet exist in paramount reality, though it guides and directs behavior. Burt Nanus (1992) wrote, "There is no more powerful engine driving an organization toward excellence and long range success than an attractive, and worthwhile, and achievable vision of the future, widely shared" (p. 3)[8]. That vision originates in the imagination, where it has influence on what transpires. One might say that a leader's vision serves the same function as the imago. If we can speak intelligibly of a leader's "vision" for the future, then why not also of an "imago"? An imago is simply the vision one has of oneself as a leader.

Neuroscience indicates that the human brain operates in part by comparing reality against an expectation or ideal, thereby learning whether to adapt accordingly (see Peterson, 1999, ch. 2). The brain compares what I want (Part 1) according to what I have (Part 2). It compares where I am hoping to go with where I am right now. It checks progress by overlaying one version upon another. Discrepancies are grounds for negative emotion, spurring a person to respond, in the hope of bringing them into rough alignment. Here again, we see the model of two "images" developing across time, repeatedly being compared to one another, until (one hopes) they mirror one another.

An etymological journey

The term "imago" derives from the same root as the word "image" – a semblance, representation, likeness, or mental picture. There are at least four contexts for its usage. First, in entomology, the term was adopted for the perfected form of an insect, which Linnaeus regarded as the fulfillment of a process of realization (OED (Oxford English Dictionary), citing *Systema Naturae,* ed. 12, (1767) I. II. 535). Second, in psychology, Jung was to adapt the term to refer to images in the mind of a person that influence one's behavior – usually at a subconscious level (OED, citing *Psychology of the unconscious,* 1916). Third, in the

8 On visionary leadership, see more recently van Knippenberg and Stam (2014); Taylor et al., (2014).

study of group dynamics, Eric Berne (1966) then applied the concept to a "group imago" which is the individual group member's latent image of the group as a group – what does he or she picture the group to be? – for this image will to a great extent determine how that member chooses to behave toward the group and within the group. Finally, in religion – primarily the Christian religion – the *Imago Dei* is literally the image of God, as for example the iconography in Byzantine theology (see, e.g. Pelikan, 2011), but often tied to accounts in the book of *Genesis* (1:26–27) where humankind is reported to have been created "in the likeness of God" – an ancient phrase in the Hebrew that has been interpreted to mean different things. It is reported later that Jesus used the same idea (*John* 14:7–11) when he told his disciples that "if you have seen me, you have seen the Father"; thus, Jesus of Nazareth claimed to be the imago of God. We are then admonished by the Apostle to bear that likeness, to grow into a semblance of the Christ (e.g. *Colossians* 1:27): an imago of the imago, as it were.

The idea behind these four uses is that within the mind – just as within the insect – is a form of what will come to pass later in a mature form. A caterpillar can be said to realize the imago of the butterfly. It was there all along, hidden within the organism, shaping its growth and transfiguration, to be recognized at the last.[9]

Aristotle was to capture this sense in his reference to a formal cause, that-which-is-yet-to-be, the model of a chair in the carpenter's head, for example, that guides his craft as he approximates and achieves the actualization of a chair made of wood (see generally Taylor, 1955, pp. 50–54). What he (the carpenter) thought from the outset is coming forth. But note, even here, the imago itself might require revision alongside the work. The builder might adjust what he can expect based on the condition of the materials or the availability of certain tools. Nevertheless, the objective is for the causes to come together into a finished product that had once originated in the imagination. Thus, if there is an artisan, then there is a formal cause in the mind of that artisan – even if you are the artisan of yourself!

The psychologist Jordan Peterson writes about this in *Beyond Order* (2021), where he urges his patients and students to "imagine who you could be, and then aim single-mindedly at that" (ch. 2). There, he explicitly urges the reader to ask, "Who are you? – and who could you be" (pp. 51–54)? The difference between your answers will inform your ambition. No doubt, your imago will change over time. Sometimes, it will come into focus as you draw nearer. Sometimes, it will lead you to a point where you discover a version of your best self that you would

9 The role of DNA in shaping one's development may pertain as well to leader development. Recent research has turned to genetics as an important predictor of leadership (Murphy & Johnson, 2011, p. 462), almost as though one's DNA bears this elusive "imago" in its coding, in much the same way that DNA influences whether a human being is tall, quick, or blonde.

never have guessed, even if it arises alongside what you had originally hoped. Maybe you won't become a lawyer, for example, but a paralegal. Maybe you won't become a physician, but a respiratory therapist. What you truly want lies in the vicinity of your dreams. In actual practice, maybe you have to draw toward the one in order to find the other.

Consonant with these uses, I propose defining the term "imago" in this context as the latent representation of oneself as a leader, influencing one's choices as part of the development into becoming a leader. What exists in the imagination shapes behavior. And even though with time the imago itself will evolve, imago and reality eventually converge or "merge" into a full-blown expression or manifestation, such that one embodies the imago in a mature form. At which point the term "imago" is no longer necessary. It can be said thereafter that the leader *is* the imago.

The social sciences speak

Leadership identity is an essential requirement for leader development to occur (Day et al., 2009; Lord & Hall, 2005; see Murphy & Johnson, 2011, p. 464). One must possess some idea of oneself as a leader. There may be evidence of an implicit leader image (or ILI) in children, but of course the maturing human being will continue to revise and upgrade that image sporadically, depending on a variety of factors. Leader development exists to make this process explicit, informed, and adaptable.

We do know that conceptions of leadership do change over time. For example, children in 6th, 7th, and 8th grade rate personality, dominance, popularity, and physical appearance as important to leadership (Lease et al., 2002). For adolescents, integrity, listening skills, and knowledge are rated as important leader characteristics, whereas compassion, consistency, and flexibility are rated as less important (Morris, 1991). As such, leader identities might also change to mirror those developmental changes in young persons' ideas of what it means to be a leader. For example, Komives et al. (2006) suggest that as young people's leadership identity develops, their conceptions of leadership shift from independent to interdependent, as they realize that effective leadership requires collaboration among leaders and followers.

Robin Eileen Sacks (2009) found that 29% of high school students believe that a person is born a leader (p. 74). Therefore, some of them already accept the basic framework of an imago, even if scholars might prefer to label this belief a product of folk psychology (e.g. Lewis, 1996). We know that at some point in the process of leader development, regardless whether they believe that leaders are born or made, the student starts to imagine himself or herself as a leader (van Linden & Fertman, 1998). But they come to that conclusion over time, as their image of what it means to be a leader evolves (Sternberg, 2008). That is, they develop an image of themselves as a leader in coordination with their emerging realization of what leadership means. The image of leaders and of themselves emerge together and sometimes merge together.

A doctoral student in organizational leadership named R. Lewis Steinhoff recently offered the opinion that "society wants to believe in natural born leaders" (2015, p. 19). He agrees that folk psychology can be compatible with the idea of a leadership imago. Given the fact that, in his research, *scholars* (unlike the population at large) have "concluded there is no such thing as a natural born leader" (2015, p. 21) – he nevertheless argues that by tweaking the inquiry slightly, evidence does suggest that many individuals do possess leadership *capabilities* and simply require awareness and attention in order to develop these capabilities. They must imagine themselves first as becoming leaders in order to take deliberate steps to realize what they might become. After all, the field of neuroscience is telling us that given the plasticity of the brain, even if you do not start out with the mind of a leader, you can grow toward one (Swart et al., 2015). What this implies is self-concept. Self-concept shapes the choices that people make. They undergo what are known as "identity maintenance and enhancement," making comparisons to their ideal self (Wood et al., 1997, p. 524).[10] The extent to which a person successfully approximates that ideal self will be reinforcing (Wood et al., 1997, p. 533). Another way of saying this is that the image one has of one's possible future shapes decisions in the present. The question is whether being a leader is included.

What we see therefore is the emergence of several images, in varying degrees of clarity. There is a descriptive self-concept, for example. And this is probably not one homogenous image, but a blend of several sub-images (daughter, athlete, student, girlfriend, employee). There is the ideal self. There is also the image of what it means to be a leader. These various images presumably sharpen with maturity, but they can also change dramatically. Over time, the discrepancies among these images will become more and more apparent. And as a student works with these discrepancies, intrapersonal conflict ensues. Decisions will probably have to be made.

- Who am I?
- What am I becoming?
- Do I need to alter my behavior in order to become something I prefer?

These are existential questions young people frequently ask themselves as they prepare to take their place in the adult world. Variations on these questions make mid-life poignant.

10 For an explication of the concepts of an ideal self and an ought self, see Higgins et al. (1994).

One might say that young adults become artisans of themselves in part by working on these images. Seen in this light, rites of passage can be seen as *poiesis*, a rendering in the workshop of one's imagination. What then follows from this understanding for leader development? And what does this way of looking at leader development mean for leadership educators? To sustain interest for the months and years required to develop and practice complex leadership skills, it is likely that a leadership role needs to become part of one's self-identity. (Lord & Hall, 2005, p. 592). Over time, leadership skills and knowledge become inextricably integrated with the development of one's self-concept as a leader (Lord & Hall, 2005, p. 592). As one's identity as a leader solidifies with increasing experience, a self-view as a leader should become a more central aspect of one's identity (Lord & Hall, 2005, p. 596).

When exploring new roles, such as "leader," individuals often adopt "provisional identities" which allow them to try out new behaviors (Lord & Hall, 2005, p. 599). As leadership identities develop, it is also likely that individuals will become increasingly motivated to attempt new leadership activities, creating the potential for learning new leadership skills and further identity development (Lord & Hall, 2005, p. 602). Thus, they begin by play-acting, trying it on for size, as it were, as a kind of experiment. Through experience, of course, their understanding should improve, as I have said more than once, but I would contend that the original image, no matter how mistaken or vague, is the imago toward which the individual is moving. The goal of leader development should be to bring that imago to the surface, improve it, and impress upon the student that whatever it is today, it must remain adaptable over time.

One word of caution at this point. Self-consciousness may be desirable, but it can also be debilitating, as for example when the piano player suddenly becomes "self-conscious" – needlessly fixated on how they might be perceived during the performance. A person can withdraw mentally from performance and become literally distracted by focusing on the self, when the moment requires a letting go, a forgetfulness. Too much inward scrutiny, constantly looking within when action is required, can frustrate leadership. I am not urging leaders to gaze at their proverbial navel constantly, whether in harsh judgment or admiration at what they find. Consulting and then upgrading the imago should be periodic, assigned to an appropriate time. A commander gets nowhere during a battle wondering whether he should have become a dentist instead. There is a time and a place for these meditations.

Concluding thoughts

In this chapter dedicated to images of individual human beings, we transitioned from crude templates or stereotypes toward more fine-grained images. In the process, we had to acknowledge the hall of mirrors in which human beings try to manage the impressions that they have of one another. In fact, one of the stranger facts is that people adopt different images of another person based in part on how they believe that other person perceives them.

The primary purpose of this chapter, however, was to begin examining the possibility that each of us has an image of himself or herself – an image (and probably multiple images) that can change. One task therefore in leader development is upgrading those images and integrating them. Are they accurate? Do they capture the reality, warts and all? Students often take inventories for class in order to get further insight. They inventory their likes and dislikes, strengths and weaknesses, their core values. That is one task. Another task is to suspend certain features at moments requiring only part of oneself, which is as much as to say that periodically we have to bracket a part of ourselves in order to be more effective in the moment. We must become cognitive angels in order to think clearly. A third task is to use avatars of oneself by submitting them to possible future scenarios, telling brief little stories about what might happen if we choose one course of action or another. Surely, Julius Caesar had contemplated beforehand what might occur if he were to cross the Rubicon. His avatar had leapt the river beforehand.

The fourth task, however, was the most important to mention. Prospective leaders develop themselves in accordance with an imago they possess (no matter how flimsy) of some future self as a leader. They use this imago not unlike a blueprint or guide. Part of leader development then is populating the imagination, enriching the possibilities, opening up new and invigorating directions. This can be done by means of studying history or the arts or simply entering into the hurly-burly of actual life, bumping up against a panoply of neighbors. What we are intimating here – and developing in greater detail in a separate chapter – is the importance to leader development of imitation. In any case, that imago will take shape while at the same time the prospective leader is pursuing it.

Many a leader has drawn near to an imago, becoming what they envisioned for themselves, only to be repulsed by the reality, forcing them to re-think their ambition in light of the circumstances. In a similar fashion, some students aspire to become surgeons until they discover they can't stand the sight of blood. Up close, leadership may not look so much like the fairy stories. On this, Machiavelli was refreshingly candid. Maybe the sooner they see this dark side of leadership, the better their choices along the way.

A final word seems appropriate. The process of leader development often entails somebody in the role of teacher, mentor, instructor, guide. I play this role at my university. I would be remiss not to point out that our responsibility to prospective leaders is to embody in ourselves what we prefer our leaders to become. We are populating their imagination with our very lives – our manner, our style, our character, our choices. The responsibility weighs heavily on me, I confess, because many years from now, when the classroom lessons have been forgotten and I am long dead, it may be the case that my example as a role model still influences my students, for better or worse.

Imagine that! I will live on in the imagination of those I teach.

References

Appiah, K.A. (2014). *Lines of descent: W.E.B. DuBois and the emergence of identity*. Harvard University Press.

Appiah, K.A. (2010). *The honor code: How moral revolutions happen*. W. W. Norton & Co.

Berne, E. (1966). *Principles of group treatment*. Grove Press.

Campbell, J. (2008). *The hero with a thousand faces* (vol. 17). New World Library.

Cawthon, D. (2002). *Philosophical foundations of leadership*. Transaction.

Collay, M. (2006). "Discerning professional identity and becoming bold, socially responsible teacher-leaders." *Educational Leadership and Administration: Teaching and Program Development*. *18*: 131–146.

Davis, B. (2004). *Inventions of teaching: A genealogy*. Routledge.

Day, D.V., M.M. Harrison, & S.M. Halpin. (2009). *An integrative approach to leader development: Connecting adult development, identity, and expertise*. Routledge.

Fry, L.W.J., & Wigglesworth, C.G. (2013). "Toward a theory of spiritual intelligence and spiritual leader development." *International Journal on Spirituality and Organization Leadership*. *1*(1): 47–79.

Gardner, H., & E. Laskin. (2011). *Leading minds: An anatomy of leadership*. Basic Books.

Gladwell, M. (2005). *Blink*. Back Bay Books.

Goffman, E. (1978). *The presentation of self in everyday life*. Harmondsworth.

Harter, N. (2017). "No one, everyone, anyone." *Leadership and the Humanities*. *5*(1): 41–50.

Harter, N. (2014). *Leadership and coherence: A cognitive approach*. Routledge.

Harter, N. (2008). "Great man theory." In Marturano, A. & Gosling, J. (eds.), *Leadership: The key concepts* (pp. 67–71). Routledge.

Higgins, E.T., C.J. Roney, E. Crowe, & C. Hymes. (1994). "Ideal versus ought predilections for approach and avoidance distinct self-regulatory systems." *Journal of Personality and Social Psychology*. *66*(2): 276.

Hillman, J. (2019). *Uniform edition of the writings of James Hillman* (vol. 4). Spring Publications.

Hillman, J. (2017). *The soul's code*. Ballantine Books.

Kegan, R. (1982). *The evolving self: Problem and process in human development*. Harvard University Press.

Kolb, A., & D. Kolb. (2013). "The Kolb learning style inventory, Version 4.0: A comprehensive guide to the theory, psychometrics, research on validity and educational applications." *Experience Based Learning Systems, Inc.*

Kolb, D. (1971). *Individual learning styles and the learning process*. M.I.T. Sloan School Working Paper no. 535–571.

Komives, S.R., S.D. Longerbeam, J.E. Owen, F.C. Mainella, & L. Osteen. (2006). "A leadership identity development model: Applications from a grounded theory." *Journal of College Student Development*. *47*(4): 401–418.

Krispin Jr., K.R. (2020). "Christian leader development: An outcomes framework." *Christian Education Journal. 17*(1): 18–37.
Lease, A.M., C.A. Kennedy, & J.L. Axelrod. (2002). "Children's social constructions of popularity." *Social Development.* 11(1): 87–109.
Lewis, D. (1996). "Desire as belief II." *Mind. 105*(418): 303–313.
Lord, R.G., & R.J. Hall. (2005). "Identity, deep structure and the development of leadership skill." *The Leadership Quarterly. 16*: 591–615.
Mazlish, B. (1990). *The leader, the led, and the psyche*. Wesleyan University Press.
Morris, G.B. (1991). "Perceptions of leadership traits: Comparison of adolescent and adult school leaders." *Psychological Reports. 69*(3): 723–727.
Murphy, S.E., & S.K. Johnson. (2011). "The benefits of a long-lens approach to leader development: Understanding the seeds of leadership." *The Leadership Quarterly. 22*: 459–470.
Nanus, B. (1992). *Visionary leadership*. Jossey-Bass.
Neumann, E. (2015). *The origins and history of consciousness*. Routledge.
Northouse, P. (2021). *Leadership: Theory and practice* (9th ed.). Sage.
Pelikan, J. (2011). *Imago Dei: The Byzantine apologia for icons* [*The A. W. Mellon Lectures in the Fine Arts*]. Princeton University Press.
Peterson, J. (2021). *Beyond order; Twelve more rules for life*. Penguin.
Peterson, J. (1999). *Maps of meaning: The architecture of belief.* Routledge.
Piaget, J. (1961). "The genetic approach to the psychology of thought." *Journal of Educational Psychology. 52*: 275–281.
Polanyi, M. (2009). *The tacit dimension*. University of Chicago press.
Rothausen, T.J. (2017). "Integrating leadership development with Ignatian spirituality: A model for designing a spiritual leader development practice." *Journal of Business Ethics. 145*(4): 811–829.
Sacks, R. (2009). "Natural born leaders: An exploration of leadership development in children and adolescents." Doctoral dissertation, Department of Human Development and Applied Psychology, Ontario Institute for Studies in Education, University of Toronto.
Seemiller, C., & K.L. Priest (2015, Summer). "The hidden 'who' in leadership education: Conceptualizing leadership educator professional identity development." *Journal of Leadership Education. 14*(3): 132–151.
Steinhoff, R.L. (2015). "Natural born leaders: Use of a self-assessment tool and benefits to coaching and development." *Journal of Practical Consulting. 5*(2): 19–28.
Sternberg, R. (2008). "The WICS approach to leadership: Stories of leadership and the structures and processes that support them." *The Leadership Quarterly. 19*: 360–371.
Swart, T., K. Chisholm, & P. Brown. (2015). *Neuroscience for leadership: Harnessing the brain gain advantage* [*The Neuroscience of Business*]. Springer.
Taylor, A.E. (1955). *Aristotle*. Dover.
Taylor, C., C. Cornelius, & K. Colvin. (2014). "Visionary leadership and its relationship to organizational effectiveness." *Leadership & Organization Development Journal. 35*(6): 566–583.
Trigg, R. (1999). *Ideas of human nature: An historical introduction* (2nd ed.). Blackwell.
van Linden, J., & C. Fertman. (1998). *Youth leadership: A guide to understanding leadership development in adolescents*. Jossey Bass.

van Knippenberg, D., & D. Stam. "Visionary leadership." In Day, D. (ed.). (2014). *The Oxford handbook of leadership and organizations* (ch. 12, pp. 241–260). Oxford University Press.

Wilber, K. (1999). *The marriage of sense and soul: Integrating science and religion.* Harmony.

Wood, W., P.N. Christensen, M.R. Hebl, & H. Rothgerber. (1997). "Conformity to sex-typed norms, affect, and the self-concept." *Journal of Personality and Social Psychology. 73*: 523–535.

Yukl, G. (2013). *Leadership in organizations* (8th ed.). Pearson Education.

5

ARTIFEX, EXEMPLAR, AND GUIDE

Using metaphors of the labyrinth in leadership studies

Introduction to the chapter

Students and practitioners of leadership operate from images they have of themselves and of one another. This includes images they have of collectivities, such as groups, teams, organizations, and entire societies. As with images they have of individual persons, which I addressed in the previous chapter, their images of collectivities are partial, misleading, and to some extent false. Also, the reality which an image is attempting to represent is changing all the time, so that people must periodically update their images just to stay current.

Images of collectivities, like images of individual persons, can be divided into descriptions and prescriptions. Descriptions try to represent the way things are. Prescriptions represent the way they ought to be. The interior perspectives, from the inside-out, I have addressed in the preceding chapter. The interior perspective for collectivities usually describes the culture of that collectivity, what Michael Polanyi would refer to as the tacit dimension of our social life (2009).[1] My purpose here is to talk a bit about this interior perspective, but also, I am hoping to talk about the exterior mode as well, i.e. models, diagrams, charts, and other analytical tools so often used to imagine people together, objectively, from the outside-in, about those persons with some kind of shared identity as members of a club or congregation, brigade or community.

Since we all walk around with an image of collectivities, albeit tentative and incomplete, we can improve them in any one of several ways. To begin with, we can make them explicit. That is a useful starting point. We can certainly obtain

1 I address the topic in *Cultural Dynamics and Leadership: An Interpretive Approach* (2022).

DOI: 10.4324/9781003374831-5

more knowledge about the collectivity. We can observe what is going on from different perspectives. We can switch out the templates we are using and overlay any one of a number of alternatives. Are we interested in demographics, crime, economics, home ownership, religious affiliation? We can try adopting a variety of metaphors (e.g. Alvesson & Spicer, 2011). Notwithstanding what I call our conceptual elasticity, however, the results will always be less than complete. Nevertheless, we still treat a collectivity based upon these images. Do I picture group X as rivals, enemies, allies? Am I drawn to them or repulsed? Do I want my group to be similar or different? In what way?

For another book, I wrote about the academic attempt to depict relationships – and especially leadership — as a sociological form, in the spirit of Georg Simmel (1971; see generally Harter, 2007). I see no reason to repeat myself here. At different magnitudes, we can adopt any one of a number of images to make sense of what is going on. Pertaining to the standard organization, there is the organizational chart laid out in a pyramid. Edgar Schein playfully created a three-dimensional cone. Some scholars like to invert the hierarchy or subdivide the functions or spread out the various roles more as a network. Elsewhere, I have argued that systems thinking is one of the most fruitful ways to imagine social entities (Harter, 2007, ch. 12). In short, there is no scarcity of options (see generally Morgan, 2006).

Remember that many of these images are **static** models, frozen at a given point in time, showing the elements of the system as well as the interrelationships among them, not unlike a diagram of soccer players distributed across the pitch. Perhaps the most elaborate image we possess for a collectivity is bureaucracy. Yet it is also possible to imagine collectivities as **dynamic**: pulsating or flowing or growing or making progress. We now know that groups mature, for instance, passing through the phases popularly known as forming, storming, norming, and performing (Tuckman, 1965). Historians once presumed to describe civilizational life-spans, destined to undergo the rise and fall of ages (e.g. Spengler, 1923; contra Toynbee, 1948). A recent attempt to analyze leadership using a dynamic model is LMX (Leader-Member Exchange), which provides for degrees of acquaintance, as followers are brought into the in-group … or not (Northouse, 2021, ch. 7).

The philosopher Charles Taylor published a book in 2004 about what he called social imaginaries. Here, he was trying to write about large-scale collectivities, such as the modern nation-state. He was inspired to do so by Benedict Anderson, who had apparently invented the idea of imagined societies. Anderson had written the following: "[M]embers of even the smallest nation will never know most of their fellow-members, meet them, or even hear of them, yet in the minds of each lives the image of their communion" (Taylor, 2004, p. 6). You will notice that here Anderson was using the interior mode, from the inside-out. Taylor took this idea of the social imaginary to represent not some abstract theory devised by an intellectual, but instead what ordinary folks accept to be true, often without thinking about it (2004, p. 23). This includes the legends and stories and social practices we accept as "the way we do things around here."

More precisely, Taylor has defined the social imaginary as "the ways people imagine their social existence, how they fit together with others, how things go on between them and their fellows, the expectations that are normally met, and the deeper normative notions and images that underlie these expectations" (2004, p. 23). He called it "background" awareness and "an implicit map of social space…" (2004, p. 25). Taylor was familiar with images that are false or unfair. He was also aware that the false or unfair images could still influence people to act a certain way. What he cautioned against was relying on imaginaries that are inoperable, that have no real-world impact on day-to-day behavior. For him, a social imaginary is not just "an insubstantial dream" (2004, p. 183). It has to have some impact on its members.

Taylor explains in his book that these imaginaries shape what we consider to be the legitimacy of our government. They influence how we display ourselves to one another and how we argue. They influence what sort of person we prefer to be, let us say, our elected public officials or our jury foremen. In brief, we might infer that for Taylor these imaginaries determine what constitutes leadership. A social imaginary does not involve itself with us in solitude or in intimate relationships or when we are anonymous, passing through the crowd. It becomes relevant only in certain activities involving our public selves and our shared projects (2004, p. 169).

From the exterior mode (or as I like to call it, from the outside-in), one of the most famous dynamic models is the circulation of elites, discussed at some length by Vilfredo Pareto (1991), who wrote about minorities who occupy positions of privilege and responsibility. Members rise into and fall out of the elite one at a time, but then an entire ruling class can be swept out of power, as for example after a successful *coup d'état*. Later, we will encounter Gabriel Tarde's imagery of the water-tower effect, in which an elite draws innovations up from the bottom to enjoy and exploit, only for these innovations to cascade back down to the bottom as the cost of production goes down and the rate of envy increases.

The purpose of this particular chapter is to illustrate the role of social imaginaries by referring to an image well-known in Western literature and lore: That image is the labyrinth. What is a labyrinth? And what can it contribute to our imagery of the social spaces where leadership takes place? We will find that the labyrinth can work either from the inside-out or the outside-in, a versatility that can be useful, but it can also make things confusing. First, though, we have to understand what it is.

What is a labyrinth?

Penelope Reed Doob (1990) published *The Idea of the Labyrinth from Classical Antiquity through the Middle Ages*, beginning with the Cretan myth of Theseus and the Minotaur and extending through archaeology, religion, and literature. Frequently, one finds implications for philosophy, especially logic and ethics. The metaphor has been a recurring theme in the West. Its appearance in the literature for Leadership Studies has pertained mostly to women and their difficult and almost convoluted pathways to positions of leadership, which scholars such as Alice Eagly and Linda Carli (2012) promise to advise others how to pass through.[2] The following chapter suggests that the metaphor offers a broader array of lessons for leaders and students of leadership.

The imagery of leadership as some kind of journey was reduced to abstraction by Kurt Lewin in his three-stage schema of unfreezing, moving, and re-freezing (2009), where the middle phase entails considerable deviation and uncertainty in a state or condition that has come to be known as liminality (see Thomassen, 2014). The simplicity of the model should not obscure the complexity of the reality it was meant to describe. Hersey and Blanchard (1969) offered a similar four-stage process indicating that leadership has a discernible direction requiring leadership to manage several eventual transitions. Leadership scholars draw on these and similar abstractions in their study of historical and literary figures such as Moses and his wandering in the wilderness (e.g. Wildavsky, 2005; see Doob, 1990, pp. 279f, 298). They are linear images, portraying movement of some sort, from point A to point B. Leadership assumes the framework of a journey. One has to wonder how fruitful it might be to resort to imagery of the labyrinth itself.

Imagery determines how one thinks. One thinks in terms of images. Archetypal psychology depends on this insight (see generally Hillman, 2019). Boulding (1961) urged the creation of an entirely new field of study for just this reason. Professional photographer Lois Farfel-Stark (2018) does a beautiful job explaining and illustrating the extent to which dominant images have shaped culture down through the ages. It stands to reason that adopting an imagery of the labyrinth would influence how one thinks about reality. We already see writers in the field of Leadership Studies struggling to think in terms of complexity.

The literature on leadership attempts to recognize conditions of complexity by investigating an idea known as Complex Adaptive Systems. Virginia Schein (1989/1995) wrote explicitly about the capabilities of women as leaders

2 The invocation of a literature about women in leadership mirrors the fact that many female writers identified in this article have written on this theme (e.g. Virginia Schein, Margaret Wheatley, Mary Uhl-Bien, Barbara Kellerman, Mary Douglas, Agnes Horvath, Lois Farfel Stark, Gill Hickman, and Georgia Sorenson), and the idea of a labyrinth has associations in archetypal psychology with the Divine Feminine. The association of labyrinths with the feminine dates back at least to the ancient Etruscans (Evans, 2009, p. 117, citing Udo Becker).

managing to operate within labyrinthine organizational structures. Margaret Wheatley (1992) urged readers to embrace the complexity. Mary Uhl-Bien (e.g. 2008) has tried to make sense of it. Barbara Kellerman (2016) complained recently that Leadership Studies had not done enough to take the idea seriously. It was toward this purpose that the following chapter was written – not so much to untangle the many threads as to see them whole, as a conceptual knot, and to see what that knot might signify.

The title of this chapter suggests that the labyrinth is a metaphor of some utility. Metaphors frequently enable a person to understand one thing if they already understand something else. One might say, "X is similar to Y." In this sense, metaphors aid in comprehension. Metaphors serve another function, however, as set forth by Hans Vaihinger (1911/2015) and practiced by subsequent thought leaders such as Kenneth Boulding (see Kerman, 1974) and Kwame Anthony Appiah (2017), which is to suggest affinities, i.e. that the same principles that pertain to one phenomenon might also pertain to another. Another scholar making similar assertions was Michel Serres (see generally Watkin, 2020). In this fashion, one might say, "X and Y obey the same basic laws." For instance, scientists can adopt fluid dynamics to study both water and wind. So the question presents itself about the extent to which the lessons pertaining to labyrinths might pertain as well to leadership. Perhaps it can be said that the reality under investigation in Leadership Studies is in fact labyrinthine. If this happens to be so, then the question needs to be asked: what can we in Leadership Studies import into our investigations from the rich literature that already exists regarding labyrinths? The most prominent example from that literature was written by Penelope Reed Doob.

In a manner of speaking, therefore, Doob's research serves as an example about how to navigate the labyrinthine structure of the nature of labyrinths.

The wisdom of Doob

Not only have different cultures preserved examples of the labyrinth in art and architecture, on coins and in tombs, but the idea of the labyrinth has appeared in a variety of texts writing about labyrinths or presenting their own implicit labyrinthine structure. Most significantly for present purposes, the idea has helped investigators trying to make sense of phenomena such as geography, the brain, and religious experience. Others see it more as a fitting image for womankind, or for one's own convoluted private thoughts, or for hell. Here, it is not so much the literal labyrinth as it is the metaphor that can be useful. The imagery can be overlaid to explain social space, conceptual space, historical developments, poetry, and God's will. But then, that range of applications should not surprise anyone; part of the durability of myth is its versatility in a variety of contexts. The idea of the labyrinth has had many uses.

Throughout the ages, the imagery of the labyrinth has been used to depict the handiwork of certain social creatures such as ants and bees, through whose engineering one discovers something of the handiwork of their Creator (Doob, 1990, pp. 67, 135). The cosmos can be portrayed as one vast, all-encompassing labyrinth. The imagery has also been used to depict the intricate products of human arts such as architecture, landscaping, and dance (Doob, 1990, p. 68). Also, the city is often symbolized as a labyrinth (Doob, 1990, p. 138) – a metaphor exploited by writers such as Franz Kafka (see generally Bolzoni, 2012). Furthermore, many have relied on the same imagery to depict the written word, such as the Bible and poetry (Doob, 1990, p. 69; see Douglas, 2008). A book can be labyrinthine. Well-known writers have not been unmindful of this fact. Doob singles out Virgil, Boethius, Dante, and Chaucer for special investigation.[3]

Doob (1990) emphasized repeatedly that labyrinths can be experienced in one of two ways – from the inside, so to speak, as you try to pass through it; and from the outside, as you stand above it and see it whole. These are complementary perspectives on the same complexity, not unlike the hermeneutic circle (see Heifetz & Laurie, 1997, pp. 125ff). The former perspective ordinarily induces frustration and suffering, whereas the latter induces admiration and a certain satisfaction – a satisfaction that the whole bewildering tessellation represents an order that would not be easy to appreciate from inside.[4] Gazing down from above one can see that the complexity ultimately makes sense.[5] In many instances, the purpose of the labyrinth is to bring the wayfarer up out of the complexity to see that what might seem to be cruel fate is in actuality part of providential order (Doob, 1990, p. 130). The judgment about any labyrinth depends on one's perception, which in turn depends on a person's vantage point (Doob, 1990, p. 144).

Consequently, the range of feelings from adventure to perplexity, agitation, foreboding, despair, relief, triumph, and aesthetic gratification can each accompany the experience of labyrinths, depending on one's vantage point and context. Is it chaos or a complex order? It can be both. And that is not a trivial point, inasmuch as the study of labyrinths entails making many distinctions and then recognizing the both/and character of reality. Part of what makes a labyrinth so

3 A volume in *Bloom's Literary Themes* edited by Blake Hobby (2009) goes further to include Spenser, Borges, Marquez, Dickens, Allende, Coleridge, Ovid, Shakespeare, Eco, Milton, Yeats, and James Joyce.

4 Doob (1990) cited Dante for the proposition that the amphitheater in Paradise is a version of this imagery of being situated above the drama, seeing it from all around so that you are not caught in the querulous drama unfolding on stage but instead appreciate a lofty perspective that gives you a sense of appreciation (p. 285).

5 Doob admitted that in several instances, one must look upward to behold the labyrinth, as for example by gazing at the underside of trees (1990, p. 157). The point is neither "up" nor "down" so much as removed, from a point outside or beyond the pathway. Today, one might call that point of view "meta."

perplexing is its both/and character. Prior to that, though, we must make some preliminary distinctions.

Doob distinguishes two types of labyrinth: the **multicursal** and the **unicursal**. The multicursal labyrinth admits of many pathways, with multiple choices for the wayfarer. In systems thinking, this is known as multifinality. Some of these pathways are blind alleys, of course, or false leads. In many labyrinths, the wrong choice can lead to ruin. Quickly, one can get turned around in a multicursal scheme and become lost, even if the smartest move is to retrace one's steps and try again. Leaders, we might note, are often loath to retreat. For purposes of comparison, the unicursal admits of only one path, which might sound simple enough, but the circuitous route that it takes can discourage the wanderer. It takes persistence to wind around repeatedly.[6] In a multicursal maze, the wanderer believes that he has only himself to blame, since he made all the so-called "bivial" choices.[7] In the unicursal, the wanderer will likely curse the artifex for all of the convolutions (Doob, 1990, pp. 48–50). It is somebody else's fault that this is taking so long.[8] The unicursal requires diligence; the multicursal, good choices (Doob, 1990, p. 249). In either case, a maze represents what Doob calls "the vagaries of earthly life" (1990, p. 155).[9]

Doob (1990) makes another preliminary distinction, between (a) labyrinths that are "good" such as carrying you toward the treasured gold or the captive virgin and (b) those that are "bad" such as lead nowhere or worse: leading to a horrifying beast such as the Minotaur or a dragon.[10] Most labyrinths have a center or destination of extraordinary value, whether extraordinarily good or extraordinarily bad (Doob, 1990, p. 54). This presupposes that the labyrinth is in fact possible to trace to reach such a destination, whether for good or ill. Sometimes, however, it can seem not to be possible to get anywhere. A labyrinth that is impossible to escape from the inside-to-the-outside is inextricable and

6 Hermann Hesse illustrated this dynamic in the novel *Journey to the East* (1932/1956), when Leo the leader takes the narrator H.H. on a meandering circuit to various shrines and temples before arriving at his destination.

7 Robert Frost describes the experience poignantly in his poem "The Road Not Taken." See also Gray, 2009, regarding Jorge Luis Borges. Morlier (2009) writes that the range of choices is usually more complicated than just two. In addition to choosing between two possible paths, the person could stop and stand still or turn back around and retrace his steps (p. 96). In fact, writes Andrew Shipe (2009), sometimes the purpose of the metaphor is to bring the treader to a standstill, to pause and ponder (p. 205).

8 A recent version from popular culture would be the film "Mother!" by Darren Aronovsky (released in 2017), in which the creator known only as Him subjects his young wife to a bewildering ordeal in order to say of the experience that it made for a wonderful story. See https://www.imdb.com/title/tt5109784/.

9 Anthony Lee (2009) insists on the distinction between mazes and labyrinths – a distinction it seems unnecessary to revisit in these pages (p. 61).

10 Needless to say, in archetypal psychology, the dragon lies where the treasure awaits. A classic both/and.

futile; a labyrinth that is impossible to enter from the outside-to-the-inside is impenetrable and likewise futile. Often, for the person in the corridors of the maze, he (or she) does not know what lies ahead, whether it is a good outcome or a bad outcome. Or for that matter just an endless series of twists and turns. And so the journey continues down these "darksome galleries" with mounting anxiety (Doob, 1990, p. 80). In the cases when the labyrinth has been designed to teach the wanderer something (Doob, 1990, pp. 82–90), it can be both good and bad. If everything goes according to plan and the student does not lose heart, he or she graduates from confusion and ignorance to enlightenment. Something similar explains the medieval labyrinths intended to represent to the illiterate the so-called harrowing of hell that Jesus made extricable for the rest of us. In a few rare instances, the maze is thought to be preferable to a complete wilderness: because at least with a labyrinth one has pathways to choose that do lead *somewhere* (Doob, 1990, p. 76)![11] A labyrinth is not the trackless void. To that extent – and maybe only to that extent – it is good.[12] Frankly, wrote Doob, when judging better or worse, labyrinths are inherently dual in nature (1990, p. 102).

Doob populated the literature surrounding labyrinths with variations on the original characters in the Cretan myth. For example, **King Minos** the Cuckold becomes the enraged tyrant. Poets will convert him into a severe judge of the damned as they are consigned to Hades. His unfaithful queen **Pasiphae**, who inveigled the artisan Daedalus to construct a wooden cow that she might mate with an actual bull, thereby conceiving the Minotaur – she represents unbridled lust. And not just spontaneous lust, succumbing to the throes of passion, but conniving, premeditated infidelity. She will be held forth as the insistent demands of bodily desire. The **Minotaur** too is bestial, as human beings no doubt are, a monstrous both/and intended to contrast with Theseus/Jesus who is a divine both/and. The Minotaur is that which lies in wait, lurking around the next turn, waiting to devour the hapless. He abides to torment the damned in the afterlife. **Theseus** is the one who enters with a plan, searching out the Minotaur equipped with two devices, one to disable the foe and one to make his way back out of the labyrinth after he kills him (i.e. the thread given to him by an admiring

11 Having too many pathways is seen to be better than having none at all (Doob, 1990, p. 177; see also p. 183). In effect, the same reality that

- appears **trackless** initially, not unlike the Sinai desert to the wandering nation of Israel (Doob, 1990, p. 279)
- reveals itself to be **multicursal**, giving the wayfarer choices; but then with persistence and perspective, the wayfarer
- discovers that in fact with the right guidance there is only one proper way to travel and reach the grail or the Promised Land (a **unicursal** labyrinth), even if that course is circuitous and long.

That is to say, the one reality should be perceived in different ways (Doob, 1990, p. 185).

12 For an investigation into the anthropology of walking in a trackless void, see Szakolczai and Horvath (2017).

Ariadne). He succeeds and celebrates, but then he rejects Ariadne despite her aid and scorns her.[13] Christians will redeem his character as a pagan version of Jesus (Theseus = God Good), the God-man who enters the underworld, slaying the Devil and releasing its hostages. Or he is Joshua circumambulating the walls of Jericho. **Daedalus** himself, the creator of the maze (at his patron's insistence), eventually must flee his situation, what with a lustful queen recruiting him to help her fornicate with an animal and a vengeful king demanding that he imprison the monster in an elaborate maze. Daedalus eventually masters the power of flight and famously escapes with his son **Icarus**, who represents his own story. In fact, Ariadne and Daedalus represent the two means of managing to make one's way through the maze: one requires retracing one's steps in a systematic fashion (ponderous logic and backtracking); the other rises above it and sees its layout from a superior height (stunning revelation) (see Serres, 1995/2018, p. 104f; Doob, 1990, p. 258).[14] Doob then paralleled these two methods with our conventional choice between handwriting (in a linear form) and drawing (in a gestalt, or imagistic form) (Doob, 1990, p. 269). They are in fact complementary modes.

Later, with specific reference to the saga of King Arthur, the labyrinth walkers would be known as Knights Errant (the word "errant" having a double meaning as both "wandering" and "error-prone"). In fact, one of the cruelties of the labyrinth is to think you have come so close, so near to your destination, only to be directed away again from the desired end (Doob, 1990, p. 179). Back you must go. This theme, by the way, can be traced to Plato in more than one place, where the tantalizing proximity to the goal makes the necessity of moving further away again that much more heart-breaking (though necessary). But then Odysseus on his voyage back from the Trojan War had come nearly home, only to be blown out to sea all over again for many more years of wandering. Aeneas saw the end of his world, so far as he was concerned, as the Greeks demolished his ancestral home. But then, as Doob was to put it, Troy must fall that Rome be founded (1990, p. 231). The setback might be a necessary precursor to one's destiny. The objective can be close enough to touch, yet we must venture some more before we are found to be worthy of obtaining it. And let us not forget that

13 Doob drew the fascinating parallel between Ariadne and Rahab, the prostitute who helped Joshua take the battle of Jericho (1990, pp. 280, 303f).

14 It may be that a focus on the center, the goal, the grail – whatever it is –induces a person to enter into the maze, but eventually the maze itself is the true beauty and an apt object of desire, as seen from above (Doob, 1990, p. 188). That is more so the case with poets, whose craftsmanship is on display, unlike preachers and teachers for whom the purpose may be a direct and clear message (Doob, 1990, p. 213). But even then, sometimes the lesson – the didactic purpose – *requires* a circuitous route. That is, sometimes the student is too dull to apprehend the lesson, or isn't ready yet, or otherwise unworthy (Doob, 1990, p. 215). Doob calls this kind of labyrinth a "productive difficulty" (1990, p. 216).

Moses comes sufficiently close to see the Promised Land with his eyes, but only from a distance, from high upon a mountaintop. He was not allowed to enter. One can come tantalizingly close and never reach the goal.

For simplicity, Doob (1990) identified at least three roles pertaining to the experience of the labyrinth, namely the **Artifex** as one who designs and builds mazes; the **Exemplar** as one who goes first into and through the maze, modeling how it's to be done or taking us along vicariously; and the **Guide** as one who offers advice and encouragement to those trying to make their own way through the maze. Each role represents a kind of leadership. The one we are calling the artifex can be said to be responsible for the experience to begin with. They designed and built the apparatus (Daedalus). Sometimes, the labyrinth exists in order to hide and protect something of value. Other times, it imprisons. Then again, the labyrinth sometimes offers an opportunity for adventure, spiritual meditation, or education.[15] As often as not, the labyrinth simply displays the ingenuity of the creator, as a work of art. Regardless of its purpose, the maker of the pathway shapes the ensuing journey (see, e.g. Doob, 1990, p. 176), and this is one kind of leadership. In recent popular culture, we might identify Dungeon Masters in the role-playing game known as Dungeons & Dragons.[16]

By way of contrast, the exemplar (or role model) leads exclusively by example, as the word implies, i.e. a wayfinder or pioneer, oftentimes enacting the hero's quest.[17] The exemplar shows that it can be done. The third role, as a guide (or shaman), assists others in their journey, providing knowledge at key moments along the way. Often, the same person plays multiple roles. The guide sometimes learns the pathways because of prior experience walking the maze or because he or she created it to begin with. Or the leader may accompany a people through a labyrinth as a conductor, sharing in the journey while at the same time possessing insight and wisdom about the best way to go. Maybe the leader is the one with a map. The character Leo in Hermann Hesse's *Journey to the East* plays each role in turn (1932/1956). It is not insignificant that the Christian Trinity aligns with the same three-part structure of Jehovah the Creator (artifex); Jesus the first-fruit to pass from death to everlasting life (exemplar);

15 Doob (1990) indicated that at one time mazes were designed simply as recreation for aristocrats (p. 112). Wikipedia indicates that the first corn maize as a popular tourist attraction was created in Pennsylvania in 1993. https://en.wikipedia.org/wiki/Corn_maze. As stated previously, in Christianity, the labyrinth was often intended to remind illiterate parishioners of the harrowing of hell, when Jesus died and – before ascending into heaven – ruptured the labyrinthine structures of the afterlife in order to release the pious dead (Doob, 1990, p. 127).

16 The academic field known as Design Thinking contributes a lot to an understanding of what it means to be an artifex (see Lockton et al., 2010). They consider what it means for a design to be useful, beautiful, or otherwise worthy.

17 The literature on labyrinths overlaps considerably with the literature regarding the hero's quest (see Campbell, 2008).

and the Holy Spirit who accompanies, communicates, and empowers mortal man on his own pilgrimage (guide). Toward the end of her book, Doob pointed out the extent to which, in his epic poem *The Divine Comedy*, Dante plays each role himself, having constructed the labyrinth of his poem, depicting his journey through it, and thereby guides his reader along his or her own trek (Doob, 1990, p. 305).

To be fair, sometimes the artifex is needlessly cruel or has an evil intent in imposing the labyrinth. And sometimes, the guide is there at the wayside to mis-lead the wayfarer (see Doob, 1990, p. 224).[18] But then just as often the artifex is God himself, or at least certainly god-like. And the guide can be transcendently good and kind, such as the character of Beatrice in *The Divine Comedy*. The fact that the one in the depths of the journey doesn't know which is which just adds to the confusion from within the adventure: who can be trusted? How is he or she to know "what should be followed and what should be fled" (Doob, 1990, p. 236)? The confusion is part of what the imagery of a labyrinth is intended to convey. Making matters worse, not only must the traveler try to figure out who on the pathway is friend and who is foe, the traveler may find that the journey reveals the ambiguity in oneself. It may be the case, for example, that in order to go slay the loathsome beast, you become loathsome yourself. Doob even wrote, "Do not become the monster you [would] destroy" (1990, p. 241). It could be that the world that seems so disordered is that way only because our own minds are disordered (Doob, 1990, pp. 259, 261, 266). This is not a trivial point. Viewed from the right altitude, it can all make sense. The imagery of the labyrinth sometimes says more about our minds than it says about the world.

Not so fast, say several Christian writers such as Dante. No matter how much distance you achieve to scan the labyrinth as a whole, beyond a certain point, the intricacy becomes too dense for human comprehension. At the center of it all is a knot so tight that it cannot be untied, an interlacing of infinite intimacy known as the Trinity (Doob, 1990, p. 292) – a labyrinth beyond tracing, a Gordian knot never meant to be penetrated or escaped. The closest we get in this life to experiencing this wholesome kind of tangle is in community, and probably most vividly in the welcome snares of romantic love, a love that serves as a foretaste of divine love, where the believer finds himself or herself suspended forever in a web of infinite signification. Ultimately, some theologians argue, we are called to abide in the labyrinth and quit striving to transcend it. His ways are not our ways. And in truth, it rises to impertinence for Job to expect anything more.

18 The Greek god Hermes, charged with conducting dead souls to the Underworld, often provided direction to the living, although not without a degree of mischief (see Hillman, 2007, ch. 11).

Leadership in labyrinths

Leaders create labyrinths. They also show us the way through. And they sidle up alongside their followers in order to guide them on their own journey. When doing so, they can often explicitly resort to imagery of labyrinths, perhaps even evoking popular depictions in the arts to help others understand the situation they find themselves in. Labyrinths capture the nuance of complexity, systems thinking, and liminality. A labyrinth suggests that there is a path, no matter how convoluted, and that path leads to somewhere. The following section indicates a few ways that leaders and students of leadership can use this imagery profitably.

a. At a superficial level, trainers and teachers can use some of the literary accounts of the labyrinth from Doob and others in order to offer a rich, fictional sense of what leadership might look like (Denning, 2011; Warner, 2011; Harvey, 2004). Harold Bloom wrote about the "labyrinth-haunted genius of Yeats, Joyce, Kafka, Calvino" – with arguably the ultimate literary labyrinth, he noted, of Shakespeare's *A Midsummer Night's Dream* (Hobby, 2009, p. xv).

We can adopt the labyrinth more readily as a governing metaphor (Alvesson & Spicer, 2011). For instance, a leader can describe the forthcoming challenge as entering into a labyrinth. "It leads us both into and through a strange and confusing new place …" (Evans, 2009, p. 113). This is to acknowledge that the imagery pertains both to certain objective conditions, such as a bureaucracy, and to subjective experiences, including stupefaction and perplexity, regardless of the reality (Swaim, 2009, p. 187). It may not be a labyrinth in fact, but it can seem to be so to the uninitiated.

b. Another way to capitalize on Doob's analysis is to adopt her taxonomy of artifex, exemplar, and guide, which are distinct roles, each of which qualifies as leadership. What follows might be helpful in teasing them apart.

Those who assume responsibility for the space in which followers are to play the role of the artifex. This includes founders and those responsible for the perpetuation of an organization or system, doing work on the conditions within which the rest of us function. Abraham Lincoln pictured himself doing this work when trying to preserve the Union. Ron Heifetz had something similar in mind when he wrote about holding environments. Instructors design courses of study, and mentors set out a regimen for the protégé. So also journal editors, assuming responsibility for the vineyard wherein writers labor. Wilfred Drath (2001) would say that such leaders serve to set direction.

Those who show the way by doing it first, who demonstrate how a thing is to be done, also lead from the front, setting an example for the rest of us to follow. Imitation, after all, lies at the heart of society (Tarde, 1903) and of education (Warnick, 2008). Oftentimes, followers apprentice by watching and absorbing the master's practices. In battle, this type of leader plunges into the maelstrom, calling out to the soldiers, "Follow me, boys!" Even when imitation is not possible, the exemplar represents the fact that it can be done. This conveys assurance to the uncertain. In some sense, followers are responding more to the image of the leader, the *imago*, very much in the same way that a child might resolve consciously or subconsciously to grow up to become just like a parent. Heroes serve an equivalent function. Drath (2001) would say that such leaders meet adaptive challenges.

During the struggle, whatever it might be, followers become discouraged. They lose heart or lose their way. They take the wrong path or threaten to quit altogether. At such moments, a leader might emerge to encourage and urge them onward, to offer words of solace where needed, but then to set folks back on the needful path. A guide can be even more concretely useful telling the follower which way to go when they stop on the trail perplexed. In this role, the leader can be said to accompany the follower, injecting only enough to keep the cavalcade moving … and moving in the right direction. These leaders do not stand outside of the enterprise, watching from above. Neither do they dash ahead on their own. Rather, they remain alongside the followers through the perils. Drath (2001) would say that such leaders create and maintain commitment on the journey.

On the fabled Oregon Trail in the nineteenth century, streams of ordinary people set out from Independence, Missouri, in order to cross the unmapped prairie for the far coast of America. These companies were organized by leaders, who brought hopeful wayfarers together, provisioned them, and gave them impetus as discrete units. Folks were also led by those who had previously made the trek and knew the best path, being aware about what lay further ahead. They were assisted along the way at stations such as forts, sometimes to re-stock or rest or catch up on gossip. One can find the same assortment of roles in the daily crossword, which one person created (artifex), with a completed version the following day in the newspaper (exemplar), and of course the many clues (guide).

Theories in Leadership Studies often pertain to only one or two of these roles. By differentiating them, we create separate opportunities to conduct research. Also, we distribute credit for leadership's successes and avoid the trap of thinking that one person must have done all of these things (Hickman & Sorenson, 2013). Not only that, but models of leadership based on only one role such as Transformational Leadership (Exemplar) and Servant Leadership (Guide) recede in significance.[19] Or, to put it another way, prospective leaders can become more intentional about which role it might be advisable to adopt at any given

19 In fact, Transformational Leadership has suffered from the felt need to make it incorporate all three roles in the same person, when that was always unrealistic and unnecessary. There is a degree of expectation with Transformational Leadership that leadership be heroic in this narrow sense, overlooking the tradition in writing about the hero's quest that the hero is none of these things but instead the one who steps into the labyrinth for the first time *in need of leadership from others*. Only in the re-telling does the hero serve as an exemplar, in the figurative sense (Warnick, 2008).

moment. "Is it my job at this moment to devise an experience for others to grow, to show people how it can be done because I've been through it myself, or to offer help in increments, in limited portions?"

The literature on systems thinking, while similar, emphasizes the system as a complex structure, from multiple points of view, not unlike looking down upon the labyrinth as a whole from a vantage point overhead (see Pavlock, 2009, p. 142). The idea of the labyrinth uses similar imagery, although it adds something else: it emphasizes the dynamics that participants undergo along different dimensions, the actual processes from a single point of view during encounters with complexity. It could be the steps for working through the bureaucracy in order to get permission, for example, or a single person's career path, or the stages of project management. Being the leader during such a linear experience, no matter how convoluted, from that person's point of view, can draw from our understanding of labyrinths. And so the two ways of imagining complexity, i.e. systems thinking (which is more ontological) and labyrinths (which is more phenomenological), offer complementary perspectives.

In education, one can see instructors moving seamlessly through these various roles, creating a curriculum (as an artifex writing a syllabus, selecting required texts, specifying learning objectives, setting a timetable, arranging the desks, and so forth), modeling learning (as an exemplar lecturing, living out the values one is hoping to inculcate, answering difficult questions to give students an opportunity to witness critical thinking, and so forth), and tending to the morale of students as the occasion arises (as a guide giving feedback on assignments, using tactics of motivation, personalizing instruction, accommodating disabilities, and so forth). We might speak of these roles as different, complementary modes in the overall process of education.

c. At a deeper level, the integrated character of labyrinths, which this chapter has been labeling as "both/and," contributes to a more sophisticated ethic in which the follower or student or protégé or ward surpasses the need for simple binary judgments. A leader need not be all good or all bad, enjoying only success all of time or otherwise becoming a failure. Leadership is a mixture of both. In another both/and, each participant in the leadership process can engage in both leading and following. Likewise, a mission can draw from both the past (e.g. enduring principles and lessons learned) and the future (e.g. hope and vision). A leader can belong within a given order and also step outside of it periodically to think afresh (Spoelstra, 2018). Also, in one of the most astounding feats, the dreaded threat – dragon or monster – can be transformed into an opportunity, sometimes in the twinkling of an eye. The apparent either/or often turns out to be a both/and.

Ultimately, scholars can transition away from depicting leadership as a finite game, in pursuit of tangible outcomes and their corresponding rewards. Instead, they can begin to address what James Carse (1986) refers to as the infinite game, the long-term purpose for any leadership in the first place. From this perspective, leadership is less about episodic results (quarterly profits, election cycles, and classroom grading) and more about the long, unending pageant that makes leadership genuinely worthwhile (value, community, and lifelong learning). Yet leadership will always consist of both, as Aimable Twagilimana (2009) points out. Leaders are needed for both the finite and infinite games.

> In ancient times a story could end only in two ways: having passed all the tests, the hero and heroine married, or else they died. The ultimate meaning to which all stories refer has two faces: the continuity of life, the inevitability of death
>
> *(p. 84, citing Italo Calvino).*

Toward the end of a long and astonishing career, Leonardo da Vinci used his notebooks to contemplate the properties of turbulence. With his powers of imagination, spatial logic, and elaborate craftsmanship, he continued to be fascinated by the flux. He had himself designed a number of extremely intricate labyrinths, unmatched in complexity; yet the chaos subsequently known as the Deluge drew him back repeatedly. The phenomenon resisted a simple design. The artist with the prodigious ability to depict birds in mid-flight could not break it down completely. The engineer who could visualize flying machines from different angles could not do anything more with complexity than scribble. Instead, by tirelessly tracing the contours of froth and spray and circular eddies, he found himself captivated (see Zwijnenberg, 1999). Even he, in the midst of life's labyrinth, could not master the structures that betoken vitality. Neither could he look away.

References

Alvesson, M., & A. Spicer. (eds.). (2011). *Metaphors we lead by: Understanding leadership in the real world.* Routledge.

Appiah, K.A. (2017). *As if: Idealization and ideals*. Harvard University Press.

Bolzoni, E. (2012). *The city as labyrinth: How a myth was rewritten between 1950 and 1980,* [Dissertation thesis], Alma Mater Studiorum Università di Bologna. *Dottorato di ricerca in Le letterature dell'Europa unita - Les littératures de l'Europe unie,* 22 Ciclo. https://doi.org/10.6092/unibo/amsdottorato/5052.

Boulding, K. (1961). *The image: Knowledge in life and society*. University of Michigan Press.

Campbell, J. (2008). *The hero with a thousand faces* (vol. 17). New World Library.

Carse, J. (1986). *Finite and infinite games: A vision of life as play and possibility*. Free Press.

Denning, S. (2011). *The secret language of leadership: How leaders inspire action through narrative* (ch. 5). John Wiley & Sons.

Doob, P.R. (1990). *The idea of the labyrinth from classical antiquity through the middle ages.* Cornell University Press.

Douglas, M. (2008). *Thinking in circles*. Yale University Press.
Drath, W.H. (2001). *The deep blue sea: Rethinking the source of leadership*. Jossey-Bass.
Eagly, A., & L. Carli. "Women and the labyrinth of leadership." In W. Rosenbach, R. Taylor, & M. Youndt (eds.). (2012). *Contemporary issues in leadership* (7th ed.; ch. 14, pp. 147–162). Routledge.
Evans, R. "Kubla Kahn." In Hobby, B. (ed.). (2009). *The labyrinth* [Bloom's Literary Themes] (pp. 113–123). Infobase Publishing.
Farfel-Stark, L. (2018). *The telling image: Shapes of changing times*. Greenleaf Book Group.
Gray, J. "The garden of forking paths." In Hobby, B. (ed.). (2009). *The labyrinth* [Bloom's Literary Themes] (pp. 29–36). Infobase Publishing.
Harter, N. (2022). *Cultural dynamics and leadership: An interpretive approach*. Cambridge University Press.
Harter, N. (2007). *Clearings in the forest*. Purdue University Press.
Harvey, M. "Literature." In G.R. Goethals, G.J. Sorenson, & J.M. Burns (eds.). (2004). *Encyclopedia of leadership* (pp. 915–918). Sage Publications.
Heifetz, R., & D. Laurie. (1997). "The work of leadership." *Harvard Business Review*. *75*: 124–134.
Hersey, P., & K. Blanchard. (1969). "Life cycle theory of leadership." *Training & Development Journal*. 23(5): 26–34.
Hesse, H. (1932/1956). *Journey to the East* (H. Rosner, trans.). Picador.
Hickman, G.R., & G.J. Sorenson (2013). *The power of invisible leadership: How a compelling common purpose inspires exceptional leadership*. Sage Publications.
Hillman, J. (2019). *Uniform edition of the writings of James Hillman* (vol. 4). Spring Publications.
Hillman, J. "Hermetic intoxication." In Hillman, J. (2007). *Uniform edition of the writings of James Hillman* (vol. 6.1, ch. 11, pp. 259–275). Spring Publications.
Hobby, B. (ed.). (2009). *The labyrinth* [Bloom's Literary Themes]. Infobase Publishing.
Kellerman, B. (2016). "Leadership – It's a system, not a person!" *Daedalus*. *145*(3): 83–94.
Kerman, C. (1974). *Creative tension: The life and thought of Kenneth Boulding*. University of Michigan Press.
Lee, A. "The history of Tom Jones, a foundling." In Hobby, B. (ed.). (2009). *The labyrinth* [Bloom's Literary Themes] (pp. 57–69). Infobase Publishing.
Lewin, K. "Quasi-stationary social equilibria and the problem of permanent change." In W. Burke, D. Lake, & J. Waymire Paine (eds.). (2009). *Organization change: A comprehensive reader* (ch. 5, pp. 73–78). Jossey-Bass.
Lockton, D., with D. Harrison, & N. Stanton. (2010). *Design with intent: 101 patterns for influencing behaviour through design*. Requisite Variety.
Morlier, M. "In this strange labyrinth how shall I turn? #77." In Hobby, B. (ed.). (2009). *The labyrinth* [Bloom's Literary Themes] (pp. 93–102). Infobase Publishing.
Morgan, G. (2006). *Images of organizations* (updated ed.). Sage.
Northouse, P. (2021). *Leadership: Theory and practice* (9th ed.). Sage.
Pareto, V. (1991). *The rise and fall of the elites: an application of theoretical sociology*. Transaction Publishers.
Pavlock, B. "Metamorphoses." In Hobby, B. (ed.). (2009). *The labyrinth* [Bloom's Literary Themes] (pp. 137–161). Infobase Publishing.

Polanyi, M. (2009). *The tacit dimension.* University of Chicago press.
Schein, V. "Would women lead differently?" In Wren, T. (ed.). (1989/1995). *The leader's companion: Insights on leadership through the ages* (ch. 27, pp. 161–167). Free Press.
Serres, M. (1995/2018). *Geometry: The third book of foundations* (R. Burks, trans.). Bloomsbury Academic.
Shipe, A. "Ulysses." In Hobby, B.(ed.). (2009). *The labyrinth* [Bloom's Literary Themes] (pp. 205–214). Infobase Publishing.
Simmel, G. (1971). *On individuality and social forms* (D. Levine, ed.). University of Chicago Press.
Spengler, O. (1923). *The decline of the West.* Alfred A. Knopf.
Spoelstra, S. (2018). *Leadership and organization: A philosophical introduction.* Routledge.
Swaim, K. "Paradise lost." In Hobby, B. (ed.). (2009). *The labyrinth* [Bloom's Literary Themes] (pp. 183–195). Infobase Publishing.
Szakolczai, A., & A. Horvath. (2017). *Walking into the void: A historical sociology and political anthropology of walking.* Routledge.
Tarde, G. (1903). *The laws of imitation* (E.C. Parsons, trans.). Henry Holt & Co.
Taylor, C. (2004). *Modern social imaginaries.* Duke University Press.
Thomassen, B. (2014). *Liminality and the modern: Living through the in-between.* Ashgate.
Toynbee, A. (1948, October). "The study of history in the light of current developments." *International Affairs. 24*(4): 555–564.
Tuckman, B.W. (1965). "Developmental sequence in small groups." *Psychological Bulletin. 63*(6): 384–399.
Twagilimana, A. "If on a winter's night a traveler." In Hobby, B. (ed.). (2009). *The labyrinth* [Bloom's Literary Themes] (pp. 81–92). Infobase Publishing.
Uhl-Bien, M., & R. Marion (eds.). (2008). *Complexity leadership: Conceptual foundations.* Information Age Publishing.
Vaihinger, H. (1911/2015). *The philosophy of "as if": A system of the theoretical, practical and religious fictions of mankind* (C.K. Ogden, trans.). Random Shack.
Warner, N.O. "Leadership in literary perspective." In R.E. Riggio, & M. Harvey (eds.). (2011). *Leadership studies: The dialogue of disciplines* (ch. 14, pp. 171–183). Edward Elgar Publishing.
Warnick, B. (2008). *Imitation and education: A philosophical inquiry into learning by example.* SUNY Press.
Watkin, C. (2020). *Michel Serres: Figures of thought.* Edinburgh University Press.
Wheatley, M. (1992). *Leadership and the new science.* Barrett-Koehler.
Wildavsky, A.B. (2005). *Moses as political leader.* Shalem Press.
Zwijnenberg, R. (1999). *The writings and drawings of Leonardo da Vinci: Order and chaos in early modern thought* (C. van Eck, trans.). Cambridge University Press.

6

FOLLOWING AS IMITATION

Recovering the sociology of Gabriel Tarde

Introduction to the chapter

Leadership Studies is a confluence of many streams, such as political science, management, social psychology, and ethics (see Harvey & Riggio, 2011; Wren et al., 2009). Scholars continue to link their efforts back to seminal thinkers from antiquity such as Plato, Aristotle, Confucius, and Plutarch and also incorporate important figures along the way such as Max Weber, Peter Drucker, Sigmund Freud, and Hannah Arendt from various, evolving disciplines. Occasionally, the literature introduces fresh streams from across the academy, from systems thinking, for example, as well as from design, critical race theory, and feminism, all of them in order to sustain the interdisciplinary nature of this field of study. Each incursion adds to the overall turbulence and momentum, requiring custodians periodically to integrate what is being said into some kind of coherent whole. The project has not been easy, and it would appear that in principle it will never end (Goethals & Sorenson, 2007).

With due apologies to these overworked custodians, the following chapter introduces yet another stream from the early days of sociology based on the neglected work of Gabriel Tarde, which has subsequently influenced more recent scholarship to explain social dynamics as a recurring process of imitation. One finds explicit in Tarde's work, originally published in 1890 and translated into English by Elsie Clews Parsons in 1903, intriguing references to leadership, which it will be my purpose here to identify.

First, this chapter will summarize many of the primary themes in Tarde's most famous book regarding the centrality of imitation in accounting for social dynamics. Second, this chapter will identify a couple of scholars who have

DOI: 10.4324/9781003374831-6

borrowed profitably from Tarde's work, extending his research in new directions. Indeed, they can be said to have "imitated" him. In the process, the chapter makes the case that it is time to recover this man's insights from over one hundred years ago and import them where they can do the most good.

Tarde's laws of imitation

Biographical sketch

Gabriel Tarde enjoyed an illustrious career in nineteenth-century France before sinking into relative obscurity because of a misbegotten rivalry with that titan of early French sociology, Émile Durkheim.[1] Terry Clark used words such as "dismissed" and "stigmatized" to describe his standing in sociology (1969, p. 1). Tonkonoff (2017) says that for a long time, Tarde was "absent" from the field of sociology (p. 25). Clark explained that pockets of interest did arise in the interim, among legal scholars, some Americans (especially at the University of Chicago), and anthropologists (1969, pp. 6269). Only lately has his work influenced academe once again, in the writings of such scholars as Henri Bergson, Bruno Latour, Gilles Deleuze, and René Girard.[2] Not incidentally, I notice a strong resemblance between Tarde's sociology and the works on social morphogenesis by Margaret Archer, which I've "imitated" in a previous book (Harter, 2020; see, e.g., Archer, 1996).

Born in 1843, Tarde himself began in the legal profession, rising to the bench and then conducting statistical research into criminal law. His more theoretical writings gradually placed him among the early sociologists, and he rose to the chair of philosophy at the Collège de France – three years after Durkheim tried and failed to obtain the post. Durkheim and his followers strenuously undermined the man's stature, continuing to do so after Tarde died in 1904.

Subsequent to several articles tentatively exploring his theme, Tarde had published the first edition of *Les Lois de l'imitation* in 1890. The second edition followed 15 years later (Giddings, 1903). The book inspired a formal debate between Tarde and Durkheim in 1903, which Tarde was unable to prosecute fully because of his death soon after. Durkheim, on the other hand, lived and worked for many more years. An increasing number of scholars are starting to believe that Tarde won that historic battle in 1903 on the merits and just couldn't win the war among the professionals in thrall to Durkheim (Szakolczai & Thomassen, 2019) – an outcome that several writers are hoping to correct today.

1 The story in this paragraph is informed by Szakolczai and Thomassen (2019, ch. 2). Terry Clark indicated that Tarde actually ran up against a point of view that was already ascendant at the time, even before the emergence of Durkheim as its champion (1969, p. 9).

2 Sergio Tonkonoff (2017) implies that it is probably an overstatement, however, to call what is happening today "Tardomania" (p. 145, citing L. Mucchielli, 2000).

The laws of imitation

Tarde began his investigation by observing regularities in social dynamics. What happens repeatedly? And more importantly, why? For in his estimation, society is comprised of the field where imitation takes place. That is, imitation is what constitutes society. To the extent one can discern laws of imitation, we have the beginnings of a science. Tarde once wrote that "though of course the laws of imitation are not the whole of social science, they constitute its first chapter" (1969, p. 104). In this, he was preceded by none other than Plato himself (O'Brien, 2020, p. 92).

Cultural dynamics depend on two things: **innovation**, which is rare, and **imitation**, which is everywhere.[3] Tarde wrote, "Socially, everything is either invention or imitation.... [that is to say] individual initiative followed by imitation" (Tarde, 1903, p. 3). Furthermore, the roots of innovation lie in imitation, because one cannot innovate without incorporating that which has been (and will continue to be) imitated (pp. 45, 49; see Clark, 1969, p. 25). Tarde added, "The most original invention is never more than the synthesis of previous inventions..." (1969, p. 90). What Tarde alleged is that "imitation plays a role in societies analogous to that of heredity in organic life" (p. 11). Imitation, therefore, "is implied in all social relationships whatsoever [and] is the common bond of these relationships" (1969, p. 95). He added that "every elementary social relationship [is] a transmission of, or an attempt to transmit, a belief or desire" (1969, p. 95).[4] Even "social kinship [consists] in having common models" (1969, p. 98).

Innovation then is equivalent to genetic variation, which has an opportunity to pass on to others. He asked the reader to imagine each innovation as a center that radiates outward. Some innovations, of course, have no success whatsoever. We might say they are still-born. A few have limited success, like small circles in a pond. Even fewer become truly successful and part of the culture. At one point, Tarde used language of diffusion (p. 17) and refraction (p. 22). Society is crisscrossed with multiple innovations radiating outward from multiple centers, as the waves of imitation spread at varying speeds and with varying strength (p. 19). As Clark summarized Tarde's thinking, he wrote, "These imitations spread...regularly progressing toward the limits of the system until they come into contact with some obstacle" (1969, p. 21). The mission in Tarde's book was to start making sense of these patterns.

Later in the book, Tarde will point out that as populations grow, gather, and interact with greater frequency, the incidents of innovation will multiply and

3 Clark (1969) acknowledged that Tarde tried to conflate the idea of invention with discovery and cover them both using the term "innovation" as any new thought or technique or device capable of being imitated (p. 23, n. 34; see Tarde, 1969, ch. 6).

4 Regarding belief and desire generally, see Tarde (1969, ch. 11).

compete in a far more confusing web of imitation (Clark, 1969, p. 26).[5] But first, for simplicity's sake, he asked the reader to begin with only two innovations in rough proximity to one another (p. 24). Think of two inventors in neighboring counties each tinkering with the same inspiration. Let us call their inventions, respectively, A and B. As these innovations take hold, they radiate outward. If they are to have any success at all, people will imitate either the one (A) or the other (B). Soon, these waves of imitation will collide, creating conflict. Here we encounter a third centerpiece of Tarde's sociology, in addition to innovation and imitation, and that is **opposition** – not opposition between two or more people, but opposition between innovations (see, e.g. Tonkonoff, 2017, p. 29).[6] Which one will prevail? Will the consumers, for instance, adopt audiocassettes or 8-track tapes as the technology for listening to their favorite music? He called this first phenomenon in which the innovations clash **interference-conflict** (p. 30). It would appear that in these situations imitators must choose either A or B, in a competition between them.[7]

These waves of innovation might collide in just this fashion, perpendicular to one another, but as with ripples in a pond, they will also spread outward at a tangent in the same basic direction as one another, reinforcing one another. A series of inventors were developing the idea of heavier-than-air flight before the Wright Brothers took off at Kitty Hawk in 1903. Their various contributions cumulatively helped to propel the invention of the airplane. Tarde would write that they are in one sense compatible (p. 26), mutually strengthening a trend that they share – validating one another and intensifying pressure to imitate (p. 28). In the same way, the competition between audiocassettes and 8-track tapes, ostensibly opposed to one another (A or B), altered the cultural expectations of transportable mechanisms for personally selecting music to listen to, resulting in such devices

5 Tonkonoff (2017) then observes that for Tarde, when people gather into confined spaces, instead of rapidly diversifying what they do and who they are, given so many unique individuals to imitate (as they do in concentrations such as cities), by compressing further the crowd tends to reduce the number of flows to one or two, which is why they transition toward becoming mobs (Tarde, 1903, p. 56). They imitate only a few things with increased furor. "With greater simplicity comes greater intensity, greater acceleration and expansion; with greater acceleration and expansion, greater simplicity and intensity" (Tarde, 1903, p. 56).

6 Tonkonoff (2017) explains that even though the idea of opposition is nearly coeval with innovation and imitation, opposition itself does not drive social behavior. It is instead the *result* of the flows of imitation and causes nothing itself, unless (he admits) it causes the destruction of the opposition (p. 58; see also p. 138; Tarde, 1969, p. 81). Further, he writes, "If imitations, by spreading, homogenize the social space, inventions diversify it and prevent it from closure. This is why they are the true agents of progress or evolution" (Tonkonoff, 2017, p. 74). The only obstacle to any innovation being imitated universally is the existence of contrary innovations (1969, p. 98). On "opposition" generally, see Tarde (1969, ch. 7).

7 Clark (1969) points out that in Tarde's opinion, conflict can result in consuming time and energy, as well as destroying possibilities, but it also induces people toward greater exertions on their behalf (p. 33).

as the CD, iPod, and Sony Walkman (A and B). He called this second phenomenon in which two innovations magnify one another **interference-combination** (p. 30). Innovation A might be opposed to B, but together they push society in the same basic direction. Each of these phenomena (**interference-conflict** and **interference-combination)** could be occurring simultaneously, according to the so-called laws of imitation.[8]

Part of leadership begins with the management of these bewildering ripples, inviting conversations about new ideas, weighing the alternatives, figuring out how to integrate appropriate novelty, without completely disrupting the system as a whole (p. 33; see Introna, 2007). One might say that leaders help to decide what gets imitated and what does not. Then, if they are successful as leaders, they will in turn be imitated by others.

One of the objections leveled by Durkheim against Tarde was the attempt to explain that this process originates in the mind of an individual human being (p. 30). Durkheim did not believe that sociology should concern itself with such psychological phenomena (see Harter, 2020). Nevertheless, Tarde alleged that imitation as a tendency "to avoid the trouble of inventing, a tendency which is born of instinctive indolence, is an absolutely natural thing" (pp. 50, 74). He wrote that "it is always more fatiguing to think for one's self than to think through the minds of others" (p. 84).[9] In fact, the human brain adopts a state of mind not unlike being hypnotized or (as Tarde put it) **somnambulance** (pp. 77, 81, 85), gliding through decisions by deferring to others who seem to know what would be best in a given situation. We readily suspend our critical powers and fall into line, both with regard to something so mundane as fashion trends and something so acute as mob psychology. And like those being hypnotized, we accept the influence of others without necessarily being aware of it (Tonkonoff, 2017, p. 48).

Imitation is an impulse, a tendency. "Any act of any one of our fellows inspires us who are lookers-on with the more or less irrational idea of imitation" (p. 79).[10] "Things are not born alike," Tarde insisted, "they become alike"

8 Much later, E.M. Rogers (2010) would address these emerging patterns in his popular book *Diffusion of Innovations*, now in its fifth edition.

9 A claim that has been validated by neuroscience (see Swart et al., 2015).

Michael Conforti (2013) added a dimension to this idea of imitation by asserting that people readily imitate themselves, which is to say that they perform repetitive acts, often as habits, and thereby create recurring patterns in their lives; nevertheless, the significance of his contribution exceeds the scope of this chapter and falls prey to Durkheim's objection that such an understanding does not belong in sociology.

10 Tarde attempted a definition of imitation as "the mental impression from a distance by which one brain reflects to another its ideas, its wishes, even its ways of feeling" (p. 1969, p. 94). In other words, it is a "special type of action exercised from a distance by one mind on another, a mental imprint given or received, which is propagated in this way by a type of contagion…" (1969, p. 96). Tonkonoff relays the hypothesis of Tarde that the processes of interest to sociology can

(p. 71). He wrote about the "tumultuous originality of elements…the radical and innate diversity that bursts out…" (p. 72). The similarity may be transient, trivial, or imperceptible. The young man seeing an old man stooped over at the bus stop suddenly stands up straighter. The young girl catches a waft of perfume and thinks to herself that she should try some as well tomorrow. The housewife notes that her neighbor's hydrangea is doing better than her own, so she begins to wonder why. Is there some trick she can learn?

Tarde was unafraid of interjecting what would become hypotheses that likely belong to the field of psychology. He suspected, for example, that anxiety is an emblem of one's stubborn refusal to accede to imitation. One's comfort with a novel situation only means that you have successfully imitated. To resist imitating is fundamentally to be afraid (p. 86).[11] The judgment sounds quite harsh, but those who seem most at ease in a novel situation are probably the most susceptible to this latent type of hypnosis. So, yes, society requires a considerable degree of widespread somnambulism. "Society is imitation and imitation is a kind of somnambulism" (p. 87). To a surprising degree, then, society depends on us almost sleepwalking through life – not because we are mindless zombies or automatons. Instead, while sleepwalking through daily tasks, we get the opportunity to turn our brains to better things, to our dreams and schemes, or jobs and our family cares. We are smart enough to let society channel our behavior so that we can spend our energies on more important topics. We drive on the right side of the road, in America, because we decided a long time ago that by adopting this convention, we don't have to negotiate with everybody else repeatedly

---

be tracked to an inter-mental action between one person and another. The interconnected persons will resemble one another as a result, although he hastens to add the following qualifier: "only in certain aspects, in a certain way, and to a certain extent" (p. 47). Tonkonoff says of this process that it is a non-reciprocal, inter-psychological transmission from one person to another (2017, p. 48). Certainly, the same thing could be happening in reverse regarding some other aspect. Each transmission is one-way, even though the two of them are going in opposite directions. Over time, then, each human being is comprised of thousands of these imitations, great and small, "simultaneously irradiating from very diverse foci (p. 51)".

Raymond Aron (1970) credits Durkheim with acknowledging the role of imitation in shaping society, but he had wanted to differentiate three different kinds of imitation (p. 30). One is a fusion of consciousness, in which two or more persons share the same purpose, as for example in a mob. We might say that they are of one will, so of course their behavior will resemble one another's. Another kind of imitation is mere conformity, outward imitation without sharing the same inward state of mind. We might say that they are not of the same will. A third involves a sequence of events in which one person does something, and immediately somebody does it also, such as yawning. We might say that the imitation does not involve anybody's will. It is more of a reflex, like tapping the brakes on your automobile because the person in front of you just did. Tarde's hypothesis is that the *kinds* of imitation do not matter; together, they shape society.

11 For a more current and detailed analysis of the psychological process of imitation, see Peterson (1999, pp. 7478), where he wrote that human beings "are extremely (uncontrollably) imitative, overwhelmingly social and interminably exploratory"(p. 75).

where to drive a car. We just know to drive on the right, and the brain can be left to think about what to purchase at the grocery. Imitation helps the human brain become more efficient. It also carves out more freedom from petty decision making, allowing us a greater degree of freedom to choose how to occupy our minds. Imitation in this sense is actually liberating.[12]

It is wrong to think that each person does not do this daily. We may forget why we do things the way that we do, because it has become a habit,[13] or we pick up from the example of the people around us so rapidly and smoothly that the imitation barely registers, not unlike figuring out where to stand in line at the store. It would be a mistake to think that somehow human beings have evolved away from acts of imitation, given how prevalent it has become (p. 77). One might say that as we mature, the art of imitation is beneath notice, second nature. Today, multiple possibilities are competing for a person to imitate, so you can choose. Having multiple models to pick from is more rational than being stuck with one role model for every decision. Even so, you still imitate. Being put into a new situation, for example, a person can feel uncertain what to do, but quickly he or she adapts largely by imitating others (p. 83). It's just that there is a variety of examples to choose from.

Looking at the process of ordinary human development, it is true that as we grow up, we imitate a greater variety of people and not just our parents or teachers. We spread our deference around freely, almost promiscuously, because it is the best way to function in a crowded, modern world. Different people show us how to behave in different contexts. We learn from all sorts of role models. Exemplars are everywhere, especially now in the media. In addition to which, after a person grows up, the flow of imitation goes back and forth. It is no longer in one direction, from the model to the imitator. The influence becomes mutual, reciprocal (p. 79). I can imitate you in one respect, but you can imitate me in some other respect. Just because the influence is mutual does not make it any less a process of imitation. Tarde was not trying to say that a single human being is entirely held in thrall to a single master. In our childhood, however, that was likely the case.

In pre-history, probably entire villages took their cue from the resident prophet or the strong man, by means of imitation through fascination or awe

12 Bryan Warnick (2008) adds that imitation does not foreclose choosing, in part because you get to choose what and whom to imitate. Surrounded by exemplars doing all sorts of things, you have the freedom to pick. Think about it this way: no individual person imitates literally everything in the social field; there will be some role for individual discernment.

13 Sigmund Freud (1914/1963) would go so far as to claim that the mature adult will continue to function with reference to childhood authorities, e.g. carrying on household practices learned as child and still trying to live up to parental expectations long after the parents have died. The imprint of imitation will persist, even at a subconscious level. Freud wrote that "psychoanalysis could explain nothing current without referring back to something past [i.e. in childhood]" (p. 45).

(p. 80; see also p. 310). Under these conditions, great leaders were understood to overwhelm their followers. This experience of awe is an "atavistic phenomenon to plunge us into the remote past..." (p. 80). The remote past, maybe, Tarde admitted, but it is a temptation even today, when we succumb to idolatry and fawning over celebrities. We might even describe history as a succession of thralldoms, passing from one type of leader to another, during which human beings were repeatedly susceptible to these moments of deference, known to us today as the cult of personality or even falling in love (p. 83).[14] Because Tarde was addressing leadership, let me quote him in full here.

> Thousands of centuries ago the human species might have been reduced to a negligible number of individuals [who] ceased to progress, had not some man of genius arrived from time to time...to stimulate its reproductive power, either by opening new outlets to human activity through industry or colonization or, as a religious reformer, like Luther, by reviving or, rather, by rejuvenating in an entirely new form the religious zeal of the community and its general belief in Providence as the protector of all the birds of the air
>
> *(p. 123).*

Later in his book, Tarde elaborated on this phenomenon, as follows:

> An energetic and authoritative man wields an irresistible power over feeble natures. He gives them the direction which they lack. Obedience to him is not a duty, but a need.... People obey for the same reason that they believe; and just as their faith is the radiation of that of some apostle, so their activity is merely the outgoing of some master will. Whatever the master wills or has willed, they will; whatever the apostle believes or has believed, they believe. And it is because of this that whatever the master or apostle subsequently does or says they, in turn, do or say or are inclined to do or say
>
> *(p. 198).*

As he looked back in time, Tarde sounds very much like an advocate of the Great Man Theory of leadership. Fortunately, he recognized that such disparities of dominance happen rarely to adults in the modern age. With a population increase and greater concentrations of people, more of these so-called "great men" walk among us. Likewise, we enjoy wider access to them through travel and the media (p. 137). Not only that, but as imitation becomes more generalized throughout the population, it "has also become mutualized and specialized" (p. 233; see also p. 369). We don't all look to the same person to lead us. Or we look to

14 It is helpful to remember that he was writing this long before the rise of Mussolini, Hitler, Stalin, and Mao.

different people to lead us for different purposes. Accordingly, imitation of some kind is still going on, but it no longer resembles the Great Man Theory.[15] Tarde did believe that certain social actors have a disproportionate impact on society. Not everyone is a Leonardo da Vinci or Sir Isaac Newton. Tarde saw no reason to deny this fact. Even then, every individual person contributes something to the flow of imitation, no matter how slight. Deny the genius, he wrote, and you have to deny us all (1969, p. 101). Of what possible scientific use is it to do that? The so-called "Great Man" is only a more vivid, a more pronounced example of something we all do, to one degree or another.

We should be able to see that imitation is a form of following.

Tarde concluded that culture is "an untold store of blind routine and slavish imitation which was constantly being added to by successive generations" (p. 75). In fact, he defined society in this way: "Society may therefore be defined as a group of beings who are apt to imitate one another, or who, without actual imitation, are alike in their possession of common traits which are ancient copies of the same model" (p. 68). Imitation is what signifies our sociability. We go along to get along. We fall into patterns, because doing so makes everything easier. One might say that sociability of this kind is the force; society is the resulting form (p. 70). A thousand subtle acts of leadership shape the spontaneous order by which we all live, as we adjust ourselves to one another.

The structure that emerges Tarde referred to as terraces and cascades (p. 84). A thousand little ripples of varying intensity, traveling in a variety of directions, gradually taking shape in hierarchies. "Societies are organized according to the agreement or opposition of beliefs which reinforce or limit one another. Social institutions depend entirely upon these conditions" (p. 146).

Toward what end? Tarde explained the motive to imitate in this way: the goal originates in a "desire for a maximum of strong and stable belief" (p. 50). "The true and final object of desire, then, is belief" (p. 147). We seek a greater repertory of beliefs, beliefs that are integrated with one another, integrating everything "widening and deepening" (p. 148). Thus, one of the reasons we imitate is because these beliefs help us in some fashion. We watch how things are done. We copy successful responses to similar problems. This is a logical use of imitation (ch. 5). If there is more than one possible response to a problem, then these alternatives engage in what Tarde called playfully a duel.[16] First, the individual who must make a decision experiences this "duel" in his or her own mind. Sec-

15 Clark (1969) pointed out that Tarde did provide a fairly extensive version of what sociologists call Elite Theory, in which certain social classes predominate (p. 48f; see generally Tarde, 1969, ch.14).

16 Tarde explained that these duels are based on a simple binary schema. Ordinarily, there are two – and only two – options (1903, pp. 155–162).

ond, once the individual makes a decision, he or she becomes a partisan for A or for B against those who make a contrary choice. Thus, "social irresolution begins when individual irresolution ends" (p. 166; see Clark, 1969, p. 34).[17] In the game of tennis, for example, coaches disagreed on the relative utility of the one-handed backhand and the two-handed backhand. Once a player selected one or the other, he or she brought pressure to bear – however slight – on other young players to do the same, if only by example. With greater success at the backhand, more and more players took notice. Here in sum is the engine of social change. By now, culture is littered with the residue of prior duels (p. 170).

The outcome of any such duel will be (a) victory for one side or the other or (b) some kind of compromise or reconciliation (p. 169). As these duels eventually become resolved, one way or another, minor struggles create contradictions at the next level (p. 186). Even once a duel is resolved at the local level, participants will find that folks in other localities resolved them differently. Or once one social class resolves a duel, other social classes will be found to have made contrary decisions. At which point, the duels resume afresh. So up and down the hierarchy of abstraction, these little duels shape social dynamics, as people struggle to adopt beliefs that work best.

At any given point in time, society is undergoing a thousand little duels about what to eat and what to wear and what to watch on television. People confront a multitude of choices about how to live. Imitation is one way that we consult each other in order to make increasingly prudent choices. Such decisions might be conscious or unconscious, deliberate or spontaneous, voluntary or involuntary (p. 192). Nevertheless, Tarde was clear that imitation has its non-logical side (ch. 6). Selecting rational solutions to life's problems is one thing, but that's not all.

Tarde noted that all other things being equal, a human being is likelier to imitate someone who is regarded as **superior**, whether they are actually superior or not. Reputation is a mighty thing. A lesser-known person off in the corner may have a superior answer, but without a sufficient reputation, nobody will listen to them. A reputation is not proof of greater competence. Fortunately, in contemporary society, there are numerous forms of superiority: who is better at plumbing, who is better at masonry, who is better at horticulture? The relevant question, therefore, is superior at what?

Also, a human being is likelier to imitate someone nearby than somebody far away. The role model is right under your nose, for immediate consultation. Tarde called this law "the imitation of the nearest" (p. 224). Obviously, **proximity** has

17 Clark (1969) explained that at the individual level, when a person is undecided how to choose, this is an experience of **internal** conflict. Once the decision is made, this increases the likelihood of **external** conflict. Clark then asks, does this mean that the individual person finally making a decision risks societal peace in exchange for personal serenity (p. 35; see Tarde, 1969, p. 169)?

little to do with competence, so again, this is a non-logical basis for imitation. Yet we often simply look around at those who happen to be at hand.

Another non-logical feature is the **social class** of the person being imitated. A human being is more likely to imitate his or her betters, even if that person of higher status knows very little about what they are doing. We just figure they must know more than we do. Out of these examples, one can infer the pattern of society that emerges, as we resemble those in proximity and esteem those of a higher class or with a greater reputation.[18]

We can gather four broad reasons to imitate, only one of which is, in Tarde's estimation, logical:

- Utility (logical)
- Reputation (non-logical)
- Proximity (non-logical)
- Social status (non-logical)

As imitation increases, there will be a subtle leveling of these disparities. It will become harder and harder to differentiate. Those who are figuratively below will increasingly resemble those who are figuratively above (Clark, 1969, p. 32). An awareness of this tendency will motivate those in power to keep their status, perhaps by frustrating apery ("you must obtain a license to do that") or by changing that which is valued. "So you resemble me with regard to X. So what? What really sets me apart is Y." This energy to distance oneself from lesser persons also contributes to social dynamics. Tarde called it "a kind of social water-tower" sucking up innovations in order to generate distinction and then indirectly distributing these innovations back down to the masses (p. 221). Only rich people can afford the early versions of new technology. They buy them in part to exhibit their superior wealth, which in turn creates demand for the same technology among those with fewer resources, and so by buying the more expensive versions first, they enable the manufacturers to bring down costs and make newer versions that are more affordable, such that by the time the item can be obtained by the masses in large numbers, the wealthy have moved on to other, more elaborate gadgets, toys, and conveniences.

This recurring impetus to differentiate oneself from one's inferiors is why the winds of fashion blow first through the privileged classes. "The social function of aristocracies is to initiate populations into an admiration and envy of foreign things, and thus to cut a way for fashion-imitation as a substitute for custom-imitation" (p. 220 n. 1).

Without this **water-tower effect**, imitation will gradually not only collapse the distinctions that led people to imitate their betters, but the attraction of imitation

18 Tarde acknowledged that influence could flow in the opposite direction, but the social impact of these "unimportant back eddies" is negligible (1903, p. 217).

itself diminishes. Once a people are adequately similar, they will exert themselves to imitate less (p. 210). For this reason, under these conditions, one will notice an opportunity for leadership. "The qualities which a man superior in any country and at any period are those which enable him to understand the group of discoveries and to make use of the group of inventions which have already appeared" (p. 235).[19] In this way, leaders sustain themselves by inspiring those who seek distinction to take advantage of the latest breakthroughs. By the same token, however, they are likelier to succeed at this to the extent they can convince their followers that what they are doing is in fact restoring something customary (p. 361), inasmuch as the ultimate goal is to arrive at stable and enduring beliefs. A leader would be advised to traffic in a series of novelties as though they were customary. Followers will find these offerings reassuring. In this way, a smart phone assures those who can afford them that in this way you stay in touch with family and preserve memories, all at the same time that you can access the accumulated knowledge of humankind. That is, you sell the novelty as a means of perpetuating that which is familiar.

Patterns in history

Although Tarde's philosophy of history is not especially well regarded (Clark, 1969, p. 33), it does illuminate his overall sense of the flow of imitation that preoccupied him. Tarde tried to explain that across time, civilizations will undoubtedly resemble one another. For one thing, they are all trying to do similar things under comparable constraints, such as feed themselves (1903, p. 38f). Common problems are likely to yield to the same simple solutions, especially among the poor, i.e. being poor the world over is more or less the same (p. 54). Nevertheless, much of that which is similar can be attributable to imitation, as peoples learn from one another, especially among those who are cosmopolitan (p. 54). They help one another know how to prop up their social status, such that they imitate one another in trying to set themselves apart from the rabble. One way to do that, of course, is for them to be proximate to one another, to be seen among one another. To invite one another to exclusive parties. To spend their vacations at the same exclusive resorts. It is said that aristocrats from different countries have more in common with one another than with the lower classes in their own countries.

Zooming out, so to speak, a sociologist will notice that innovation tends to originate in cities and diffuse into the hinterlands. Also, innovations will tend to

19 Once an elite plays it safe and stops generating and displaying innovation, that elite will soon be replaced by another (Clark, 1969, p. 30). These innovations could very easily originate among non-elites, so that it is in the leader's interest to pick some of these and offer them to the elite as a way to legitimate the innovation and also keep the elite in its higher position (Clark, 1969, p. 31). In this way, useful innovations get to circulate, no matter where they begin. Leaders are, in this sense, brokers of innovation.

originate in dominant capital cities and expand to lesser cities (p. 229). Again, this is not because there is more of worth in these cities to imitate, so much as cities bring people into proximity and attain a rough status of superiority to outlying districts. When farmers become really sick and need specialized care, they usually drive into town. They assume that local docs aren't up to the challenge. When small town couples want to see a top-notch show, they buy tickets to the theater in the city rather than the high school rendition of "Beauty and the Beast." It was in this regard that Tarde made an interesting assertion. He wrote that "the classes or nations which are most imitated by others, are those within which the greatest amount of reciprocal imitation goes on" (p. 239). Whereas imitation at one time might have signified a person's inferior status, demonstrating a dependence on superior models, in today's society imitation is being conducted across all levels of society, back and forth. Imitation is if anything a sign of one's astuteness in learning. As a result, innovations will more readily arise and find a niche.

Having said this, one might suppose that the goal is to create a climate of novelty and almost frenetic or assiduous attention to what one's neighbor is doing. In such a community, fashion would be king. Think for example of the fastidious attention to fashion in the court of Louis XIV at Versailles. Yet Tarde does not hold that the goal is to create such a community, except as a means to an end. Remember, the ultimate goal is to form stable and enduring beliefs. That is, people seek a configuration or constellation of customs that work. Fashion blows through to differentiate ourselves from others, yet it has the water-tower effect of strengthening the community overall. Seasons of fashion come and go.

The broadest categories for imitation – which we might refer to as the macro level are **fashion**, which tends to be transient, dependent on a sense of novelty, and **custom**, which tends to be enduring and more predictable. Fashion transmits across space, from one place to another, whereas custom transmits across time, from one generation to another. Tarde suggested that these two (fashion and custom) swap prominence in a cyclical model of history (Clark, 1969, p. 29). Although the two will seem to work at cross-purposes, according to Tarde, each is an example of imitation. Also, with the passage of time custom tends to swallow up certain fashions and make them customary (ch. 7). Another way of saying this is that fashion auditions to become customary. Tarde would describe a rhythm to these macro categories by which fashion disrupts custom for a time, only to subside.[20] Each novelty that emerges, grows in popularity at first and then becomes entrenched, in a pattern familiar to many theorists. Thus, what is fashionable today becomes vulnerable to each subsequent fashion, over and over. And the residual effect is to construct a panoply of customs, many of which are

20 In a time of fashion, people seek to be compared *to one another*. When these times subside, people seek to be compared *to their ancestors* (Tarde, 1903, p. 318).

not even conscious. Fashion commands attention, but custom ultimately governs. He wrote that "imitation…that is engaged in the currents of fashion is but a very feeble stream compared with the great torrent of custom" (p. 244).

Recovering the laws of imitation

Bryan Warnick

Bryan Warnick, professor of the Philosophy of Education, published a book in 2008 titled *Imitation and Education*, where he states that "questions of human exemplarity, modeling, and imitation have been largely ignored" (p. 2). He acknowledges there has been work in the cognitive sciences on these questions, such as mirror neurons, but unfortunately they had not been migrating into the social sciences (p. 5). He then devotes a chapter to the historical tradition in the West, going all the way back to Homer, explaining why the methods of teaching by example have tended to disappear from formal education in modernity, despite the fact that we continue to imitate one another just as frequently today.

Under what he calls the **standard model**, there would be three steps to the process. First, the person must notice (or have his or her attention drawn to) another person's actions. Second, that first person (whom we might designate as a follower) must believe that the other person's actions result in some kind of benefit (or avoidance of some detriment). In other words, it causes a preferable outcome. Third, the benefit must be sufficiently appealing to the follower that he or she will conclude that doing the same action themselves will result in the same benefit (p. 15).[21] One way to imagine what is going on is that the model exhibits something that the follower can foresee as an aspect of his or her own future self (pp. 32, 36). "If I were to imitate, I would look like that."[22]

Warnick explains that the social sciences indicate that people still imitate one another, even if they do not realize it. And they still advise others to imitate those who know what they are talking about in order to acquire knowledge, skills, and abilities as for example in apprentice programs or YouTube instructional videos. The standard model has been challenged of late, but it still applies widely to modern life.

21 Warnick gives examples of this standard model in Plato, Plutarch, Livy, and Isocrates, plus Christianity (2008, pp. 2, 17). With John Locke, we start to see qualifications and exceptions, further complicated by the work of Descartes, Rousseau, Kant, Emerson, and Nietzsche (ch. 2). Regarding Freud and imitation, see Warnick (2008, p. 56).

22 Warnick (2008) admits that we are less likely to imitate another person if what that person does is incompatible with the story we tell ourselves about our own future life (p. 77). I cannot foresee myself dancing professionally, so I'm not inclined to imitate the professionals when I watch television. In addition, a person is less inclined to imitate something they consider to be impossible for themselves. I could not imitate giving birth.

Warnick points out that some models are types, i.e. representative of a class, such as fathers or lawyers or tennis players. If you want to know what lawyers do, go observe one. Warnick refers to these as models of **convention**. But then Warnick adds that in many cases the ones we most readily notice are definitely NOT typical. In fact, they are extraordinary, exceptional. Warnick refers to these as models of **differentiation**. So we scan the social horizon noticing both the typical and the exemplary (pp. 34, 39). One tells us what it means to belong; the other tells us how to excel.[23] Each of these is imitation. As Warnick put it, "Examples must be similar to the group in significant ways, while possessing differences that focus our attention on the exemplified features" (p. 50).

In both cases, however, the model draws attention to some certain aspect or feature and not literally everything about them (p. 37). Telling children to grow up to be like Abraham Lincoln does not mean urging them to buy a stove-pipe hat and wear chin whiskers. Even here, there is a degree of freedom to choose, which we might think is a version of selectivity. I notice how this lawyer dresses for court and remember that for future reference; you might notice how he or she interacts with the client. We pick up on different things, depending on our interests and purpose.[24]

Tarde had asserted that imitation takes place in a state or condition of somnambulance, like hypnosis, whereas Warnick introduces the element of choice, as though we go around all day making selections using the executive function in our brain. Warnick credits Tarde with the insight that we seek to imitate and often do so without much (if any) conscious thought (2008, p. 55). We might even think of this tendency as impulsive, instinctual, or constitutive.[25] Nevertheless, there is room for consciousness, he argues, a possibility of choosing, as for example (a) choosing to adopt a mode of somnambulance in certain novel circumstances such as walking into a strange venue and looking around wondering where to start or (b) choosing whom to imitate and then lapsing into somnambulance while following them around all day, as with job-shadowing. We can elect to enter into and leave these modes of somnambulance, almost at our discretion.[26]

23 On this distinction between recognition/belonging and esteem, see Appiah (2010).

24 Warnick does caution the reader that people might say that they are imitating a model X, when in actual fact they are imitating model Y. The selection he is talking about can be done at a subconscious level (2008, p. 3). Tarde made a similar point when he wrote about "the illusion that their ideas, all of which have been suggested to them, are spontaneous.... Did not ... people think, like us, that they were autonomous, although in reality, they were but the unconscious puppets whose strings were pulled by their ancestors or political leaders or prophets, when they were not being pulled by their own contemporaries?" (p. 77).

25 Warnick (2008) invokes the discovery of mirror neurons that fire in the brain as though we were undertaking the activity we are witnessing in another human being (p. 59; see Swart et al., 2015).

26 Warnick does note that consciousness does tend to "break" the somnambulance and interrupt the imitation, if only for a moment (2008, p. 62). But in those instances, what he is referring to is

Choosing what and whom to imitate sends a kind of signal about our values (2008, p. 124f). Warnick then lists many of the social implications of imitation. The act of imitation has some combination of many possible consequences. The most obvious perhaps is to exert social pressure to perpetuate the practice in others, increasing the likelihood that somebody else will adopt the same practice. That is, they become likely to imitate you. Imitation increases overall momentum toward the practice becoming widespread. By imitating, we are passing it along to others. Imitation also might signal respect for the person being imitated, endorsing their status – unless, that is, the imitation is intended to mock (pp. 84, 89). Imitation can signal to others that you belong to their group, because you are conforming to their norms. And so you dress like they do, talk like they do, ingratiating yourself with them (p. 84).[27] At the very least, it shows that you are interested in what they do (p. 86). Imitation can create a sense in the other person that you are kindred in some way, simpatico, so that you form a subtle bond that makes it easier to influence them, as for example in face-to-face salesmanship (p. 86). In these instances, imitation makes it likelier that you would obtain favor, approval, and rewards (p. 89). In addition, imitation gives the teacher or instructor an opportunity to check your work and make corrections (p. 90). This too is a social function of imitation.[28] In short, imitation says something about what you think of the model, or of what the model is doing, or even of yourself, such as your disposition to conform (pp. 91f). What a person imitates tells others about what that person values. "I am doing what these folks do. Please think of me as one of them."

Relevant to Leadership Studies, Warnick reports that when children perceive the leaders in their midst, they select the ones more likely to imitate other people and not the mavericks or freethinkers (p. 89). Accordingly, those who go through life sleepwalking would appear to have social advantages. This is why educators bear some responsibility for selecting role models, including role models who themselves were known to think for themselves (ch. 8). Educators might invite students to bring their imitating to the surface, making them explicit and being conscious of their role models – and what it is about them that would be worthy of imitation. In this way, students can learn to become the curators of their own selections.

---

consciousness of oneself and one's choices. Imitation often requires acute consciousness of *what the other person is doing*.

27 Warnick (2008) acknowledges the risk to groups of imitation tearing groups apart when they adopt practices, the cumulative effect of which is to destroy the basis of belonging, such as gossip (p. 97) or groupthink (p. 99).

28 Tarde himself wrote that imitation "can proceed from sympathy or even animosity, from envy or admiration, from servile docility or a free and intelligent calculation; it makes no difference…" (1969, p. 114).

Deleuze and Foucault

Recently, in 2017, Sergio Tonkonoff published a study of Tarde's influence on two French postmodern thinkers, Gilles Deleuze and Michel Foucault. He groups the three of them together under the label "infinitesimal" because to them the social is an infinite field of infinitesimal differences (p. 5). What does he mean by that? Very small and subtle things are happening all the time, colliding or reinforcing one another, to varying degrees, from the slightest nod to the color of one's turtleneck. Tonkonoff calls these nearly inscrutable phenomena part of a thousand little flows, going this way and that, both for and against nearly everything. The human individual is in one sense a point of intersection for these many flows (2017, p. 105) or a crossroad (2017, p. 121). Tonkonoff then adds, "Each of these flows has diverse and changing intensities and velocities, and comes from different places and eras" (p. 105). Each person is a manifold – and the social groups to which he belongs even more so. Tarde referred to "imitative radiation" and said, "Our social life includes a thick network of radiations of this sort, with countless mutual interferences" (1969, p. 171).

A countless multitude of people send and receive social cues — many of them unconsciously, only some of them accurately, passing through people so wildly different from one another that they respond differently to the exact same stimulus. Even when two persons attempt to imitate the exact same thing, such as a dance move, they will do so differently (p. 137). The cumulative effect of all of these little flows will be overt behavior, newsworthy events, and the gradual formation of our social institutions, which are merely "aggregates of inventions" (2017, p. 75). He wrote that "the social world appears before us as myriad heterogeneous and singular elements in constant movement" (2017, p. 11). Thus, sociology must begin with plurality, mutability, and variety.

Tonkonoff points out that these bewildering flows change and transmogrify constantly, yet they do assemble into recognizable configurations long enough to deserve a name. Tarde called such a configuration an **ensemble** – "an open set made of moving elements whose origins are diverse and its future uncertain" (2017, p. 12). A team, an organization, a family, a faculty: each of these is an ensemble. The three theorists (Tarde, Deleuze, and Foucault) describe a recurring series, from a condition of multiplicity and difference contributing to innovations that are subsequently imitated (or not), which in turn clash with other innovations, jumbling up the original multiplicity without resolving much of anything (2017, p. 20). The human being is to be regarded as the conduit for these flows, more of a copy than an original. Even the creative act of innovation is a lot less creative than it appears. The innovator is the locus of a strange (and happy?) confluence of pre-existing flows, so that the imitations downstream can be depicted in sequence as rays from a single point (even though that "point" is in fact where many prior innovations came together under unique circumstances) (2017, p. 30; see also 2017, p. 73). Tonkonoff summarized the process in this way: "[A]ll social phenomena, all current forms of acting, feeling, or thinking, were once born of a spectacular or discrete example, and spread themselves as fashions, to finally become established institutions, and repeated as custom" (2017, p. 33).

The more successful "flows" increase in speed and intensity, as more and more people jump on board the proverbial bandwagon (2017, p. 54). I remember as a kid seeing automobile owners affix little orange Styrofoam balls on the tip of their radio antennae, in order to be able to spot their car quickly in a crowded parking lot. The irony is that soon so many people imitated that practice that you could step out of a mall to find literally hundreds of cars all sporting the little orange Styrofoam balls, thereby nullifying their purpose. When something catches on, we say it catches fire.

Tonkonoff (2017) captured the theory of Tarde succinctly in the following passage, which is worth quoting in full:

> Tarde begins by understanding social life as an enormous number of small, simultaneous, and specific human activities which he classes into three types: imitations, [innovations], and oppositions. What makes these activities social is that they are modes of inter-mental relation in which beliefs and desires are communicated by repetition, co-adaptation, and confrontation. For Tarde, societies, groups, and individuals are made and transformed through these communicational processes. Here the production, reproduction, and mutation of any social system (including the individual) takes place in that multiple field made from the constant influx, convergence and divergence of currents of inter- or trans-individual beliefs and desires
>
> (p. 72).

References

Appiah, K.A. (2010). *The honor code: How moral revolutions happen.* W. W. Norton & Co.

Archer, M. (1996). *Culture and agency: The place of culture in social theory* (revised ed.). Cambridge University Press.

Aron, R. (1970). *Main currents in sociological thought* (vol. II). Anchor Books.

Clark, T. "Introduction." In Tarde, G. (1969). *On communication and social influence: Selected papers* (pp. 1–69). University of Chicago Press.

Conforti, M. (2013). *Field, form, and fate: Patterns of mind, nature, and psyche* (revised edition). Spring Journal Books.

Freud, S. (1914/1963). *The history of the psychoanalytic movement and other papers.* Collier Books.

Giddings, F. "Introduction." In Tarde, G. (1903). *The laws of imitation* (pp. iii–vii). Henry Holt & Co.

Goethals, G.R., & G.J. Sorenson (eds.). (2007). *The quest for a general theory of leadership*. Edward Elgar Publishing.

Harter, N. (2020). *Leadership across boundaries: A passage to aporia*. Routledge.

Harvey, M., & R.E. Riggio (eds.). (2011). *Leadership studies: The dialogue of the disciplines*. Edward Elgar.

Introna, L. (2007). "Maintaining the reversibility of foldings: Making the ethics (politics) of information technology visible." *Ethics and Information Technology*. 9: 11–25.

O'Brien, J. "Plato's statesman: Defending *phronesis* from coding." In A. Horvath, A. Szakolczai, & M. Marangudakis (eds.). (2020). *Modern leaders: Between charisma and trickery* (ch. 5, pp. 88–104). Routledge.

Peterson, J. (1999). *Maps of meaning: The architecture of belief*. Routledge.

Rogers, E.M. (2010). *Diffusion of innovations* (5th ed.). Simon and Schuster.

Swart, T., K. Chisholm, & P. Brown. (2015). *Neuroscience for leadership: Harnessing the brain gain advantage* [*The Neuroscience of Business*]. Springer.

Szakolczai, A., & B. Thomassen. (2019). *From anthropology to social theory: Rethinking the social sciences*. Cambridge University Press.

Tarde, G. (1969). *On communication and social influence: Selected papers*. University of Chicago Press.

Tarde, G. (1903). *The laws of imitation* (E.C. Parsons, trans.). Henry Holt & Co.

Tonkonoff, S. (2017). *From Tarde to Deleuze and Foucault: The infinitesimal revolution*. Palgrave Macmillan.

Warnick, B. (2008). *Imitation and education: A philosophical inquiry into learning by example*. SUNY Press.

Wren, J.T., R.E. Riggio, & M.A. Genovese. (2009). *Leadership and the liberal arts: Achieving the promise of a liberal education*. Palgrave Macmillan.

7

MAKING DISTINCTIONS

Hazel and Hawthorn

Introduction to the chapter

The literature in the field of Leadership Studies offers a bewildering variety of distinctions. One finds distinctions between types of leader (task-oriented v. people-oriented), types of leadership (transactional v. transformational), types of power (personalized v. socialized), types of empirical research (quantitative v. qualitative), and so on. Differentiation turns out to be more than helpful: it is in fact necessary yet insufficient for understanding the phenomenon. Nevertheless, as students of leadership, we can take things too far. David Collinson (2019) writes that "even the most influential ideas in leadership studies can be prone to over-dichotomization" (p. 260).

The following chapter takes up comparable words of caution from Agnes Horvath (2013) against an excess of differentiation. Instead, one must adopt a dynamic model in which making these distinctions is only a phase or stage in a process of comprehension, and it goes like this

compact reality > differentiation > integration

As a way of illustrating how anthropology describes the process, this chapter refers to the seminal work by van Gennep on rites of passage (1908/1960), when children (in compact reality) are brought through a liminal phase (differentiation) before becoming adults and thus integrated into the larger community.

Archetypal psychology relies on this same schema for a variety of its investigations, suggesting that maybe the process is itself archetypal, as human beings transition from one phase of life into another. We might say that we journey from a point of departure, by means of uncertain travels, toward a destination. Change

DOI: 10.4324/9781003374831-7

is often depicted as a crossing over. Perhaps the mind is constituted to structure its experience of the change process in just this way, as a journey, from point A to point B, by way of some circuitous path. We saw this in a previous chapter on the imagery of labyrinths.

Mythology, which often serves as the raw material of archetypal psychology (Hillman, 2013, p. 14), presents an interesting story about the boundary that we cross from one phase into another. The boundary itself serves a purpose, admitting wholesome changes and blocking unwelcome changes. Ancient Rome designated the two-faced god Janus to represent the passageway, the gate or door or archway, gazing both inward and outward at the same time. In Celtic lore, the permeability of the boundary through which one passes is represented by two trees, the hazel and the hawthorn. One of these trees enables passage, whereas the other filters what may pass. In systems thinking, one speaks of a membrane or sensorium, a surface such as one's skin presented to the environment for bounding the system and interacting with other systems. The imagery of boundaries and borders can be extended into other examples. That is, even here, the process of differentiation and then integration serves to discern the way forward in the midst of uncertainty, helping us to navigate.

This imagery of a "passing through" puts the emphasis on the wayfarer, the one who undergoes the journey from point A to point B. There is another frame of reference. Those on the far side of the boundary have a vested interest in what passes through the gate into *their* domain. Other systems present their surfaces to you. To some extent, those on the other side of the fence line participate in choosing what can be admitted (see generally Douglas, 1966). The boundary is a liminal space where authority is shared, a veritable no-man's-land, betwixt and between.

Ultimately, the community is right to police its perimeter for the sake of its enduring integrity. Someone standing at the gate seeking entrance requires some kind of screening. This principle applies not only to human beings in a concrete form (viz. the stranger) but also to strange ideas, innovations, and novelty. Not to mention a literal virus. Often, the task of judging who or what may enter falls to leaders, yet it is my contention that leadership rightly understood will also be experienced by the community as an incursion from beyond the enclosure, something literally extra-ordinary, as being "from outside the prevailing order" (Spoelstra, 2018). Thus, in addition to enforcing the status quo, firming up the borders, patrolling the gate, leadership also sometimes threatens the status quo, importing something new. The chapter concludes with another dichotomy that leaders and their scholars would be advised somehow to integrate. To an extent, leadership as a process can be imagined using the botanical metaphor of the hazel and the hawthorn. But let us get to that metaphor in stages.

An excess of differentiation

Even though the practice of making distinctions has been evolutionarily necessary for survival, Agnes Horvath (2013) expresses a concern about this tendency to make distinctions. Of course, some distinctions present us with false dilemmas. In our haste to sort anything we encounter into two, we fail to consider the possibility that they are not in fact opposed at all. A beer company once made light of this tendency by depicting a quarrel between those who argued that its product tastes great and those who argued that it is less filling. Back and forth they squabbled. The joke was that the brewery wanted the consumer to realize it could be both. Asking somebody to decide whether a button is either red (on the one hand) or round (on the other) makes no sense. They are entirely different dimensions (see Foucault, 1966/1994).

Let us suppose, however, that the distinction does make sense. Suppose the goal is to sort by color. We have one pile for white buttons and one pile for reds. Even then, in our haste to split the world into two categories, we overlook the extent to which examples might be both. We set up a polarity in our minds and then assign objects to one or the other, like sorting buttons into separate piles. That is, differentiation ignores the fact that reality is from the beginning compact. And some objects might belong in both piles at the same time. A leader, for instance, can be both task-oriented and people-oriented. In sociology, Robert Merton (1976) had called this both/and possibility by the name of Ambivalence. A button can be half red and half white, in alternating patterns. Or it can blend the two into shades of pink. The original attempt to differentiate into two piles or categories might be infeasible.

But then some false dilemmas omit the possibility of the neither/nor; maybe there is a third alternative, neither white nor red, but green. Being forced to choose between A or B overlooks the C option. In electoral politics, plenty of eligible voters prefer to vote for none of the above. "Are these really our only options?" Perhaps not.

Even assuming that the differentiation between two piles makes some sense, Horvath pointed out that once these distinctions have been made, we have a tendency to read into them more than is necessary. For example, we tend to treat one pole as more valuable, good, right, normal, while treating the other as less valuable, bad, wrong, or abnormal. We take multiple distinctions and align them. For instance, in literature, we associate distinctions as to color (white/black) and illumination (light/dark) with morals (good/evil), even though these dimensions have nothing whatsoever to do with one another. The differentia become metaphors for one another. We find this problem at work in the perceptual error known as Halo/Horns, whereby we associate one feature about a person with other aspects of them, so that if we (from an earlier generation) disliked tattoos, let us say, we made assumptions about the person's character as well.

In Leadership Studies, something of the sort has occurred regarding the famous distinction by James MacGregor Burns (1978) between transforming leadership and transactional leadership, as scholars and educators quickly presupposed that one is better and more important than the other. Burns himself (2003) seems to have done this later in his career, as though transactional leadership is lesser, slightly less than moral, and perhaps not even leadership at all. Yet in his original statement, he gave equal importance to both.

Back of all that logic-chopping, in Horvath's imaginary, is what the appetite for making distinctions will become. There is in principle no end to the distinctions a person can make. If we persist, we show ourselves to be endlessly clever, but then we lose the perspective of the whole. We forget the integrity of the larger image. We fish the sea waters for short-term profit at the expense of the overall supply. We focus on our pet political project and ignore the well-being of the polity. We specialize, narrowing our attention, without periodically zooming outward to take in the system of which it is only a part. You might say that we fail to continue our way around the hermeneutic circle. This tendency to make distinctions without stopping now and then to integrate our findings can result in a state or condition of liminality, a conceptual twilight of shards (2013, p. 57ff). Agnes Horvath cites Norbert Elias favorably that in modernity we have erred on the side of detachment, making distinctions promiscuously to the detriment of our eventual involvement. We become as ghosts in our own skin, recoiling from immersion into the stream of life, consumed only by novelty and resentment, as though purity (and self-esteem) demands withdrawal from the encompassing mess. (These are pretty big claims.)

Hers is an unfamiliar diagnosis, yet in my opinion strangely plausible. The necessity of making distinctions becomes an obsession with purity, finding fault and heresy. What did I eat yesterday that I should not have? What remark by that comedian last night offends? Which neighbor's property reduces the value of my own house? Which play call by the coach cost my team the championship? A person can feel rewarded for noticing discrepancies, differences, all while straining at gnats (*Matthew* 23:24).

What this attitude generates throughout modernity is what she calls liminoidality, a state or condition of belligerent crisis (Horvath, 2013, p. 132). If things are not unsettled, then something is wrong. The only acceptable posture is standing aside. The only gaze, askance. The only speech, irony. We encounter the world only so long as we can keep it at arm's length. In short, Horvath laments the direction we as a civilization have taken – a direction that begins with our considerable powers of differentiation. We become so adept at gaining critical distance that we back away completely from life itself.

The problem with her diagnosis is that we simply have to make distinctions in order to function. We have to know which berries are poisonous, which sounds are menacing, which sky is forecasting rain. And lest Horvath lay this entirely at the feet of modernity, preliterate societies were also exhaustively differentiated. At least they had the virtue of being mindful of the ways that one negotiates these differences, by paying due respect to each. One sees how traditional communities negotiated these distinctions in the example of rites of passage, culminating in making a fundamental distinction between childhood and adulthood. So let us look closer at that particular rite of passage.

Rites of passage

Arnold van Gennep (1908/1960) spearheaded the anthropological investigation into rites of passage as basically a three-stage process of (a) separation, (b) liminality (or transition), and (c) unification. This is a version of the dynamic model introduced previously

compact reality > differentiation > integration

Children are set apart from their familiar context and submitted to disorienting conditions. They find themselves outside the circle of their own community. If they want to be admitted back into the circle, they must cross a threshold into adulthood.

Certain rituals were necessary whenever crossing thresholds – geographic boundaries, such as territorial borders, to be sure, but also changing classifications within a given community, such as birth, initiation, marriage, and death. van Gennep noticed the same basic pattern continues today when joining a fraternity or a profession or when converting to a new religion. These experiences are imbued the world over with "magico-religious" significance (1908/1960, p. 16). They entail danger, both to the one making the transition as well as to the ones about to receive the stranger into their midst. And make no mistake, the uninitiated pubescent child is always a stranger … and a threat.

Central to van Gennep's analysis is the focus on the intermediate phase known as liminality. Liminality is a buffer zone, an extended gateway filled with ambiguity. There, one is between two worlds (1908/1960, p. 18). In order to pass, therefore, one must contend with the "guardians of the threshold" (1908/1960. p. 21) which we often refer to as gatekeepers. These could be literal guards, standing watch, but they could also be magic forces invoked by the host to protect the integrity of their enclosure. During this liminal phase, the individual outside of the enclosure is truly solitary and has no group, having already left one grouping and not yet belonging to another (1908/1960, p. 26). They are beyond the law and therefore outlaws. This status means that the individual is temporarily vulnerable, in a kind of limbo; but then in many instances this capacity to make the solitary passage back into the community suggests an uncanny strength. One must fight to get back. Until the situation is resolved, however, the individual out there is a potential foe to his village. We won't know until the process resolves itself. For rites of passage, there is no guaranteed outcome.

Often, when somebody bearing this ambiguous status appears at the gate, "the chief, alone or with his warriors, goes before the strangers as a representative of his society, since he is better immunized against this contact than ordinary inhabitants (van Gennep, 1908/1960, p. 28)." This is not a trivial observation, especially for those of us in Leadership Studies. The leader, by virtue of being the leader, possesses the power and the duty to encounter the strange. Let me repeat that. The leader, by virtue of being the leader, possesses the power and the duty to encounter the strange. The chief apparently was thought to have a stronger constitution, whether that strength is physical, psychological, or spiritual. After all, the threshold exists to prevent pollution or contamination of some sort (1908/1960, p. 25). The community relies on someone or something to possess the power to manage the border.

Over and over, the experience for the individual undergoing the transition was akin to dying and then being reborn. One puts away the things of youth in order to become a man (1 *Corinthians* 13:11), or one renounces the old religion and emerges from the baptismal waters a new creation. But what, pray tell, is going on *during the interim*? Here, van Gennep drew our attention to the bizarre turn, as you "run through Hades" or suspend all rectitude or dip into the Underworld (1908/1960, p. 91). The Amish call this phase Rumspringa. These unsettling experiences will recur throughout one's life, as it happens; life can be seen to entail the rhythm of letting go and reaching forward, over and over (1908/1960, p. 189). The cycle never ends, yet with each iteration, something is different. We can all be said to engage in a rhythm of differentiation and integration.[1] The rite of passage into adulthood is a universal example of this.

It is but a small leap to ascribe much the same consideration to the transmission of messages from beyond the horizon: having been uttered in an alien place, transported to us somehow, and then deciphered or interpreted here. Proclamations from on high (Eliade, 1959), news from abroad, demands from the menacing horde (Voegelin, 19401941/2000), overtures from a romantic swain, secrets of a cabal – again, we see the same basic tripartite structure. Somebody must obtain the message. Somebody must construe it. And throughout, one finds the

1 The psychologist Robert Kegan (1982) organized his developmental model around this same rhythm, in which the self is constituted by making distinctions and then establishing a relationship with that which is separated. One passes through phases of a present equilibrium, then disequilibrium, and finally a more encompassing equilibrium. And although this current chapter on leadership is not intended to address individual psychological development, the pattern is equivalent. Furthermore, Kegan's approach can inform the leader who assumes responsibility for the followers' progress, by guiding folks through the traumas of maturation. Kegan offers a word of caution, however, that followers sometimes need to be *protected from* a leader's hopes for their future (1982, p. 296). Ultimately, they have to make their way alone and decide for themselves. Finally, Kegan himself applied his theorizing along these lines to group development (e.g. Kegan, 1982, p. 213).

same apprehension that in some way the communication will disrupt the status quo and throw things into upheaval. Messages, like unwelcome strangers, can cross over boundaries and threaten the peace.

The extra-ordinary threatens the status quo and yet promises invigoration. It heralds change. It introduces turbulence.

Something significant plainly happens at the portal. It matters a great deal that Julius Caesar crossed the Rubicon. We must be mindful of the significance of the act of crossing. In this way, we preserve the prevailing order while remaining open to alarms and epiphanies from beyond. Archetypal psychology would recognize an elaborate structure of metaphors, stories, gods, and taboos surrounding these liminal spaces – many of which operate just below consciousness, when leadership presumes to intercede.

The metaphor of a boundary

Implicit in making distinctions would be the presence of a boundary or border demarcating the space between the two sides. We use imagery of "sides" in conceptual space in order to preserve the fact that we have made a distinction. In ordinary language, we say "on the one hand, on the other hand" or we refer to "two sides of the same coin" – representing in some fashion our effort to sort reality. Venn diagrams do something equivalent, although they also provide for the possibility that two sets can overlap. The circles represent conceptual boundaries, aiding us with spatial imagery.

Niklas Luhmann spoke about this imagery during his lectures on systems thinking in the winter quarter of 1991–1992 (2013). There, he said quite simply that "a system is a form with two sides" (p. 52). One must begin with that most basic of distinctions between a system and its environment. He adopted a symbol from the work of George Spencer Brown, and it looks like this:

$$\urcorner$$

For this purpose, one might represent the distinction between system and environment by writing "system $\urcorner$ environment." The symbol suggests that the focus now will be on the near side of the boundary, on the system (2013, p. 47). As a practice, then, "we must always indicate to which side of the distinction we are referring" (2013, p. 146). To make a distinction of any kind is to identify a plurality, an inside and an outside, a this-but-not-that, such that what appears on the lefthand side of the symbol will occupy our attention for the time being. We might say that we are temporarily bracketing everything to the right. We know that something is there, outside the system, and it is certainly important, but we must get back to it later. Right now, we pay attention to whatever appears on the left of that symbol, i.e. the system. As Luhmann was to state, "When handling a distinction, you always have a blind spot or something invisible behind your back" (2013, p. 104). Dirk Baecker (2015) put it this way: "observe the mark 'a' [on the left] in the context of its distinction from something indeterminate, basically from all that is 'not a'" (p. 2). When mapping systems, the portion on the right is represented by a cloud.

James Hillman referred to this practice of making distinctions as a "fantasy of opposites," which is useful for the mind, given our bounded rationality, but contrary to the reality we are trying to understand, where everything is interconnected (1971, p. 89).

Derek and Laura Cabrera (2015) explain systems thinking as a process beginning with the making of distinctions (ch. 3). They state: "Any idea or thing can be distinguished from the other ideas or things it is with" (p. 52). By paying attention to one of these, a person is not paying attention to the rest, for that is what it means to pay attention. (This does not mean the rest does not exist, of course.) Having done so, then, the next step is frequently boundary testing; is there in fact a hard-and-fast difference between the two ideas or things (p. 59)? We could be mistaken, for instance. There might be some blurring of the lines. It helps to be confident that one has drawn the boundary correctly and that it actually means something.

In most organizations, participants differentiate those who belong from those who do not. Their IT specialists erect firewalls to preserve the integrity of the organization's information. Often, an outsider has to wear a badge just to walk through the building. New hires undergo a process known now as "onboarding" before they can be welcomed fully into the group. Lawyers help businesses police the boundaries that distinguish the organization from its rivals, as for example noting trademark infringement and industrial espionage. Experts must obtain certain credentials before practicing their craft or profession, where they are subsequently set apart by titles and even uniforms, so there is no mistaking who is qualified to do a thing and who is not. Organizational charts depict hierarchies, which imply their own (internal) boundaries. The entire concept of bureaucracy has been constructed of distinctions, from one office to the next. One might even call bureaucracy the triumph of differentiation.

The nation-state has evolved a number of ways to separate itself from everybody else. Obviously, there is a physical border, often monitored by security forces. Some are to keep outsiders out. Some (like the Berlin Wall) to keep insiders in. Culturally, patriots display flags, pledge allegiance, sing anthems, and cheer for the national soccer team. Legally, citizens have rights and obligations that others do not. In some systems, this status must be represented by an ID card or papers, such as a passport. Certainly on the battlefield, each nation-state must know promptly who belongs to which side in a conflict. Otherwise, chaos ensues. And battles are confusing enough without being able to tell who's on which side.

In Leadership Studies as an academic pursuit, the lines are not so clear, especially given that it is an interdisciplinary undertaking. Nevertheless, with the formalization of the field comes the office of gatekeeper, whether that means editors and reviewers at assorted academic journals or hiring and tenure committees where Leadership Studies is taught. The boundaries are frequently contested, as partisans take sides for and against. For example, some scholars and journals regard the *ne plus ultra* to be quantitative analysis, with statistical sophistication, such that anything less "rigorous" (such as history, case studies, literary interpretation, ethics, and memoirs by famous leaders) is considered to be unsatisfactory. Efforts have been underway to formalize even further. This possibility has been urged on both leadership educators and practitioners. Barbara Kellerman (2018), to cite one example, wondered aloud whether leadership ought to be treated as a profession, with threshold criteria and some form of certification. The International Leadership Association has investigated accrediting educational programs in Leadership Studies, in an effort to define what would be legitimate.[2]

Defining any set, if it is to have any meaning, requires a boundary. Some of these sets can conceivably be empty, but the fact that we refer to it as a set presupposes that there is a boundary of some sort. For purposes of continuity in social sets, then, there must be some effort to police the boundary, monitoring who comes and who goes. Leadership has responsibility for that boundary, which we might think of as the surface, the membrane that stands adjacent to the system's environment. Boundaries can shift. They can collapse altogether. They can resist or admit things from outside. They can eject things into the environment, spewing what had been inside to the outside. In open systems, by definition, things can be said to pass through the system, entering and leaving (Luhmann, 2013, pp. 3033), in the way that raw materials arrive at the loading dock and finished products depart from the loading dock. Or pastries pass through one's digestive system. Much depends on where the boundary is and what exactly happens there.

Archetypal psychology

The field of archetypal psychology has examined the tendency to imagine differentiation (boundaries) and their crossings. Here too one sees the effort to make

2 See http://www.ila-net.org/communities/LC/GuidingQuestionsFinal.pdf. Not to put too fine a point on it, but the ILA as an organization also differentiates between members and non-members.

distinctions. The theoretical founders of this approach laid out a series of polarities not unlike cardinal points that orient the traveler. Carl Jung, for instance, famously set forth the four dimensions of personality popularized (and distorted) in the Myers-Briggs Personality Test (e.g. Hillman, 1971). James Hillman noticed that in ancient Greek and Roman pantheons, the deities tend to operate in a matrix of contrasts (e.g. Hermes and Hera, Senex and Puer). Mircea Eliade wrote about *The Sacred and the Profane* (1959). Rudolf Otto put the process of making distinctions at the center of *The Idea of the Holy* (1923/1958), inasmuch as holiness means having been set apart, higher and therefore available for comparison.

In fairness, these eminent scholars warned against many of the dangers of making distinctions promiscuously, just as Horvath fears. Hillman (1980) especially descried the temptation of therapists to slot patients into diagnoses for ease of managing treatments. He also credits Jung with tracing the origin of neurosis back to a one-sidedness (2010). So it is not as though one remains stuck at one end of the polarity. That would be pathological. The interesting thing for archetypal psychology is the relationship between the poles, the fact that both are present in the psyche and that they ultimately depend on one another. For instance, each person is both introverted and extraverted, both judging and perceiving, both sensing and intuiting, and both thinking and feeling. Again, for the sake of psychological well-being one must move in one's imagination from compact reality, through the process of differentiation, en route to a comprehending integration.

Archetypal psychology does tend to personify the two poles as gods (Hillman, 1976, ch. 1). This is true. But it also finds other useful means of portraying them, going all the way back to the four elements of earth, wind, fire, and water. One thinks of the more abstract taxonomy of choleric, sanguine, melancholic, and phlegmatic temperaments. Hillman (2010) has written about the importance to Jung of alchemical studies. Hillman's uniform edition includes an entire volume dedicated to using animals and even bugs (2008). So it would not be a stretch of the imagination to turn as well to the plant kingdom. A metaphor representing the twin features of the boundary itself, admitting novelty without tolerating undue disruptiveness, can be found in an archaic combination of two wild florae.

Hazel and Hawthorn

The pairing of two sacred trees, the hazel and the hawthorn, occurs in *Sir Gawain and the Green Knight:*

> Over a hill in the morning in splendour he rides
> Into a dense forest, wondrously wild;
> High slopes on each side and woods at their base

Of massive grey oaks, hundreds growing together;
Hazel and hawthorn were densely entangled,
Thickly festooned with coarse shaggy moss,
Where many miserable birds on the bare branches
Wretchedly piped for torment of the cold (see Anon).

This pair of unlikely weeds in particular connotes more than a thicket in the dark heart of the forest through which the hero must ride. In European folklore, they also had complementary magic properties. What presents itself to Sir Gawain as an obstacle on an inhospitable passage is actually full of wonders, imbued with mysticism and redolent with symbols relevant to themes in this chapter. Terry Mabbett (2003) wrote, "No other trees native to these islands [UK] are more deeply steeped in our history and culture than hazel and hawthorn" (p. 47). So, let us take a closer look at each.

Hazel

According to Niall MacCoitir (2016, pp. 7282), the hazel's wood, for instance, connotes divine sanction. It gave shelter and shade to both the Holy Family fleeing Herod to Egypt and to King Arthur and his knights on their sojourn. In Celtic culture, a hazel stick was kept by the bedside to ward against terrors in the night. In addition, the hazelnut was thought to be poisonous to snakes.[3]

The hazel nut provides insight to those who consume it[4] – except to the snakes, apparently. The nut represents wisdom that drops into a pond or sacred well and brings bubbles of inspiration to the surface "to be drunk by people of many arts" (MacCoitir, 2016).[5] In much the same vein, then, the hazel tree supplies revelation, the portal where another world irrupts into our own and imbues human beings with fresh and provocative knowledge. It elicits poetry, music, and vision.

It is interesting to note, still relying on MacCoitir, that the very word "hazel" derives from the Anglo-Saxon for "authority."[6] When a certain legend speaks of the three peoples as the Plough, the Sun, and the Hazel, the plough represents the laboring class, the sun represents the noblemen who conduct war and manage territories, and the hazel represents the priestly caste which mediates

3 In Christian lore, St. Patrick used a wand of hazel to drive out the snakes from Ireland (Skinner, 1911, p. 133).

4 Robert Graves (2013) explained that the hazelnut symbolizes concentrated wisdom, compact, not unlike the brain itself.

5 Its connection to springs of water appears in the folklore of several peoples. Hazel is used, for example, as a dowsing rod. The analogy of springs of water to the issuing forth of spiritual insight is not accidental.

6 Mabbett (2003) wrote that the term literally meant "big stick" (p. 48).

between the sacred and the mundane. If among the trees the oak suggests stately governance, the hazel evokes the otherworldly basis for rulership – the mystery behind the majesty, as it were.

Charles Montgomery Skinner (1911) cites the etymological kinship of the words hazy (as in bewildering) and hazing (as the process of initiation into secret rites). Perhaps not surprisingly, the wood appears as the caduceus of Hermes, the god who mediates between Olympus and humankind and oversees commerce. Hermes, you will recall, was the messenger of the gods. Hazel therefore accompanies the herald, innovation, and the orienting word. In actual practice, its branches do communicate in a mysterious manner, for they are used as water diviners (also known as dowsing rods) (Mabbett, 2003, p. 49).

Hawthorn

The thorny hawthorn presents a contrast to hazel. Again, according to MacCoitir (2016, pp. 5258), it symbolizes the little pixies that human beings would be right to fear and respect. Rather than nourishing man's spiritual hunger, the hawthorn warns against interference. Its powers are set to punish all who abuse its peace. Not for no reason was the hawthorn believed to be unlucky. You don't mess with the hawthorn! You do not gather its branches for your usage. Rarely was it used for building anything or eating. You do not burn it. You do not so much as bring a sprig into the house without incurring mischief or worse.

Given its irascible properties, a shrewd shaman could use the hawthorn as a hedge against incursions of evil, such as witches, so that it pays to encircle your home with them. The herdsman used it as a living fence line to keep farm animals in a confined space (Mabbett, 2003, p. 49). Later, the superstitious would pluck hawthorn blossoms in May and hang them in the house as a charm against misfortune. Like the hazel, the hawthorn was associated with wells of water – not so much to endow those who drink with new knowledge, but instead to guard against disease.

Skinner (1911) tells of hawthorn as the branch woven as a crown for a number of eminent personages such as Jesus of Nazareth, Charlemagne, and Richmond, King Henry VII of England, denoting a type of humble sovereign. While it protects its wearer – again, a defensive role – its thorns also pierce the scalp and draw blood, suggesting the price of sovereignty. Leadership lacerates the one who leads.

More recently, after the epoch of lore, the hawthorn proved to be a tough wood used for walking sticks, tool handles, and cutting boards (Mabbett, 2003, p. 50).

Pairing the hazel with the hawthorn

As with so many myths, the symbols pile up in a kind of hyperlinked labyrinth. For instance, according to the pagan calendar, hazel month is May, a veritable springtime of bursting forth from the long cruelties of April, suggesting an abundance; whereas the month for Hawthorn is December, with its plucky berries as a reminder of the powers of life even during seasons of darkness, cold, and scarcity. The cultic powers that are so profligate in preparation for the summer solstice, in times of plenty, promising bounty, they also persist even in measured array as we await the winter's solstice. Classic both/and figures.

If the hazel is associated with King Arthur (who ascends to power and initiates the quest), then hawthorn is associated with Merlin (who watches over and preserves, as something of a gatekeeper).

To summarize, then, hazel serves a function in the liminal space between two worlds, bearing gifts to human beings of heightened consciousness. It symbolizes a crossing over from there to here. Hawthorn, on the other hand, also serves a function in the liminal space between two worlds, but its function is to thwart, to assert the boundaries and keep separate worlds apart.[7] If hazel intrudes from elsewhere, hawthorn retains the differentiation, defining what to humankind is holy in the original sense of the term as wholly other, removed, set aside, consecrated or sacerdotal. Mary Douglas wrote, "For us sacred things and places are to be protected from defilement" (1966, p. 7). The wisdom from a higher plane would not seem strange and bear no authority if the worlds had been intermingled promiscuously.[8] Hawthorn limits the transactions that take place at the border. Speaking gnomically, therefore: without hazel, nothing would cross over; without hawthorn, there would be nothing to cross. Together, they open what is shut and shut what is open. Ultimately, therefore, hazel suggests an infusion of welcome novelty, while hawthorn suggests purity. These twin florae – both of them dense and spiny – present us with a symbolic tension, rather than a stark opposition. Both have some bearing on the imagery of leadership as grounded in encounters from outside of the prevailing order.

7 In Roman mythology, the hawthorn serves a similar function of prophylaxis (Graves, 2013, p. 63). Robert Graves (2013) informs us that in Roman culture newlyweds used hawthorn to propitiate the jealous goddess who resists marriage (p. 169). Graves (2013) noted that the Welsh had a similar association of hawthorn with the barriers to marriage (p. 170). Again, we see that this plant was associated with a barrier to the coming together of **two** different things, in this case men and women. Graves (2013) added that hawthorn also connotes feminine sexuality, with its orgiastic, mind-altering cult (p. 171), which often proves too wild for prudence, so that maybe a little modesty suits you. To let its frenetic powers wash over a you is to lose your mind. It stands to reason that in fairy tales the rescuing hero must chafe through hawthorn in order to reach the princess (p. 412). That is to say that sexual frenzies are parallel to spiritual frenzies, to be cherished in season but not to be wantonly indulged.

8 Besides, we could not bear the plenitude of sacred knowledge if it just poured freely into our minds, for as it states in the letter known as *Second Corinthians* (ch. 3, verse 3:7) that to gaze full upon the countenance of God would burn us to cinders. The Israelites could hardly bear to look upon the face of Moses after he had held counsel with YHWH on Mount Sinai, inasmuch as Moses was to the Lord as the moon is to the sun, bearing only a reflection.

Anxiety, doubt, and resistance

It probably goes without saying that incursions from beyond instill fear. In many instances, such a fear is well founded. That which is alien might disrupt the status quo. Certain species when introduced into unfamiliar ecosystems sometimes flourish at the expense of local organisms. Something similar purportedly occurred once Europeans landed in the Western Hemisphere, as diseases that were exotic to indigenous peoples ravaged the population. It is reasonable to want to know in advance how novelties might impact existing systems. Patients of a physician wonder about side effects of a new prescription. Athletic players worry about team chemistry after a blockbuster trade. Believers are quick to detect the whiff of heresy. Manufacturers need to figure out how to combine new technology with existing methods of production. As Douglas put it, "The initial recognition of anomaly leads to anxiety and from there to suppression or avoidance…" (1966, p. 5).

Renata Salecl (2004) explained that once a person or a population has built a kind of fantasy that gives their existence meaning, they are at risk of severe anxiety should the entire edifice fall (pp. 24, 28). They are left raw and exposed – not in fear of any specific threat necessarily, but in general. Then, unfortunately, it is too late. The incursion blew it all up, leaving everyone bereft. Anxiety arises at the mere threat of this happening.

If all of this is so, and for good reason, then why do people even tolerate leadership if (as I would contend) leadership is by its very nature an incursion from elsewhere? Leadership is in part a process of bringing across and into the enclosure from outside the circle (Harter, 2020; Spoelstra, 2018). It would be tempting in those instances to disallow leadership and hear no more about it. The ancient Athenians, to cite one example, did (as a democracy) exercise wariness of promising leaders in their midst, moving to ostracize the best who, by their very excellence, posed a threat to their concord. Athens voluntarily squandered leadership talent, banishing it. For a long time, the Romans took action to prevent the imposition of a king. It is not unheard of to resist leaders precisely because they represent a change. Bureaucracy exists, arguably, to construct a system so perfect that leadership becomes unnecessary. In the literature, this has been called "substitutes for leadership." The instinct for self-preservation would seem to extinguish the prospects of any leadership.[9]

Yet leadership occurs. And in our times, it is positively encouraged. We lavish leaders with attention. We teach children about our leaders in schoolbooks. If leaders induce anxiety, yet we favor leadership, is Salecl wrong? Am I? Why would people encourage something that induces anxiety?

9 A particularly vivid example of the threat posed by leadership can be found in the novel written by Nobel laureate Naguib Mahfouz (1985/2000) titled *Akhenaten: Dweller in Truth*.

Five arguments come to mind. First, we certainly do want leaders who will *repel* threats, both foreign and domestic. We need a leader to preserve our identity, even if that means making adaptations. One could argue that Donald Trump, president of the United States beginning in 2017, promised to lead the United States of America in opposition to multiple incursions, real and imagined (immigrants, cheap imports, terrorists, and so forth). A second reason that followers might tolerate these so-called incursions from leaders is when the people already sense that the status quo is inadequate (Kegan, 1982, p. 41). Maybe they are looking for somebody who has the answers they apparently don't. If your plumbing leaks in the house, you invite an expert into your home to fix it. At that point, you are open to outside help. A third reason people will risk anxiety, I suppose, is that there is (as hazel signifies) something attractive about that which proves to be exotic. On occasion, we welcome new things simply because they are new.[10]

There is a fourth argument, however, which involves ethics. When the incursion comes from a trusted authority to whom we owe allegiance, we accept the input – albeit perhaps grudgingly. We tend to defer to those we esteem. In religious texts, when God says to do something, we should not be quick to ignore him. Jonah did and look what happened to him! Yet the historical record is strewn with stiff-necked rebellion, a whoring after other gods, and similar repudiations of divine mandates. A follower can empirically acknowledge the paramount authority of a leader and receive the message loud and clear, but that alone doesn't guarantee compliance. Nevertheless, followers often follow a trusted leader into the great maw of anxiety because they trust him (or her).

I have a fifth argument about this apparent contradiction. Why welcome the one who threatens you with anxiety? Often, the leader might not be seen as bringing something altogether new. Perhaps he or she is *restoring* something that has been forgotten or ignored. It would be new in the sense that we have lost our way and maybe forgot, such that it now seems unfamiliar. Nevertheless, what the leader proposes can be said to resonate: it hearkens to an earlier time; it brings us back to ourselves. Accordingly, in the short term, yes, this is a change, but in the long term, it is a mark of persistence, a plea for continuity, a return. Some voice beyond the gate calls us back to our selves. Perhaps that is a kind of leadership that we eventually appreciate.

Individuals can agree or disagree with the value of specific incursions. Was it really a good idea to import starlings into the Western Hemisphere? Are we foolish to persist in devising a virus with a gain of function? What hath the Internet wrought? Beyond a certain point, we must trust leaders to use their best judgment.

10 Gabriel de Tarde (1903) puts the reliance on fashion near the center of his sociology. See also Simmel (1971, ch. 19).

Concluding thoughts

Leaders can be found standing at the proverbial gate, discerning which novelties to admit. Leaders can be seen to manage what – if anything – crosses the threshold, and this includes people, technology, farm produce, and ideas. Leaders also conduct sorties into alien territory, whether in secret or broad daylight, in order to obtain what the village requires. Accordingly, part of leadership is spent at the liminal space, establishing the permeability of a given order. Symbolizing the responsibilities at the portal are two sacred plants, the hazel and the hawthorn, each serving a particular function for the ongoing well-being of the tribe.

In a recurring pattern from compact reality by means of differentiation, that tribe must integrate itself intelligently, meaningfully, in a never-ending progression toward maturity, like any open system. The future must pass through the filters of discernment. Nevertheless, being mindful of Horvath's warning against obsessive scrutiny for the sake of purity, straining at gnats, leaders must welcome the occasional incursion and trust the system to adapt and digest. That is what it means to be a resilient system. Otherwise, anxiety about everything alien and new can deteriorate into a sociological hypochondria.[11]

Ultimately, leadership is about conditioning the group for these transitions, to equip the group to manage its own negotiations with its environment, to remain open without becoming empty. Part of any group's maturity is its capacity to detect and then prudently enfold these apparent dichotomies into a more complex configuration. It is my contention that it would aid people faced with uncertainty to picture these two humble weeds as symbols of what the process going forward requires.

Before going to the final chapter, let us stop for a moment to check our progress. This book of separable studies fits an overarching pattern. After a couple of chapters dedicated to emphasizing the importance of the imagination to both science broadly (Vaihinger) and to the conduct of a good life (Huizinga), we considered the role of imagination in regarding individual human beings (including the imago), their collectivities (labyrinths), the dynamics by which they order themselves (imitation), and the boundaries where they operate (hazel and hawthorn). In the concluding chapter, we will imagine leadership taking place within a complex hierarchy of games or "theaters," in a kind of three-dimensional space. Leadership at one level is inevitably part of the dynamics at another level. Even within a single level, frequently leadership is part of multiple games at the same time. Students of leadership would be advised to consider the interlocking complexity of such games within which leaders must operate.

11 "Sociological hypochondria" is a new label for a state or condition that afflicts my own culture at the time of this writing. It is my hope that scholars can put the phrase to good use in subsequent researches.

Successful leaders are playing each of these games simultaneously, whether they know it or not. For purposes of illustration, we will consider the career of an exemplary broadcast journalist from the twentieth century by the name of Edward R. Murrow.

References

Anon. (1992). *Sir Gawain and the green knight* (J. Winny, trans.). Broadview literary texts.

Baecker, D. (2015, June 14). "Working the form: George Spencer-Brown and the mark of distinction." *Mousse Magazine*. Retrieved 6 February 2023 from https://ssrn.com/abstract=2618146.

Burns, J.M. (2003). *Transforming leadership: A new pursuit of happiness*. Grove Press.

Burns, J.M. (1978). *Leadership*. Harper.

Cabrera, D., & L. Cabrera. (2015). *Systems thinking made simple: New hope for solving wicked problems*. Plectica Publishing.

Collinson, D. "Critical leadership studies." In Riggio, R. (ed.) (2019). *What's wrong with leadership? Improving leadership research and practice* (ch. 14). Routledge.

Douglas, M. (1966). *Purity and danger: An analysis of the concepts of pollution and taboo*. Routledge.

Eliade, M. (1959). *The sacred and the profane* (W. Trask, trans.). Harvest.

Foucault, M. (1966/1994). *The order of things: An archeology of the human sciences* (Anon., trans.). Vintage Books.

Graves, R. (2013). *The white goddess: A historical grammar of poetic myth* (2nd ed.). Farrar, Straus and Giroux.

Harter, N. (2020). *Leadership across boundaries: A passage to aporia*. Routledge.

Hillman, J. (2013). *The uniform edition of the writings of James Hillman* (vol. 1). Spring Publications.

Hillman, J. (2010). *Alchemical psychology*. Spring Publications.

Hillman, J. (2008). *The uniform edition of the writings of James Hillman* (vol. 9). Spring Publications.

Hillman, J. (1980). *Egalitarian typologies versus the perception of the unique*. Spring Publications.

Hillman, J. (1976). *Re-visioning psychology*. Harper Collins.

Hillman, J. "The feeling function." In M.-L. von Franz & J. Hillman. (1971). *Lectures on Jung's typology* (pp. 73–150). Spring Publications.

Horvath, A. (2013). *Modernism and charisma*. Palgrave Macmillan.

Kegan, R. (1982). *The evolving self: Problem and process in human development*. Harvard University Press.

Kellerman, B. (2018). *Professionalizing leadership*. Oxford University Press.

Luhmann, N. (2013). *Introduction to systems theory* (P. Gilgen, trans.). Polity.

Mabbett, T. (2003, January). "The heritage of hazel and hawthorn." *Quarterly Journal of Forestry*. *97*(1): 47–50.

MacCoitir, N. (2016). *Ireland's trees: Myths, legends and folklore* (2nd ed.). Collins.

Mahfouz, N. (1985/2000) *Akhenaten: Dweller in truth.* Anchor.

Merton, R. (1976). *Sociological ambivalence and other essays*. Free Press.

Otto, R. (1923/1958). *The idea of the holy* (J. Harvey, trans.). Oxford University Press.

Salecl, R. (2004). *On anxiety*. Routledge.

Simmel, G. (1971). *On individuality and social forms* (D. Levine, ed.). University of Chicago Press.

Skinner, C.S. (1911). *Myths and legends of flowers, trees, fruits, and plants in all ages and all climes*. J.B. Lippincott Co.

Spoelstra, S. (2018). *Leadership and organization: A philosophical introduction*. Routledge.

Tarde, G. (1903). *The laws of imitation* (E.C. Parsons, trans.). Henry Holt & Co.

van Gennep, A. (1908/1960). *The rites of passage* (M. Vizedom & G. Caffee, trans.). University of Chicago Press.

Voegelin, E. "The Mongol orders of submission to European powers, 1245–1255." In Sandoz, E. (ed.). (1940–1941/2000). *Collected works* (vol. 10, ch. 4, pp. 76–125). University of Missouri Press.

8

LIGHTS, CAMERA, ACTION

The ceremonial function of hearings and trials

Introduction to the chapter

Shakespeare wrote that all the world's a stage. Maybe he was right. The sociologist Erving Goffman (1978) demonstrated, for example, how everyday life can be understood as a presentation of self, using many of the same conceptual frameworks familiar to thespians, such as being backstage and on-stage. To a great extent – even more than we seem to realize – public life manifests as one great, inchoate exhibition, filled with drama, where each of us practices some form of impression management. As we pass through our world, we are simultaneously actor and audience in a theater that is without script or director. This is most obviously the case at job interviews and first dates, but we may have underestimated the extent to which it is also true of leadership.

In a previous chapter, we examined the prevalence of imitation in social life, where each of us watches one another for hints or clues on how to behave. We pick up on gestures and fashion and language itself from the example of others. Often, we consciously select role models to mimic, the whole person as a living, breathing exemplar, a hero or mentor; but as we saw in that same chapter, we collect little tidbits like magpies, here and there, from nearly anybody we encounter, almost at a subconscious level. At such moments, it is as though we are sleepwalking through life, subtly impressionable. We could be talking about a haircut, a facial expression, the curlicue on the letter "f," even something so annoying as getting a song stuck in our head after overhearing somebody in the stairwell whistling a tune.

In politics, we are often advised that statecraft is stagecraft. Perception is reality. We have heard this adage since Machiavelli, who not only wrote the book

DOI: 10.4324/9781003374831-8

on getting and using political power, but he also wrote a successful comedy in Italian that has been performed down through the years. Politics may not consist entirely of theatrics, to be sure, but only a fool would ignore the possibility that leadership itself is a performing art. One does not have to restrict this lesson to what are regarded as politics in the conventional sense, as for example campaigns and governance, for one can speak of a "micropolitics" in everyday life, in every group and club and office. Leadership can occur on a bus, in a jury, or during a riot. Leadership arises everywhere that people work together to make a difference, at home, at school, at work, in faith communities and team sports. Leadership is everywhere. So too is the art we commonly refer to as dramaturgy, a term devised by Gotthold Ephraim Lessing which can be defined as the practice of acting out a story or narrative.

Central to the practice of leadership is the idea of a ceremony, a conscious enactment of certain rituals that display authority, enhance the stature of leaders, and remind everybody of their various roles within a larger unity. Stuart Elden has written about ceremony more than once, but most recently in 2021 in *The Oxford Handbook of Politics and Performance*, where he identifies a variety of examples, such as coronations, public executions, parades, and prescribed routines surrounding the opening of school or even tea time. A ceremony is thought to be obligatory, a device by which a collective affirms itself and acknowledges those who preside. Broadly speaking, a ceremony is a representation of an abstract principle or idea to which participants pledge their allegiance (Elden, 2021, p. 384). Nevertheless, it is significant to note that sometimes the ceremony is designed to resolve disputes, to impose a process on the contestations that threaten the collective. We might see this, for instance, in ritual combat, courtroom dramas, and political elections. The audience may not know who will win, but we attend to the rituals for channeling our anxieties and resolving that conflict. We seem to need some sort of reliable method for sorting through our contestations.

But what I want to know is this: what if the dispute pertains to the ritual itself? What if there is substantive disagreement on the meaning of our conflict resolution practices? What if we don't know how to process our various grievances? Or we no longer trust them to be fair? I would argue that especially in these liminal moments, when the accepted methods are being questioned, leadership becomes crucial to the wellbeing of the whole.[1]

The following chapter approaches this very situation step-by-step, reaching an historical moment when the public found itself confronted with grim uncertainty about how to enact their wishes and affirm their solidarity when all around

1 It is not a coincidence that I write these words when so many Americans of both political parties question the integrity of elections and view the Supreme Court as just another venue for waging ongoing culture wars.

them, the community felt as though it was threatening to tear itself apart. I speak of the Red Scare, a period of time in the United States when a minority of self-anointed tribunes terrorized the populace on the pretext that they must expose treason in their midst.[2] The leader for whom this era was named, Senator Joseph McCarthy, commanded the hybrid rituals in Congress and the media, in a bizarre combination of courtroom niceties and stump speeches, using the device known as the Senate Hearing to publicize his persecutions of suspected Communists – that is, until another character of unimpeachable integrity from within the media rose up in challenge. That leader was broadcast journalist Edward R. Murrow.

Ceremony

According to Elden (2017), the noted social theorist Michel Foucault investigated the political functions of ceremony, such as coronations, public executions, and military triumphs. At one time, the overwhelming purpose of these ceremonies was to display one's authority, establishing vividly who in fact reigns. These ceremonies manifested sovereignty. As such, they were theatrical, a living drama for the imaginations of the people. Foucault was especially intrigued apparently about ceremonies that deposed kings, demonstrating the passage of power from one person to another – and most especially, the passage of power from one person to anonymous experts who would govern behind the scenes (e.g. during the madness of King George III). This is political theater on a grand scale.

The exhibition of sovereignty can be seen vividly portrayed in a famous statue in Florence, Italy, across from Michelangelo's *David*. It is known as *Hercules and Cacus* by Baccio Bandinelli, in 1534, and it shows the mythic hero subduing a fire-breathing giant. The meaning of the figure was not lost on the people. It signals that the Medici will crush any opposition. Hercules stands with a club in one hand and a kneeling victim in the other – a victim (Cacus) that is plainly no larger than Hercules himself. Hercules is not looking at Cacus. Instead, he is looking at you, doing this for you to witness, as he is about to slay the victim. Let there be no mistake who is powerful.

On a smaller scale, then, Foucault investigated similar rituals, such as the assertion of one's power over prisoners, patients, and schoolchildren, when those in authority assume the position of legitimacy, orchestrating the moment to enhance their stature and possibly making an example of someone about an infraction. It is for these occasions that leaders engage in petty theatrics, as for example staging the encounter and wearing the costume.

Foucault penetrated even further, however, to examine the extent to which society is filled with people engaging in minor – even perhaps subliminal

2 There is no longer any doubt that at the time in question there were spies in the United States working for the Soviet Union. I would not want to suggest otherwise.

– exercises of power, in the way they board the train or order their coffee or pay for their groceries. Here is power at the level of social capillaries, in subtle (and often imperceptible) attempts to influence other people. By implication, therefore, society consists of thousands and thousands of these transient ceremonies, involving wardrobe, furniture, gestures, inflections, and the occasional flare of the nostrils. At this magnitude, we might refer to our investigations as micropolitics.

The theater itself as an institution has even circled around to depict such ceremonies. Two noteworthy examples are judicial trials and investigative/inquisitorial hearings. Some of the most famous from history lend themselves to re-creation for the stage or on film, as a space dedicated to portraying the height of conflict. One might think for instance of the trial of Socrates in Plato's *Apology*, Jesus by the Sanhedrin, Galileo by the Roman Catholic Church, Martin Luther by the Diet of Worms, the Salem Witch Trials, Amistad, the Soviet Show trials, the Scopes trial, the Dreyfuss Affair (a court martial), Leopold/Loeb, Sacco/Vanzetti, Alger Hiss, Nuremburg, the Chicago 8, and O.J. Simpson. Furthermore, the general public has been riveted by Watergate and impeachment trials, plus Senate confirmation hearings for the Supreme Court of the United States that are as much spectacle as deliberation.

Having said that, of course, the lines between theater and politics blur, to the point where they overlap and become impossible to separate conceptually. According to Stuart Elden (2017), Foucault insinuated that not only was politics a kind of theater, but also theater can be politics (p. 168; Elden, 2021, p. 383). Playwrights sometimes use their platform to advance politics by other means, settling old scores and hoping to shape politics going forward. Other fictional confrontations continue to entertain the viewing public: "Twelve Angry Men," "Inherit the Wind," "A Man for All Seasons," "Witness for the Prosecution," "To Kill a Mockingbird," and "A Few Good Men."

The function of ceremony is to a great extent to arrest and inform the imagination, to enact as ritual the mechanics of authority.

Investigative hearings: "I'm Not a Potted Plant."

On March 12, 1954, Senator Joseph McCarthy (R-WI) chaired a hearing of the Senate Permanent Subcommittee on Investigations where he was interrogating Annie Lee Moss about her possible ties to the Communist Party. At one point, an attorney attempted to speak on her behalf, only to receive this rebuke. "We will not hear from counsel. You've been told what the rule is. If you have anything to say, say it through your client." Counsel was thereby rendered mute as the interrogation resumed (Cohen, 2016).

With this as precedent, the Joint Committee of the House and Senate investigating the Iran-Contra scandal on July 9, 1987 – some 33 years later – found itself in a similar situation, when Oliver North's attorney Brendan Sullivan objected to a particular question from a sitting congressman. The chair replied as follows: "We have attempted to be as fair as we can. Let the *witness* object if he wishes to." Immediately, the attorney shot back, "Well sir, I'm not a potted plant. I'm here as the lawyer. That's my job." Those words drew an audible gasp from the audience. The impertinence! Impertinent, perhaps, but it made for terrific theater (Anderson, 1987). Indeed, hearings of this type frequently provide moments of real drama. After hours of tedious questioning, suddenly the room becomes electric. Everybody leans forward. Such moments resound in the media and sometimes even in the history books.

Here is another such moment, when a nominee to the Supreme Court of the United States was being questioned on live television by Senate Judiciary Committee on 11 October 1991. Then-Supreme Court nominee Clarence Thomas was asked during confirmation hearings whether he had an opening statement in response to the hours of accusations leveled against him earlier in the day by a woman named Anita Hill. The nominee said this:

> Senator, I would like to start by saying unequivocally, uncategorically (sic), that I deny each and every single allegation against me today that suggested in any way that I had conversations of a sexual nature or about pornographic material with Anita Hill, that I ever attempted to date her, that I ever had any personal sexual interest in her, or that I in any way ever harassed her.
>
> A second, and I think more important point. I think that this today is a travesty. I think that it is disgusting. I think that this hearing should never occur in America. This is a case in which this sleaze, this dirt, was searched for by staffers of members of this committee, was then leaked to the media, and this committee and this body validated it and displayed it at prime time over our entire nation.
>
> How would any member on this committee, any person in this room, or any person in this country, would like sleaze said about him or her in this fashion? Or this dirt dredged up and this gossip and these lies displayed in this manner? How would any person like it?
>
> The Supreme Court is not worth it. No job is worth it. I am not here for that. I am here for my name, my family, my life, and my integrity. I think something is dreadfully wrong with this country when any person, any person in this free country would be subjected to this.
>
> This is not a closed room. There was an FBI investigation. This is not an opportunity to talk about difficult matters privately or in a closed environment. This is a circus. It's a national disgrace.
>
> And from my standpoint as a black American, as far as I'm concerned, it is a high-tech lynching for uppity blacks who in any way deign to think for themselves, to do for themselves, to have different ideas, and it is a message

> that unless you kowtow to an old order, this is what will happen to you. You will be lynched, destroyed, caricatured by a committee of the U.S. – U.S. Senate, rather than hung from a tree (Thomas, 1991).

These remarks galvanized the nation and consequently ensured his confirmation. The man knew the world was watching, and he made the most of it.

Some witnesses at legislative hearings are placid, workmanlike, grinding through the ordeal. Others are surly or churlish or cute. Some crumble under the pressure.[3] Others acquit themselves brilliantly. And the ones doing these investigations, asking the questions – they can be courtly, or sly, or boring, or rude. Personality is often on full display, especially when the stakes are high, and the cameras are rolling. In such contexts, the power differences can be acute. The one conducting the investigation enjoys considerably more power and, like the sovereigns of yore, wants everybody to know it. But they are under pressure as well, perhaps from other members of the panel who disagree with them or from an absent third party, such as a president or the voting public. Rarely does the person being investigated enjoy relatively more power, but it can happen – and not a few clever witnesses such as Clarence Thomas do turn the tables, establishing power where no one had expected it. A truly gifted witness can make investigators look pretty foolish. President Bill Clinton believed he had done so when he quibbled at a grand jury proceeding over the meaning of the word "is" (see Raymond, 2007).

One journal article has said that "previous empirical studies suggest that such hearings are sometimes uninformative because the members choose to grandstand by promoting their own views rather than gathering information" (Park, 2016, p. 3). This process can indeed obtain information and raise awareness, but as one study notes, "it can also be used as a weapon" (Paulson, 2004, p. 62). Cornelia Vismann (2003) calls them "tele-tribunals," and Adam Ashforth (1990) calls them "reckoning schemes of legitimation." In such instances, the very purpose of the hearing is to influence an audience that is not otherwise participating, whether that purpose is to promote an individual politician's stature, the legislature's stature, or the issue being investigating. Or, for that matter, any combination thereof.

The theater within a theater

One of the questions that a leader has to consider is the extent to which they enter into these venues intending to exploit the opportunity for drama. Is it so

3 Special Counsel Robert Mueller testified before both the House Judiciary and Intelligence Committees in July 2019. *The New York Times* wrote that the witness "sometimes appeared confused or at a loss for words and frequently responded to questions with one-word answers – 'no,' 'true,' 'that's accurate' – [and] was a reluctant witness whose deflections sucked some of the punch out of his most damning findings…" (Hirschfeld-Davis & Mazzetti, 2019, July 24).

wrong, in other words, for a little showmanship? If impression management is part and parcel of leadership – and especially of *political* leadership – then can it be said that at least to some degree statecraft is stagecraft? Historians deplore the propaganda tactics of Joseph Goebbels, who was open and straightforward about his purposes (1928/1934), yet they compliment a John F. Kennedy for winning his televised debates against Richard Nixon in 1960 largely because of his visual appearance, not least of which was his willingness to wear makeup (see Self, 2005, quoting Hewitt, 2001). Or Franklin Delano Roosevelt because he mastered the manufactured intimacy of the radio during his so-called Fireside Chats (Lim, 2003)? They applaud Ronald Reagan for seizing the moment, as it were, when visiting the Berlin Wall (Buckley, 2004). Is it any wonder, therefore, that participants in investigative hearings likewise turn toward the proverbial klieg lights and the microphones, like plants turning toward the sunlight, in the hope of gaining or solidifying public support for their causes? Even if that "cause" is nothing more than their own celebrity?

What Foucault referred to as micropolitics takes place within a larger framework, which in turn takes place within an even larger framework, at various magnitudes. We might think of it as the theater within the larger theater, the play within a play. An encounter or exchange during an investigative hearing can be dramatic on its own, in isolation, between two adversaries, yet that incident occurs within a comprehending drama, at multiple levels. The encounter takes place within the hearing, for example, which takes place within politics broadly speaking, within the flux of history. And conflicts taking place within each magnitude can influence the conflicts in both directions, from the smaller to the larger and from the larger to the smaller. Which is as much as to say that what happens at each level can have implications at other levels. Think of it as three-dimensional chess.

A senator hoping to win an argument with a witness at the micro level might be alienating the constituency back home, at the macro level. Voters don't always enjoy watching their congressman bully and browbeat other people. (Of course, sometimes they most certainly do enjoy the spectacle.) Debates and quarrels never take place in a vacuum. Often, the participants are quite aware of these magnitudes. They enter into the fray knowing that more is at stake than the specific outcome. You can figuratively win the battle but lose the war. The senator might assail a witness exclusively because it plays well with the audience. Polling data might suggest that a politician's standing will rise if he or she can be seen to be "tough" about something. Georg Simmel (1955), for example, noticed that frequently during conflict the participants can be seen to represent people who are not present. This knowledge influences how they conduct themselves. They are mindful of the larger theater, the encompassing game. Furthermore, some participants enter in to these exchanges fully aware that by subjecting themselves to the importunities from the other side, they become martyrs.

In principle, therefore, these magnitudes – that is, the theater within the theater – resemble the schema set forth by James Carse when writing about finite and infinite games, as I had reason to mention already in these pages. In his version, if you recall, there are two types of game, the finite and the infinite, and these two are qualitatively different undertakings. Here, I would suggest that we might conceive of a gradient of games and not just two. There are smaller games and larger games, each one shaping the other. Most especially, however, we can consider the extent to which the furthest and most comprehending theater resembles what Carse said about the infinite game. Dante called it the Divine Comedy. Shakespeare wrote that the whole world's a stage. Christian theologians have indicated that creation itself is a spectator sport (*theatrum gloria Dei*), witnessed by angels, with a tremendous narrative arc culminating in the return of Jesus as Christ (see Nisbet, 2017). Each life is but a part of a much longer story, so that what we do in the moment echoes down through eternity. By conceiving of leadership – and especially the theater of leadership – as an episode in a broader epic, we can make sense of certain features that might otherwise bewilder us as students.

Gandhi, to cite one example, sought out confrontations where he would assuredly "lose" precisely because the news of it would bring his cause publicity and condemn his assailants in the eyes of the world. Perhaps more profoundly (and a part of his legacy that often gets overlooked), he did so in order to confront his assailants with an opportunity to see *themselves* in a new light. It was as much for their edification that he subjected himself to the imprisonment and the blows, for to him: the ultimate audience, the final court of appeal, was the guilty conscience of the oppressor. His vulnerability was designed in part to ask them – the colonial authorities – about their usage of power, i.e. to interrogate their conscience. "What have you become that you would treat me thus?" And so he willingly lost the narrower game precisely in order to win the broader one.

Jesus of Nazareth famously stood before Pontius Pilate, a representative of the most powerful hegemon the world had ever known, the Roman Empire. Only Pilate could exercise the legitimate authority to condemn a man to death. And despite the immediate merits of the case against Jesus, which were paltry, he calculated the political cost of judging this case on its merits. Jesus did not deserve to die. That seemed obvious, and he said so. But this trial was only a small part of geopolitical considerations, hardly a blip really. Pilate explained that he understood the larger context well enough, the political ramifications, and he was uneasy that Jesus seemed not to be cognizant of all that. "Don't you understand what is actually happening?" Jesus was doubly innocent: he was not guilty of a capital offense, and he was naïve. Jesus, however, responded that it was Pilate who was unaware that what was taking place at the trial was part of an even larger narrative, a cosmic drama, that dwarfed the politics of the day. "Don't *you* understand what is happening?" Both Pilate and Jesus were locked in a trial at level one, and Pilate understood that the trial was locked in a conflict at level two as well, but Jesus tried to assure Pilate that the entire conflict at level two was actually locked in a conflict at level three. Jesus was playing the infinite game.

The conventional approach to investigating this phenomenon is multilevel analysis. Instead, within the confines of this chapter, let me simply recount an example.

Edward R. Murrow

The idea of nested theaters, in which an encounter of some sort plays a part in a larger, encompassing drama, only to be part of an even larger one, explains a number of contexts where leadership is practiced. It certainly contributes to understanding the leadership practiced by Edward R. Murrow, an American icon. Complicating our model, however, is the fact that at any given magnitude, there may be more than one drama taking place simultaneously, such that leadership occurs within what we might think of as a hierarchy of theaters, as well as within a horizontal array of theaters. Such a framework is not foreign to analysis of organizations generally, but it will have been useful to Leadership Studies. Here then is the story of Edward R. Murrow.

A man named Fred Friendly was an integral part of broadcast journalism for many years. He was a collaborator with Murrow at Columbia Broadcasting System (CBS) in the early days of television. His account of that time was published in 1968 under the title *Due to Circumstances Beyond Our Control*. In those pages, he described Murrow and other key players in assorted dramas that were part of a larger struggle, as he saw it, between the mission of broadcast news and the economic pressures to turn a profit. Friendly accepted the judgment of the poet Archibald MacLeish that television in particular will have had a persistent influence on the hearts and minds of humanity beyond any other institution (1968, p. xxiv). It was to become an instrument for influencing millions of people, as indeed it has been. Anyone interested in leadership during the twentieth century must account for the power of this medium.

The problem, as Friendly saw it, was that, because somebody has to subsidize television, the person who pays the piper calls the tune (see also Kalb, 2021, p. 83). And the funding in the US came overwhelmingly from commercial advertising. Broadcast news was part of a business that always needed to turn a profit. Revenue was generated from advertisers, who wanted to reach the maximum number of potential customers, such that they relied on ratings to tell them where to invest their money. And the ratings favored entertainment over news (see, e.g. Persico, 1988, p. 244f; Friendly, 1968, p. 272). Not only that, but when the public was most attuned to breaking news, the broadcaster could not easily interrupt programming now and then in order to accommodate sponsors. You don't want to turn away from a rocket launch or a presidential address for a couple minutes about dishwashing detergent. Furthermore, sometimes the news addresses topics that make the general public uncomfortable – or at least will anger partisans. As a general rule, advertisers had little appetite to associate themselves with such controversies. They needed access to audiences, but only under the most favorable conditions. We cannot understand Murrow's career without appreciating this tension between commercialization and hard news reporting.

As part of the news, bare facts require interpretation and context, yet the effort to supply these can be construed as editorializing, lapsing into someone's opinion about the situation on air. Journalists constantly try to delineate what is news from what is opinion, but not everyone draws the line in the same place, especially if the news is against their interest – as for example the evidence that smoking tobacco causes cancer. The struggle to find and maintain that line between fact and opinion was –and still is – ongoing (see, e.g. Friendly, 1968, pp. 10, 198–204). Friendly himself, seeing beyond the bare recitation of facts, preferred what he called "yeasty news analysis that might make a difference" (1968, p. 191). Occasionally, the best journalism could be abrasive, especially when exposing a cover-up and holding public figures to account (1968, p. 78). In an effort to provide a degree of fairness, therefore, journalists resorted to the principle of equal time, during which an aggrieved party might receive an opportunity to tell his side of the story (e.g. Friendly, 1968, pp. 55, 61, 84, 122). At the outset, CBS tried to maintain a separation between broadcast content and sponsor preferences, going so far as to prohibit an advertiser from sponsoring programs pertaining to their industry (1968, p. 206f). Friendly and his allies in the media saw journalism as a sacred trust (Friendly, 1968, p. 197, quoting William Paley), a barrier difficult at times to maintain under enormous *political* pressures and nearly impossible under increasing *financial* pressures. While negotiating the business side of things, Friendly discovered that there were multiple games going on, so that his job as a manager was to play them all. By his own account, he won some, he lost some.

Clearly, throughout his tenure at the CBS, Friendly saw one leader who consistently played the games successfully and with integrity. His name was Edward R. Murrow. The man Murrow sitting at a desk at CBS may not have inspired confidence in the casual observer. Here was a fellow who suffered from a bad case of stage fright just before going on the air (1968, p. 36),[4] who struggled to write his own copy, who had no prior newspaper experience (1968, p. xv). Nevertheless, he was exemplary among his peers and a symbol to the nation. His leadership at each magnitude would be instructive today, despite changes to what is now called the mainstream media and the troubling emergence of social media (see generally Edwards, 2004, afterword). In his day, Murrow was almost Lincolnesque in stature.

4 Marvin Kalb (2021) revealed that Murrow refused to ad-lib on the air. Instead, he would break into a sweat and open his collar while delivering the text of his remarks (p. 24).

The very practices that made journalism effective also made it controversial, even within the network where journalism is practiced. Someone at CBS had to manage the risk, calculating the cost (in lost revenue and lawsuits, for example) and absorbing the inevitable criticism. Murrow understood this to be part of the job. He accepted it. But executives at CBS were not always supportive. At the very least, they expected him to help them cope, keeping surprises to a minimum. Murrow had to walk a fine line between his organizational obligations to the network, on the one hand, and his independence, on the other (Friendly, 1968, p. 95). Fortunately for him, Murrow had previously earned unmatched credibility. And he knew it. His power came primarily from his reputation, a reputation that CBS had paid good money to acquire, so it made little sense to undermine that reputation by bringing him to heel. Murrow could always walk away in high dudgeon and make the executives look bad. Still, he was not completely untethered to the realities of running a business.

Friendly put it this way. A man named Edward Klauber may have been the founder of broadcast journalism, but Murrow perfected it (1968, p. 168). Eric Sevareid eulogized Murrow on the air by saying "there was no basis for comparison. He was an original, and we shall not see his like again" (Friendly, 1968, p. 211; see also Kalb, 2021, p. 312). So who was this man?[5] And how did he manage the three-dimensional space known as leadership?

Murrow was born into the working class and proud of his blue-collar roots, although he could be reticent later in life disclosing just how poor they had been (Sperber, 1986, p. 15).[6] In fact, on many topics, the man could swing between two incompatible points of view, almost as though he lived in an abiding state of tension (Persico, 1988, foreword, p. 14). For example, he so assiduously pursued his education that he often thought about becoming an educator himself (or a college president), yet he expressed some resentment about the educated class that enjoyed life so much easier than he had growing up (Sperber, 1986, p. 22). He wanted to join their fraternities and exclusive societies, to the point of falling in with the loftiest aristocrats in England during the war, while at the same time hoping to reform a system that offered such privilege.[7] Politically, he was a confirmed centrist, intensely patriotic, yet eager to champion a series of proposals that struck some peers as revolutionary (Sperber, 1986, p. 38). By temperament,

5 I acknowledge three extensive biographies on Murrow written by Alexander Kendrick (1969), Joseph Persico (1988), and A.M. Sperber (1986). Also, I commend a shorter, accessible, and award-winning biography by Norman Finkelstein (2005).

6 Murrow had always been a natty dresser, even in the days when he could ill afford it (Sperber, 1986, pp. 49, 84, 94). Toward the end of his career, Murrow was handsomely compensated and ordered his suits from Saville Row, in London (Kalb, 2021, p. 14), yet he insisted on mingling with ordinary people and doing the chores himself on the farm in upstate New York.

7 Persico (1988) explained that Murrow resented *unearned* privilege. He had no such scruple with privilege that had been earned (p. 364).

Murrow admired his father, mingling happily with his brothers and the loggers at the camp, so that he always adhered to a fairly strict affinity for the company of virile men, which Sperber called "supermasculine" (1986, p. 24); yet he relied at key moments in his life on the guidance of strong women, especially his mentor Ida Lou Anderson (Sperber, 1986, p. 25f). Murrow set up his wife Janet as the first woman staff correspondent for CBS (Sperber, 1986, p. 142).

Here is another seeming contradiction. For a man devoted so much to the spoken word, who could be light-hearted at parties and contentious in debate, known the world over for his very public remarks under volatile conditions, a lively conversationalist in private (Sperber, 1986, p. 95), Murrow often lapsed into prolonged silence, brooding and inaccessible, with a dark opinion of the world (e.g. Sperber, 1986, pp. 40, 96). Biographer Joseph Persico claimed that these spells had begun during his teenage years and could last for hours (1988, p. 30). He labeled Murrow as "a loner masked by charm" (1988, p. 31). It should be noted, however, that to some extent his studied avoidance of speaking unnecessarily was captured in a motto that decorated his office and served as a daily reminder (Persico, 1988, p. 260): "Silence is a hard argument to beat." This seeming contradiction between verbal acuity and intense periods of silence led Persico to conclude, "He was magnetic at one moment and remote the next, effusive and reticent, approachable and inaccessible" (1988, p. 308).

In his native North Carolina, his ancestors had earned a reputation as contrarians – abolitionists in a slave-holding state, Republican for Abraham Lincoln in 1860. But then they were not entirely white folks: the family was part Cherokee (Sperber, 1986, p. 2). One ancestor had founded an historically black college (Sperber, 1986, p. 7).[8] Growing up, despite evidence of respiratory ailments and bouts of depression (Sperber, 1986, pp. 17, 148), he had worked on the railroad and as a lumberjack in Washington state while concentrating in school on diction, elocution, and the theater – a combination not too surprising given the topic of this chapter. Raised to be perpetually busy and work hard, he had played multiple sports and performed in several shows, becoming instantly popular wherever he went (Sperber, 1986, p. 21). He was aided in his schooling by a near-photographic memory (Persico, 1988, p. 38). Upon graduation from college, he soon found work promoting educational opportunities, including a job for the two-year old CBS lining up educational speakers for radio (Sperber, 1986, p. 36). In this capacity, he forged relationships with a dizzying array of highbrow intellectuals, such as Albert Einstein and Rabindranath Tagore, many of whom were to become lifelong friends (Sperber, 1986, p. 36f).

What brought him to Europe as a young man during the Great Depression was the prospect of educating others. He was – in the words of biographer A.M.

8 As a young man, Murrow had conspired to integrate a segregated hotel in Jim Crow Atlanta (Sperber, 1986, p. 44). On the topic of race relations and antisemitism, he was never ambivalent.

Sperber – "a pioneer in international educational exchange" (1986, p. 45). In those early days, he had had to reach out to wealthy donors, university officials, various intellectuals, and ambitious youth while creating a network throughout Europe, which necessitated extensive travel for such a young man (Sperber, 1986, p. 46f). Needless to say, he loved the adventure.

Complicating his efforts in Germany at the time was the rise of the Nazi party. Murrow was always antifascist, but he was forced to figure out how to work with them, much as he would with a bewildering variety of different regimes in the region. Here in the midst of increasing upheaval was an education in the real world that was unmatched for someone so young. Murrow had to get involved when American students ran afoul of Nazi policies, for example, but increasingly he found that many scholars in Europe began turning to his organization in order to arrange visits to America, hoping to get out from under the perils of fascism. Thus, he was ostensibly creating closer ties with the German government while secretly enabling many of its brightest and best to flee. One biographer noted that of 6,000 applicants for this program, which is a stunning number in itself, he could actually help only 335 – a percentage that would haunt him the rest of his life (Sperber, 1986, p. 64).

As Sperber put it:

> [Murrow] sifted and evaluated, acquiring a sense of global interdependence – history seen in terms of shifting demographic patterns and national power plays, a thoroughgoing, firsthand education in realpolitik at a time when most reporters of his age were still covering the [local] courthouse
>
> *(1986, p. 66).*

Murrow himself would say that these efforts were "the most satisfying thing I ever did in my life" (Persico, 1988, p. 79).

With this experience among academic luminaries, especially overseas, CBS brought him on board full-time as Director of Talks (Sperber, 1986, p. 75). He was now expected to use his multiple contacts to plan educational programming for the US, arranging for his audience to hear directly from the likes of George Bernard Shaw, Benito Mussolini, Leon Trotsky, and John Maynard Keynes (Sperber, 1986, p. 97). Murrow also gave an opportunity to Winston Churchill, who at the time was not terribly popular in Great Britain for his views (Sperber, 1986, p. 108).

It was in this capacity at CBS that Murrow had reason to experience the Anschluss in 1938, when the Nazis marched across the border into Austria. Here he witnessed firsthand the brutality of the fascists and the desperation of the Jews (e.g. Sperber, 1986, p. 120). It was also world-historical news of the first rank. After his colleague William Shirer raced back to England in order to broadcast the breaking news, nobody else from CBS was available in Austria to report back to the United States on subsequent developments, so he had to do it himself, even though he had no training in journalism, writing the news, delivering it on the air, let alone mastering the technical apparatus necessary to transmit a signal (Sperber, 1986, p. 104). He had to learn it all on the fly. His simple, calm, and factual account of that traumatic event impressed his superiors, who asked him to go do the same thing from London. He went.

Murrow's eyewitness radio reports were broadcast throughout the US as the Battle for Britain began in earnest. Listeners were galvanized by his prose describing air raids and fires and bombed out buildings, the smell and the menacing buzz of the Luftwaffe overhead. The audience could hear the sirens in the background as he told them what he saw. In time, he was allowed to join Allied bombers on their sorties across the Channel, which put him further into harm's way but made for compelling drama. At least one acquaintance noted that Murrow always had been something of an adrenaline junkie, even when driving his roadster through traffic. Nothing could be more of a rush than flying through the anti-aircraft surrounding Berlin in order to deliver explosives thousands of feet below, knowing the odds against coming back.[9]

After the war, Murrow was the first journalist to enter the notorious concentration camp known as Buchenwald. He confessed on the air that words failed him, but he tried to convey the horror. Skeletal figures clumped in tiered bunks, unable to stand, gazing at this tall and healthy American striding through the barracks. Spontaneously, they broke out into a feeble applause that sounded to him like children clapping. This experience, perhaps more than any other, convinced him that there is such a thing as evil. For such atrocities, there cannot be two sides to the story. Journalistic objectivity had its limits.[10]

9 Persico (1988) revealed that in college Murrow had been persuaded to adopt a philosophy known as Stoicism (p. 41), which contributed to his capabilities under immense strain to fulfill his obligations and not let his passions get the better of him. Stoicism recommends considerable self-discipline as a way of life.

Perhaps it becomes necessary to acknowledge that the man was not without weaknesses, of course, as it seems he got a girlfriend pregnant in college (Persico, 1988, p. 52) and after he married Janet he also carried on a long affair with a British socialite. There is also the addiction to cigarettes that plagued him throughout his life. He had lied on job applications for a number of years in order to convince people that he was older than he actually was (Persico, 1988, p. 99). This paragon had feet of clay. Yet nobody questioned his devotion to the job.

10 Marvin Kalb explained that to Murrow, analysis includes both an *explanation* of current events and some *perspective* on why it matters (2021, p. 29). Nevertheless, one could do so objectively. In fact, writes Kalb, Murrow routinely concluded broadcasts with a brief commentary (2021, p. 32). When it came to the Holocaust, however, Murrow saw no merit in granting air time to the point of view from the other side. What the Nazis had done was beyond the pale. Even so, it is interesting that at one point during the war Murrow had said, "I am finding it more and more difficult to suppress my personal convictions" – which implies that presumably he had been trying to do so (Sperber, 1986, p. 123).

Murrow returned from the war a celebrity. CBS hired him as an executive in New York City, a role he came to despise, so he returned to the airwaves. For the rest of his career, he treated managers with a kind of studied arrogance. He understood what they did for a living. In fact, he was relatively effective himself as a manager (Persico, 1988, p. 247). Nevertheless, he wanted no part of it. From his perspective, they were an infuriating necessity. The chief executive at CBS – and something of a legend in his own right – William Paley, who had befriended Murrow during the war (Sperber, 1986, p. xiv), ran interference for him during meetings.

Murrow had recruited and nurtured the careers of many newsmen, known informally as Murrow's boys or "that band of brothers" or a "gilded brotherhood" (Cloud & Olson, 1996; Kalb, 2021, p. 219, quoting David Schoenbrun; Persico, 1988, p. 240). Their loyalty to him was expressed in words of admiration, reverence, and love. Kalb (2021) wrote, "Literally, a hush would fall over the newsroom whenever he appeared" (p. 27). He added, "Clearly Murrow's impact on me, and many others, had been powerful and lasting" (p. 44; see also p. 83). The man was often praised for his tenacity, courage, moral rectitude, honesty, humility, fairness, and dignity (e.g. Kalb, 2021, p. 123, quoting Richard C. Hottelet; see also p. 312).

Celebrated in print back home, at one point Murrow was invited to run the British Broadcast Corporation (BBC) and even knighted by the Queen of England (Sperber, 1986, p. x). More than anything, he had come to be known for his integrity, as a brooding conscience (Sperber, 1986, p. xi, quoting T. White). A perfectionist, high in conscientiousness. Or as Persico (1988) worded it, Murrow has an "obsessive, compulsive nature" (p. 138). He was studiously non-partisan, rejecting belief systems that were sometimes fashionable, such as socialism (Persico, 1988, pp. 149, 335f). One biographer said of him, "Murrow was an idealist, not an ideologue" (Persico, 1988, p. 203). He continued, "[Murrow] was not really political. He was not ideological. But he was viscerally attached to certain fundamental principles which were not necessarily owned by the left or right" (1988, p. 336).For this reason, he could in good conscience sign the pledge that he was not a communist, even though his staff thought the mandate from CBS executives inappropriate, i.e. invasive of their privacy (Persico, 1988, p. 342). For one thing, Murrow never had been a communist, so he was merely attesting to the truth. More importantly, he knew to pick his battles, and he had a very big battle ahead against Senator Joe McCarthy.

Much of Murrow's reputation had been won resisting malign forces, such as Nazism (during the war), McCarthyism (after the war), as well as corporate executives who put profit above the public good. Toward the end of his career, he even challenged the entire television industry itself (Persico, 1988, p. 433). Persico wrote: "If Ed Murrow believed one thing about himself, it was that he was a man of integrity" (1988, p. 450). This is the person who decided to confront Joseph McCarthy when the terror in America was most acute.

The story of Murrow's courageous treatment on the air of the powerful senator from Wisconsin has been told better elsewhere. There is even a celebrated feature length film about it titled "Good Night, and Good Luck" (released in 2005). The point is that the junior senator had been taking advantage of a hybrid theater that was part courtroom trial and part campaign stump when he used congressional hearings to grab attention and intimidate witnesses. He was undoubtedly aware that the hearings themselves were one kind of theater restricted to the Senate, with assorted rules and conventions consistent with legislating, but that the wider publicity garnered from the media put him squarely in another, encompassing theater in which he could play the conquering hero. At CBS, Murrow waited until the last possible moment to cover the senator's behavior, and he did so largely by showing such boorish behavior to his own wide television audience. Murrow regarded his exposure of McCarthy as a defense not of any partisan position but of the principle of the due process of law (Persico, 1988, p. 8; see Sasse, 2018, p. 245; but see Persico, 1988, p. 383). That is to say that McCarthy had been using a hybrid forum to injure the reputations of citizens who were owed far more consideration in a court of law, which is where many of these hearings belonged. Murrow drove the point home by using the so-called court of public opinion that had kept McCarthy in the news. Television was Murrow's theater, after all, and he was better at using it than McCarthy, which became painfully obvious once McCarthy used his equal time at CBS a few weeks later to make matters for himself even worse.

A Senate Hearing is a ceremony where the outcome is presumably in doubt. But with Murrow, the coverage of these proceedings became a kind of ceremony unto itself, the ritual scrutiny by a disinterested journalist who relied on the public's trust to know venality when it sees it. This, he believed, was the role of broadcast journalism in democracies, especially in a time of crisis (Sperber, 1986, p. 112).

Not long after his finest hour, Murrow was repaid for his risk-taking by being marginalized in the industry for the sake of capitalizing literally on the public's apparent preference for television as a source of amusement, such as comedy and game shows, and not so much a source on the serious business of civics. According to one biographer, after his controversial broadcasts Murrow had become to the network "an ornament with sharp edges" (Persico, 1988, p. 421). The business slowly concentrated its resources on generating revenue (Kalb, 2021, p. 83). Murrow's parting shot at the squalid way he had been treated in the name of profit turned out to be a bombshell speech in 1958, delivered to the very industry that had swept him aside (Sperber,

1986, p. xviii). One might say that he had one last line to deliver before exiting the stage.

It is not without irony that Murrow chose to use a ceremony intended to honor the man by confronting his audience with a stern warning about the temptations inherent in television.

References

Anderson, D. (1987). "Attorney Brendan Sullivan: No potted plant." *UPI*. Retrieved 22 June 2023 from https://www.upi.com/Archives/1987/07/09/Attorney-Brendan-Sullivan-No-Potted-Plant/9717552801600/.

Ashforth, A. (1990). "Reckoning schemes of legitimation: On commissions of inquiry as power/knowledge forms." *Journal of Historical Sociology*. *3*(1): 1–22.

Buckley, W.F., Jr. (2004). *The fall of the Berlin Wall*. John Wiley & Sons.

Cloud, S., & L. Olson. (1996). *The Murrow boys: Pioneers on the front lines of broadcast journalism*. Houghton Mifflin Company.

Cohen, J. (2016, May 26). "I'm Not a Potted Plant; or am I?" *HuffPost*. Retrieved 16 June 2021 from https://www.huffpost.com/entry/im-not-a-potted-plant-or-_b_7443442.

Edwards, B. (2004). *Edward R. Murrow and the birth of broadcast journalism*. John Wiley & Sons, Inc.

Elden, S. "Ceremony, genealogy, political theology." In S. Rai, et al. (eds.). (2021). *The Oxford handbook of politics and performance* (ch. 23, pp. 377–391). Oxford University Press.

Elden, S. (2017). "Foucault and Shakespeare: Ceremony, theatre, politics." *The Southern Journal of Philosophy*. *35* (Spindel supplement): 153–172.

Finkelstein, N. (2005). *With heroic truth: The life of Edward R. Murrow*. Authors Guild Backinprint.com.

Friendly, F. (1968). *Due to circumstances beyond our control….* Vintage Books.

Goebbels, J. (1928/1934). "Knowledge and propaganda." From "Erkenntnis und Propaganda," *Signale der neuen Zeit. 25 ausgewählte Reden von Dr. Joseph Goebbels* (Munich: Zentralverlag der NSDAP., 1934), pp. 28–52. Retrieved 21 June 2021 from http://www.calvin.edu/academic/cas/gpa/goeb54.htm.

Goffman, E. (1978). *The presentation of self in everyday life*. Harmondsworth.

Hirschfeld-Davis, J., & M. Mazzetti. (2019, July 24). "Highlights of Robert Mueller's testimony to Congress." *New York Times*. Retrieved 5 February 2023 from https://www.nytimes.com/2019/07/24/us/politics/mueller-testimony.html.

Kalb, M. (2021). *Assignment Russia: Becoming a foreign correspondent in the crucible of the Cold War*. Brookings Institute Press.

Kendrick, A. (1969). *Prime time: The life of Edward R. Murrow*. Avon Publishers.

Lim, E. T. (2003, Fall). "The lion and the lamb: De-mythologizing Franklin Roosevelt's Fireside Chats." *Rhetoric and Public Affairs*. *6*(3): 437–464.

Nisbet, R. (2017). *History of the idea of progress*. Routledge.

Park, J. (2016). "A lab experiment on committee hearings: Preferences, power, and a quest for information." *Legislative Studies Quarterly*. *42*(1): 3–31.

Paulson, K. (2004, winter). "Regulation through intimidation: Congressional hearings and political pressure on America's entertainment media." *Vanderbilt Journal of Entertainment Law & Practice*. *7*(1): 61–89.

Persico, J. (1988). *Edward R. Murrow: An American original*. McGraw-Hill.
Raymond, M. (2007). "On legalistic behavior, the advocacy privilege, and why people hate lawyers." *Buff. L. Rev. 55*: 929.
Sasse, B. (2018). *Them: Why we hate each other and how to heal*. St. Martin's Press.
Self, J.W. (2005). "The first debate over the debates: How Kennedy and Nixon negotiated the 1960 Presidential debates." *Presidential Studies Quarterly*. *35*(2): 361–375.
Simmel, G. (1955). *Conflict & the web of group-affiliations* (K. Wolff, trans). Free Press.
Sperber, A.M. (1986). *Murrow: His life and times*. Freundlich Books.
Thomas, C. (1991, October 11). "Opening statement." Confirmation hearing of the US Senate Judiciary Committee. *American Rhetoric Online Speech Bank*. Retrieved 16 June 2021 from https://www.americanrhetoric.com/speeches/clarencethomashightechlynching.htm.
Vismann, C. (2003). "Tele-tribunals: Anatomy of a medium." *Grey Room*, 521.

9

CODA

The emergent beauty of authentic leadership

Georg Simmel once made a peculiar claim that all beauty "takes the form of those elements which are indifferent and alien to it and only acquire their aesthetic quality by their proximity to one another" (2018, p. 33). We might call this emergent beauty, much in the same way that Friedrich Hayek wrote about emergent order. The constellation is what makes it beautiful. The elements themselves do not even assemble themselves – or, if they do, they do not do so with the purpose of constituting something beautiful. It is the interrelationship that makes beauty possible. More peculiar, perhaps, is Simmel's claim that, standing alone, the elements might be absurd or disharmonious (2018, p. 35). A multiplicity of seemingly random parts can be regarded by the observer as a beautiful whole. Simmel then extends this line of thought to say that even the individual person, occupying a particular time and place, can transcend his circumstances and regard himself within context and see that he is only a participant in a larger whole. Whatever beauty an individual achieves requires being integrated in a certain fashion with the rest of the world in order to fulfill his potential to participate in beauty (2018, p. 42). The beauty of one's life – its pinnacle – requires being situated in a broader, comprehending beauty, with other people.

It is our freedom to participate consciously in bringing about such beauty.

Simmel is careful to say that he is not arguing that individual parts must all be uniform. In fact, the diversity itself contributes to the beauty. You must be you and not some flattened, fungible character (2018, p. 45). Crowning this sense of beauty is the condition that no matter from what angle one looks at the whole, it will seem beautiful, so long as you can detect the unifying theme. In the same manner, you can classify another human being by a series of generalizable traits,

DOI: 10.4324/9781003374831-9

such as height and intelligence, or you can diagnose a patient using medical taxonomies, and still know absolutely nothing about them as a living, breathing person (Simmel, 2005, p. 66f). Reducing a person to the sum of his or her traits is, in his words, like drawing a curve out of straight lines (2005, p. 80). Chartres Cathedral has been sketched from the front or back, above, at a distance, both interior and exterior – each perspective is beautiful, yet different. And together they constitute a single, irreplaceable structure. That multiplicity of facets, we might call them, goes a long way to explaining what lends any agglomeration its fascination and charm. I see it this way, for instance, yet you see it that way. Even so, we can agree that it is beautiful (2018, p. 46). One of the dimensions that we would ordinarily say keeps things apart and not unified is time; the past is not the future. Yet Simmel sees beauty as timeless, to see in the arc of development the emergence of a beautiful story (2018, p. 38f). It is beautiful at every stroke. He spoke of the unity across time, more of a dynamic model than a static model, a process into which the present is fully integrated (2005, p. 106).

In other words, a work of art unfolds beautifully.

To what extent, therefore, might we characterize leadership as the conscious effort to participate in assembling diverse parts into a unified whole that meets the criterion of beauty, i.e. a beautiful story?

Years later, Simmel acknowledged that there is a distinction to be made between that which *seems* beautiful and that which is *truly* beautiful. He contrasts the city of Venice, with its "lying beauty of the mask" and "artifice" and "precious game," with Florence and Rome (2018, pp. 55–62). He wrote that "the surface has lost its foundation" and leaves us "hypnotized by unremitting impressions" (2018, p. 60). We might call this an inauthentic beauty – "not a homeland but merely an adventure for our soul" (2018, p. 62). If we can characterize leadership as the conscious effort to participate in assembling diverse parts into a unified whole that meets the criterion of beauty, then we can add as Simmel's criterion that the beauty is more than just apparent. Leadership would be authentic social action which participates in that ongoing, comprehending, even timeless story and isn't contented with the simulacrum of beauty – the torches and the banners and the spirited songs of a fascist rally.

In his analysis of the portraiture of Rembrandt, Simmel noted that the figures being depicted do not appear in the light, as though passing toward a lamp. They are themselves the source of light. The light seems to emerge from within. Each human being, to Rembrandt, is a bearer of the light. Their authenticity shines through (2005, p. 116f). Leave it to leadership, then, that we encourage and draw together such luminosity, even if for a moment – even if for a season – to render something beautiful.

References

Simmel, G. (2018). *The art of the city: Rome, Florence, Venice* (W. Stone, trans.). Pushkin Press.

Simmel, G. (2005). *Rembrandt: An essay in the philosophy of art* (A. Scott & H. Staubmann, trans.). Routledge.

APPENDIX

A multitude of writers from a multitude of academic disciplines has tried to explain the meaning of several terms that are integral to the purpose of this book. It would be too much for me to attempt a thorough analysis of this vocabulary, which soon becomes abstruse, yet I agree with one of this book's reviewers that I owe some explanation to readers what I mean by them. The key terms are the following:

- Imagination
- Imaginary
- Imaginal

Obviously, the term "imagination" is a noun that refers to a faculty of the mind, the term "imaginary" is in popular usage an adjective that describes something that isn't there, and "the imaginal" is a noun that refers to a domain, which is a less-conventional usage that I hope to explain before we are done.

Imagination

Murphy et al. (2010) identify a number of philosophers who tried to explain what is meant by the **imagination**. They mention, for example, Burke, Hume, Kant, Dewey, and Sartre. Chiara Bottici (2019) adds Aristotle and Cornelius Castoriadis. Koliji (2015) adds Vico, Schelling, and myriad Islamic philosophers such as Al-Kindi, Al-Farabi, and Avicenna. Ultimately, Murphy et al. claim that one cannot define the term "imagination" except metaphorically.

They can however say what the imagination is not. It is not instinct, for instance, because instinct involves one's reflexes, unmediated responses, whereas the imagination is reflexive. It provides an operation of the mind that will have gained some distance from one's instincts. Instinct tends to be – if you will pardon the word – pointillesque. Human beings can also recognize the role of a symbol, for example, which indicates something else, when X stands for Y. Language itself depends on this capability to know that a certain sound conveys a message, but it requires a break from experience long enough to make that connection.

The imagination operates in that razor-thin boundary between sensibility, on the one hand, and conceptualization, on the other. Given sensory inputs, such as taste and smell, the mind spontaneously generates representations (see Hanna, 2020). A word used to capture this process is intuition. We might say that the brain's capacity to make associations instantly links sensory input with images. A famous example of this would be the *madeleine de Proust,* whereby the novelist in *À la Recherche du Temps Perdu* recounts the associations that flood into his brain when he smells a certain kind of cake from his childhood. The aroma can be said to evoke hundreds and hundreds of details from his life. Memories are not the only things that sensory input can evoke, however. The imagination can connect unrelated things and order them in some comprehensible way. It "sees" resemblances and therefore analogies that are not otherwise apparent. In order to be thought through logically, remembered consciously, and communicated to other people, these representations must be rendered ultimately as concepts, yet conceptualization operates in a different (logical, analytical) part of the brain (cf. Mosley, 2020; see generally McGilchrist, 2009). In short, for our purposes, we can rely on a tripartite structure, with the imagination ensconced in the middle as a distinct operation (see generally Koliji, 2015).

- Sensation
- Image
- Concept

As Murphy et al. (2010) remind their readers, the imagination allows us to look around corners and see into the future, generating possibilities. It would not constitute knowledge per se to foresee likely outcomes, but we anticipate many things. We have to. One way that we perform this feat is by bringing the evidence together to anticipate how it might be joined to make sense of reality, like assuming that when gazing at the cover of this book, you fully expect there to be a back cover. Until you actually flip it over, of course, this is only an expectation, albeit a reasonable one.

One of the most famous accounts of the generative power of the imagination is told of a dream that came to the chemist August Kekulé. According to Malcolm W. Browne (1988):

> Of all the cases cited by psychiatrists, psychologists and historians of science to illuminate the role of symbolism in creative thought, none is more famous than August Kekulé's somnolent vision of a snake biting its tail, a dream that supposedly revealed the true structure of the benzene ring to the German chemist.

Browne continued re-telling the story:

> The first historical mention of the snake dream appears to have been by Kekulé himself, in an extemporaneous speech at a benzene symposium in 1890. In this speech … Kekulé recounted a dream he had had in the winter of 1861–62 while dozing in front of a fire in Ghent, Belgium, where he was a professor of chemistry. The dream was that of the self-devouring snake, which, Kekulé said, led him to the benzene ring.

The important point is not whether the chemist actually ever had this dream. (Browne has his doubts.) The point of the story is to illustrate the relationship between intuition as a function of the imagination, on the one hand, with conceptualization, on the other. In this way, we would not just see things, but also see them "as" – as something useful or beautiful or good. I see an object *as a chair*. For without the recognition that they might be stars, we would behold only pinpoints of light on a dark surface and think no more about them (Mosley, 2020). And, what is worse, without the imagination, we would find ourselves incapable of empathy for other people.

An anthropologist named Philippe Descola (2013) set forth a worldview that predominated Renaissance Europe and influenced a number of other communities into the twentieth century – as well as influencing a French philosopher by the name of Michel Serres, whom I have had reason to cite in these pages. Descola called this worldview **analogism**, in which one recognizes that no two things are identical, but they do share a host of resemblances. Leonard da Vinci was thought to be a master of analogism. It does not require much imagination to recognize that one duck resembles another duck; the resemblance is what leads to the classification "duck." You require more imagination to see some cloud in the sky as a duck. The interesting question is why the two things resemble one another.

A humble deck of playing cards provides an opportunity to experience analogism firsthand. The same deck of cards can be grouped by color (red and black), suit (diamonds, clubs, spades, and hearts), numerical value (2, 3, 4, and so forth), face cards (Jack, Queen, King), and even the distinction between the front and the back of the cards. Thus, two cards can be similar in one respect (the color red) but dissimilar in another respect (diamond v. heart). It is the imagination that first recognizes and then sorts these resemblances.

Cartoonists rely on the imagination of children to recognize that the mouse named Mickey behaves like a human being, talking, walking on two legs, steering a steamboat down the river while whistling a tune. Let us not forget that the character is not even a mouse; he is a series of two-dimensional drawings. There must be sufficient resemblances from these drawings for the story to work. The brain can make connections that are otherwise not evident.

By means of the imagination, that child can watch the cartoon on television, then answer a mother's question about what happened at school, before going out to the driveway and pretend to win the big basketball game as the clock expires. From one world to another, seamlessly. We can do this only because we possess this power known as the imagination. Now, to be thorough, some have argued that the imagination is less of a power and more of a process, an epigenetic model that holds that the imagination is the method by which certain things happen (Wiltsher, 2022; Hanna, 2020, p. 59). Coleridge had supposed that only by means of the imagination did human beings even understand the world and give it meaning (Mosley, 2020). Paul Ricoeur called this capability "narrative intelligence" (Freeman, 2010, p. 40). Likewise, in an interesting turn of phrase, it is our capacity to imagine that demonstrates what it meant in Scripture that humanity was created "in the image of God" (e.g. *Genesis* 1:27), for we also can create. We take isolated data and "create" a meaning out of them.

Imaginary

The adjective "imaginary" suggests something that is not there. It might appear to be there, like an optical illusion, but in fact it is not. It could be a complete fabrication, like a fairy tale. In this sense, the term "imaginary" is supposed to mean the opposite of "real" – "outside the framework of being and existing" (Corbin, 1972/2000, p. 71). One might say to the hypochondriac, "it's all in your head" – insinuating that otherwise there would be no physical evidence of injury or disease.

The problem, of course, is that many things that are imaginary are real. A goal, aim, or purpose is not real, existing in paramount reality (or at least not yet), though it clearly motivates leaders and their followers to extraordinary exertions (Hopkins, 2019). Try telling a child that there is no bogeyman under the bed. To the parent, the child's fear is irrational. Nevertheless, the fear itself is very real. A feature-length science fiction film is designed not to portray a real world; saying this does not negate two things. First, the viewer can suspend judgment for a couple of hours to imagine that it is real. Temporarily, the story is for all intents and purposes acutely real. The body frequently reacts as though it is real: blood pumps harder, eyes dilate, the body might recoil from the monster. Second, the film itself is a real thing. *Star Trek* exists, even if the events it portrays are not. The response of the individual person to something unreal can be very real. But who's to say that what transpires in the fantastical mind of the painter is not real? It is occurring. One doesn't imagine that he is dreaming. She dreams. *What she dreams about* would be imaginary.

I would go further than this. What one imagines might in fact be altogether real. Let us say that I suspect that a player is cheating. I imagine so based on scraps of information. Is the player cheating? It might be the case that I am correct. It is a possibility. In that sense, what I imagine is more of a hypothesis. It may turn out to be the case that I was correct. What one imagines is not necessarily unreal. Scientists must infer many things about the world and rely on their imagination to explain it. They wouldn't say that a hydrogen atom is unreal, but they are forced to imagine it. Just because one imagines it does not make it imaginary in the sense I am trying to convey.

It is not unreasonable to acknowledge that often the imaginary is simply false – a distortion of reality or a complete lie. Just because one imagines something does not make it meaningful and good. Indeed, some dark imaginings qualify as evil – lurid, tempting, disturbing. For purposes of academic rigor, which Leadership Studies aspires to achieve, a scholar must routinely submit imaginings to the acid test of validity and truth. Otherwise, the fertile mind can spin off into sterile abstraction, fever dreams, and nonsense. The literature on leadership is frankly grotesque with wishful thinking, untethered happy talk, and tiny cherished idols that fit in one's suitcase. For these reasons, it is rightfully an indictment to say of something that it is imaginary when it presumes to depict the real.

The term "imaginary" does serve as a noun to describe something else, however, and it would be important to acknowledge this usage. Chiara Bottici (2019) refers to an imaginary as a context, a social frame, which people use to provide meaning (p. 434). In this usage, the imaginary is collective, whereas the imagination is individual. The United States of America is an imaginary. One's employer is an imaginary. One's family, also. When I rely on my own powers, I am using my imagination, but when I borrow imagery from my societal context, I resort to an imaginary. This usage of the term tends to be restricted to academics, but it does point to a useful distinction, and in these pages, I resort to this meaning in Chapter 5.

Imaginal

The term "imaginal" has an entirely different provenance and probably offends the hard-nosed realist. For the imaginal describes a domain or realm in which imagined things abide. Psychologists refer to it as a territory within which we move, like a dreamscape. Henry Corbin referred to it as an order of reality (1971/2000, p. 72). In the imaginal, characters cavort and morph, not unlike Toontown in the feature-length film "Who Framed Roger Rabbit?" The ancient Greeks spoke of Mount Olympus as the dwelling of the gods. Corbin also called the imaginal the topography of the visionary state, esoteric, a spiritual dimension (1971/2000, p. 74f). But another use of the imaginal would be geometric space, a place apart abstracted for the purpose of contemplating contours and shapes. The imaginal is the "where" of the imagination. What exactly is the Promised Land? Until they had physically reached it, the Promised Land was only a fantasy, a land that one could cherish without ever having set foot in it. Muslims call this domain "beyond Mount Qâf" (Corbin, 1971/2000, p. 76). One might think of it as a laboratory for thoughts and ideas, where nothing in paramount reality occurs except a lone man standing on the banks of the Rubicon, contemplating his next move. At that moment, he occupies imaginal space.

Chiara Bottici, whom I have had reason to mention already, offers a different meaning of imaginal, which is not incompatible with Corbin's, even though it provides a different emphasis. The imaginal is the production of images and not the end result. It is the process by which images come to the fore (2019, p. 436f). In this usage, images are primordial, before understanding, even before one can find the appropriate words. They flow with consciousness based upon the varied associations one possesses. Bottici wanted a name for that flow, that prodigious birthplace of images, only some of which prove accurate or useful (2019, p. 437). One might think of it as the name for a spring of water, where imagery spouts out of the very ground and then flows downward toward channels of utility. Even when one sleeps, she remarks, the images just keep coming. The human mind is a never-ending process of the generation of images. The situs for this production, which William James called the stream of consciousness, is the imaginal, which has its own textures, contours, and precepts.

References

Bottici, C. (2019). "Imagination, imaginary, imaginal: Toward a new social ontology?" *Social Epistemology*. *33*(5): 433–441.

Browne, M. (1988, August 16). "The benzene ring: Dream analysis." *New York Times*. Retrieved 20 May 2023 from https://www.nytimes.com/1988/08/16/science/the-benzene-ring-dream-analysis.html.

Corbin, H. "*Mundus imaginalis*: Or the imaginary and the imaginal (R. Horine, trans.)." In Sells, B. (ed.). (1972/2000). *Working with images: The theoretical base of archetypal psychology* (pp. 71–89). Spring Publications.

Descola, P. (2013). *Beyond nature and culture* (J. Lloyd, trans.). University of Chicago Press.

Freeman, M. (2010). *Hindsight: The promise and peril of looking backward*. Oxford University Press.

Hanna, R. (2020). "The essential non-conceptuality of the imagination." *Contemporary Studies in Kantian Philosophy*. *5*: 53–72.

Hopkins, R. (2019). From *what is to what if: Unleashing the power of imagination to create the future we want*. Chelsea Green Publishing.

Koliji, H. (2015). *In-between: Architectural drawing and imaginative knowledge in Islamic and Western traditions*. Ashgate.

McGilchrist, I. (2009). *The master and the emissary: The divided brain and the making of the Western world*. Yale University Press.

Mosley, D.R. (2020). "Toward a theology of the imagination with S.T. Coleridge, C.S. Lewis, and J.R.R. Tolkien." *Religions*. *11*: 238–247. https://doi.org/10.3390/rel11050238.

Murphy, P., M.A. Peters, & S. Marginson. (2010). *Imagination: Three models of imagination in the age of the knowledge economy*. Peter Lang.

Wiltsher, N. (2022). "Imagination as a process." *Philosophy and Phenomenological Research*. *106*(2): 434–454.

INDEX

Note: Page numbers followed by "n" denote footnotes.

For Product Safety Concerns and Information please contact our EU representative GPSR@taylorandfrancis.com
Taylor & Francis Verlag GmbH, Kaufingerstraße 24, 80331 München, Germany

www.ingramcontent.com/pod-product-compliance
Ingram Content Group UK Ltd.
Pitfield, Milton Keynes, MK11 3LW, UK
UKHW022355190926
475702UK00015B/2306

* 9 7 8 1 0 3 2 4 4 9 8 5 2 *